# Foreword

Within the Caribbean intellectu.............................................., .................my of underdevelopment and poverty, a prominent place has always been accorded, and rightly so, to George Beckford's *Persistent Poverty: Underdevelopment in Plantation Economies of the Third World* (1972). Seminal as it was, this study and the prodigious writings of Beckford and many colleagues provided a corpus of thinking and practice in which the 'dispossessed peasantry' was expected to provide creativity and resistance by which agrarian underdevelopment and rural poverty, in particular, would be overcome.

Beckford's work as a significant contribution of 'New World' scholarship, originating in the Caribbean during the 1960s and '70s, was widely sought after by academics, students, policymakers and political activists. So much so it appeared in a second edition some 17 years later (1999) with an elaborate introduction by Clive Thomas, Distinguished Professor of Economics at the University of Guyana. *Persistent Poverty* explained Caribbean underdevelopment as derived from the historical forces that subjected the colonies in the periphery to the dominant exploitative process of capital accumulation by the metropolitan powers. It was situated in the line of arguments by Andre Gunder Frank's *Capitalism and Underdevelopment in Latin America* (1967) and Walter Rodney's universal classic, *How Europe Underdeveloped Africa* (1974) and the extensive literature of the 'structural dependency school'.

In that theoretical framework applied to Caribbean rural economy and society, the 'small garden' cultivators in their struggle against the 'bitter weeds' of structural constraints were seen as the major driving force for the abolition of poverty in the rural economy of the plantation system (Beckford and Witter 1982). For this to be realized, economic and political policies have to be crafted to empower the peasantry to overcome 'dependence' and achieve 'transformation' of society as a whole. From such a perspective, the state plays a vital role in providing requisite policy and institutional mechanisms.

This publication of Theresa Rajack-Talley's *Poverty is a Person: Human Agency, Women and Caribbean Households* is a notable contribution that traces the expanded use of the 'structural dependency paradigm' by the late Professor Norman Girvan and makes links with Amartya Sen's 'enlarged freedoms'. By the author's assessment of the 'theorizing on causations' of poverty from a political economy perspective, one comprehends that the condition of the poor worldwide 'stems from the fact that they have no control over the resources of their countries.' Hence, in this line of thought, developing the capacity of the poor must be attributed fundamental importance in eradicating poverty. Counter posed to 'state-directed' policy, or complementary to that, Girvan saw the need for governments to focus on the capability of individuals and groups in society, as a way of addressing inequality and poverty similar to Amartya Sen's thesis.

Moreover, what makes Rajack-Talley's work a significant advance on the 'structural dependency paradigm' is the combination of social psychological attributes, and the class and gender relations in which human agency is grounded. It thereby becomes the transformative force to overcome 'persistent poverty'. This all-embracing understanding of 'human agency' is the potential capacity that Caribbean womanhood is regarded as having to overcome not only 'rural underdevelopment', in general, but also the gendered inequality pervasive of the contemporary Caribbean. This is the jewel of the 'theory and praxis' that the author offers for serious reflection by scholars, students, practitioners and policymakers who wish to deal with the multidimensional character of poverty that Rajack-Talley reveals for her readers to grasp.

Many aspects make this study very appealing and refreshing. It is presented in a vivid style and takes readers into the lived experience of Caribbean poverty. But, the narrative also draws on a range of current scholarship and shows how established agencies, like the World Bank, deals with 'poverty' as empty statistics when contrasted with the 'participatory poverty assessments' of the Caribbean Development Bank. By going beyond empty statistics, one uncovers a compelling narrative by which to engage on the gendered and systemic roots of poverty.

The discourse in which this central thread connects her analysis of earlier 'structural dependency' approaches with the 'agency of gender and household relations' is closely argued and lucidly conveyed in chapters 4, 5 and 6. Therein the discussion gives readers the benefit of the participatory approach to 'measure' poverty based on the experiences of the poor themselves and provides a wider perspective on the meaning of gender relations in Caribbean households and society. Those experiences illustrate the ability to overcome adversity in the face of humiliation and to grapple with the consequences of social exclusion.

Poverty is a Person

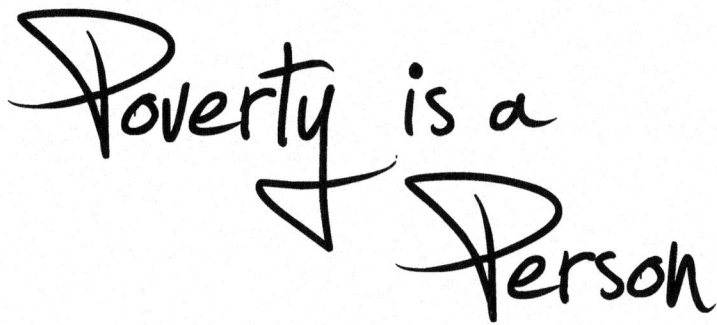

# HUMAN AGENCY, WOMEN
# AND CARIBBEAN HOUSEHOLDS

## Theresa Ann Rajack-Talley

IAN RANDLE PUBLISHERS
*Kingston • Miami*

First published in Jamaica, 2016 by
Ian Randle Publishers
16 Herb McKenley Drive
Box 686
Kingston 6
www.ianrandlepublishers.com

**National Library of Jamaica Cataloguing-In-Publication Data**

Rajack-Talley, Theresa Ann,

    Poverty is a person not a statistic : human agency, women and Caribbean households  / Theresa Ann Rajack-Talley

       p. ; cm.

Bibliography : p.

ISBN 978-976-637-895-0

1.  Poverty – Research – Caribbean Area   2.    Poor – Caribbean Area

3.  Women – Caribbean Area – Economic conditions

4.  Women heads of households – Caribbean Area

5.  Caribbean Area – Social conditions

I.  Title


362. 509729      dc 23

Cover and Book Design by Ian Randle Publishers
Printed and bound in the United States

# Contents

# List of Figures

# List of Tables

# List of Boxes

To realize that these psychological aspects of impoverishment are embedded in structures of inequality allows one to understand the 'relational aspect of poverty'. This avoids victimization, a common occurrence in 'poverty studies', and identifies the structural processes that deny opportunities to the poor and, in turn, stigmatize them from one generation to another. Within that interplay of structural and agency factors, the author develops her central arguments on the gender dimension of poverty from a Caribbean perspective that shows how women fight poverty and, in so doing, question Western/Eurocentric stereotypes of women's roles.

In the central place given to human agency, engagements in the processes for meaningful livelihoods by the 'dispossessed' indicate that both women and men negotiate and contest the power relations between the sexes in the public and private spheres. On this basis, the 'feminization of poverty' in single-female-headed households as derived from the absence of a male breadwinner is clearly dismissed with historical and contemporary evidence. Caribbean women are shown to be income earners and great contributors to the quality of life in their households and the wider society.

Quite revealing are the case studies of women-managed sheep farms in the Caribbean. These demonstrate the complexity of relations within households, in terms of gender, power and economic demands, thereby putting to rest simplistic stereotypes of the poor as helpless victims, resisters of change and as 'disadvantaged' women who willingly subordinate to the so-called 'dominant' male. The vivid portrayals of the household dynamics are revealing of the power of 'women's agency', indicating how this complex social force has its material and institutional basis in the 'household' as a vehicle of survival, embodying social capital and resources to maintain human dignity.

Dr Rajack-Talley critically discusses the concept of social capital with its potential for poverty reduction by tapping the social and economic dynamics of a community forging its own identity and drawing on the innovative energy portrayed in a brief ethnographic analysis of Tumbasson village, located in the east-western corridor of northern Trinidad and Tobago. But the limitations of the community's social capital become clear when agency is used to effect change in more permanent and structural ways. As a result, one can readily support the cautionary note addressed by the author to technocrats who wish to advocate this newly-discovered 'social capital' as an instrument in itself as a decisive factor for poverty reduction. The concept, as pointed out by the author, exists within the larger context of the unequal distribution of resources; to think otherwise is to create a false misunderstanding of the concept and an impractical expectation of its use. In the end, the poor will continue to be blamed for their limitations and gender issues marked as a simple issue of providing more resources to women.

A fundamental rethinking must be undertaken  not only in poverty studies and the approach to policymaking, but also in the inclusion of those who are essential for the policies to be effective and genuinely transformative. As a major contribution to the multidimensional, gendered understanding of Caribbean poverty and why human agency is the driving force to confront and overcome structured inequalities, Dr Rajack-Talley's work is highly commendable and makes us anxious to await her future projects.

Dr Patrick I. Gomes
Secretary General
African, Caribbean and Pacific (ACP)
Group of States

# Acknowledgements

There are many who have assisted and supported me along this journey. First, I would like to thank Dr Ralph Henry and the team from KAIRI Consultants for not only giving me the opportunity to work in the field, but for teaching me the many dimensions (quantitative and qualitative) of poverty. Additionally, there were a few faculty colleagues who read some of the earlier chapters giving positive feedback, and graduate students who helped with some of the citations. Also, I wish to express my sincere appreciation to my technical editor for her careful and painstaking editing of the manuscript and thoughtful feedback.

A very special acknowledgement to Dr Patrick I. Gomes for taking time from his very busy schedule to write such an enthusiastic foreword to the book. You have always encouraged me to write that 'earth-shaking' manuscript, so I hope that this book is a fitting tribute to that end. I would also like to thank my reviewers who took the time to read the manuscript and provide valuable comments and suggestions. Your contributions are appreciated more than you will ever know as they pushed me to a higher level of scholarship.

To the many households, particularly the women, who spoke and cried with me, and the others who I did not directly encounter but whose responses in the Country Poverty Assessments published by the Caribbean Development Bank were valuable to this project, my heartiest thanks. While this may sound like a cliché, it is true that this book would not be possible without you. I hope in some small way my work and this book will make your lives a little more humanely livable.

Lastly, to my close circle of family and friends, you have not only supported this endeavour with your valuable inputs and feedback, but you carried me with love and patience, especially in recent times. My sincere thanks, appreciation and much love I give to you.

I dedicate this book in memory of two gentlemen warriors who themselves held a strong disdain for social inequality, exploitation and oppression of all peoples; and who fought all their lives against these atrocities. I was fortunate to have them both as my dearest friends and mentors – Professor Jan Carew and my beloved husband, Dr Clarence R. Talley. Jan always believed in me and encouraged me to write; he taught me patience and how to be gracious, especially in times of turmoil. Clarence was not only my friend and mentor but my soul mate, my co-investigator and my love, so it was very difficult to complete this book without him. Some of his last words were: 'Theresa Ann, there is too much work to be done to be sad.' This book is much about him as it is about me.

# Introduction

This book looks at the multidimensional and gendered aspects of poverty; two areas that are least researched and understood in poverty studies. The content, focus and analyses are the results of years of being immersed in research on rural communities and farm households, and in the past two decades working with a team of consultants commissioned to study poverty in the Caribbean. The combination of academic research and field data collection and analysis propelled me to try and understand the humanity of the people we study. What does it mean when an elderly woman on an idyllic Caribbean island says to you that 'poverty is a crime not a sin?' Or a boy living with his family in an urban centre feels 'He really does not have a mother and father who can take care of him'. A 12-year-old girl in describing how she is treated by her schoolmates laments that poverty 'is being teased that you smell because my mother cannot afford to buy deodorant' (NALC, Cayman Islands 2006/07).

The painful words above emanate from the shores of the blue picturesque Caribbean and reflect the other side of paradise. Unfortunately, these experiences are not uncommon but are found in most underdeveloped countries, as well as among certain groups in more industrialized societies. Despite the prevalence of poverty, the woeful expressions of those less fortunate remain muffled. Poor communities are hidden in isolated pockets of the inner and/or outer city limits, in addition to rural or non-urban locations. Their voices are often muted in poverty research and excluded in the policymaking processes. As part of recent attempts to make poverty studies more participatory and effective, research and development projects should be more inclusive of the experiences and behaviours of the most vulnerable members of our society.

The stark confrontation of how women, men and children who live in least desirable conditions survive, and who amid intense humiliation even smile, led me to explore the concept of human agency. What do households, families and communities do when faced with economic hardships and socio-political exclusion from society? Are they mere victims to their environment simply responding to life conditions, or do they also act upon their socio-economic circumstances? Are they hopeless or hopeful? Because these questions are seldom addressed in both the academic literature and in technical poverty reports, this book represents an attempt to put the 'people story' back into poverty studies. The purpose of this book, however, is not to simply highlight the voices of the poor because of some romanticized impulse, but it is the firm belief of this author that listening to the subjects of poverty and understanding the role of human agency, women in particular, are key to finding solutions to persistent poverty in the region and elsewhere. It also begs for different methodological and conceptual approaches in research on poverty and on women, as well as the interrelationship between the two.

Putting people back in poverty studies changes the purpose of how statistical data are used to create policy and fashion solutions for the economically deprived and socially excluded groups and communities in society. The adoption of this perspective forces us to address the multidimensional and gendered nature of poverty, and the importance of responding to poverty in targeted, as well as in more integrated ways. It raises questions about the research approaches adopted, and the origins and relevance of the measures and theoretical perspectives used in the Caribbean context. Putting the people back in poverty studies directly addresses how human relations affect issues of social inequality and gender inequity. Poverty is not just a structural phenomenon but a process that involves networks of active human beings in households and communities.

Additionally, while at the national and regional levels, steps are adopted to address gender inequality; poverty strategies have been limited in their responses to the needs of single-female-headed households, women in resource-poor households, and women in general. As a result, following on the lead of Caribbean feminists and scholars, I pay particular attention to the gender dynamics in the home and the workplace. Rather than treating women as victims of discrimination and economic marginalization, I draw attention to the physical and psychological pain of their social exclusion and isolation from resources, but also acknowledge their strengths as social agents who employ strategic tactics because they must support their households. Thus, the book features women as a group that is most affected by economic and social limitations and, at the same time, show how they also have the greatest impact on the livelihoods and well-being of so many.

Caribbean women for a long time have played central roles in their family household economies. They continue to work and make progress, sometimes greater than those of their male counterparts particularly in the areas of higher education and professional jobs. However, these advancements are not enjoyed by all groups of women. There are those who live in resource-poor households, who continue to feel powerless and invisible, and who 'have no one to go to or no one to talk to'. Women still do face structural gender barriers as a result of manifestations of patriarchy in the workplace and in the home. Not only are their voices socially excluded in policymaking, but also in poverty studies where their lives are represented in the form of a statistical variable. As a result, it is mathematically easy to imply that single-female households are the 'poorest of the poor' and assume that this is because there is an absence of a male breadwinner. Likewise, the discussions in the chapters give you an idea why without in-depth understandings of the roles women really play, and the coping mechanisms of the less fortunate, women and men from resource-poor households and communities continue to be negatively stereotyped and stigmatized.

The book is titled *Poverty is a Person*. This title reflects the humanitarian framework within which I examine structural inequalities as well as social and gender biases that deny certain groups access to resources, dignity and a decent standard of living. I critique the dominant methodological approaches and conceptual tools used to conduct poverty studies because they are not designed and implemented to address these issues. The data that continues to be collected are useful, but the lessons learned from those who have been silenced, marginalized and socially excluded needs to be further drawn out. Without addressing the dynamics of social inequality and gender inequity in research that inform policymaking, poverty will persist and people will continue to live under rusting galvanize in clustered neighbourhoods, bordering the gated communities of the middle and upper classes.

## About the Book

The book reflects my own pedagogical standpoint of consistently linking research to teaching and community development. The information, discussions and analyses presented here are a reflection of these three areas and are, therefore, relevant to intellectuals engaged in research and education on human poverty and gender studies, as well as policymakers and practioners in the field. The eight chapters in the book collectively capture the complexity and multidimensional characteristics of poverty and social inequality. They provide a synopsis of poverty from a people's perspective and with gendered understandings. Voices of the poor resound throughout and are accompanied by case studies of households and communities. The quotes taken from poverty studies are used in a way as if the rooftops of homes were lifted and readers are observing the family dynamics in the home, and the lives of the women as they manage their household budgets, their families' continued existence, and their own psyche. The examples, discussions and analyses make obvious the importance of human agency in negotiating poor living conditions and developing survival strategies. With a growing appreciation of the role of gender and power, as well as the need to reduce poverty and achieve the United Nations Millennium Development Goals, the book is timely and fills a void in developing more appropriate research approaches, theoretical understandings and poverty strategies for the Caribbean region.

## An Overview of Poverty in the Caribbean

Following the introduction, chapter one gives both a quantitative and descriptive overview of poverty in the Caribbean. It provides data on income measures and inequality within societies and across the various Caribbean countries. In so doing, readers get some idea of the level of economic development in the region, as well as the extent to which poverty, indigence, and the gap between the rich and poor exists. This chapter helps the reader situate the discussions and case studies cited in the chapters to follow. It also provides brief descriptions of what poverty looks like in resource-poor communities, households, and among groups, including women and children. Further, it sums up some of the major discourses on why poverty exists and persists in the region, including historical debates as well as contemporary political economy arguments. In general, chapter one gives a succinct depiction of the geographical, political, demographical and geometrical make up of the Caribbean, that is, the context within which households, community-based scenarios, and women's narratives are located and analysed in the chapters that follow.

## Putting the People Back in Poverty Research

Chapter two examines the more common approaches used in the Caribbean to research poverty and indigence. It briefly describes the methods used and then highlights the weaknesses and voids in understanding the human condition, what it means, how it works, and the gender differences in the ways it is experienced and negotiated. Most of the poverty assessments adopt the income or monetary approach that centres on the resources required for individuals and households to maintain a certain standard of living. Surveys of living conditions are commonly used and are designed to capture data that determine the extent to which individuals and households live below a poverty line. The assumption is that measures of income and material assets are sufficient to understand and define whether an individual or a household is poor, and the extent of that poverty.

Although, the inclusion of human poverty indices (health, education, and gender variables among others) has broadened the scope of poverty studies, the chapter discusses how these additions are still limiting in understanding how people identify and measure themselves, how they understand their living conditions, and what recourse they take to ameliorate these conditions. In particular, the approaches are critiqued for neglecting gender analysis and the implications of how the social construction of gender roles and relations are linked to poverty. As an alternative and/or supplement to the more quantitative approaches, the chapter analyses the usefulness of Participatory Approaches in providing a more robust comprehension of gender issues, human capabilities and the social exclusion of those most affected. The chapter lends support to research approaches that rigorously conducts independent analysis of poverty based on the local experiences of people who live in resource-poor households and communities. This would entail placing the human factor (socio-psychological dimension) and gender analysis centre stage in poverty studies, rather than having a reliance on faceless data.

The next chapter, chapter three, develops from chapter two and immediately makes the argument that the humanity of people is consistently left out of poverty studies. It explores the social and psychological dimensions of poverty and deliberately sets out to highlight that poverty is not only about material deprivation and physical pain, but those who experience poverty also feel humiliation, shame and helplessness. The trauma of being shunned because of your physical appearance, or shamed for the simple reason that you cannot afford what you need, or profiled because of the community in which you live, comes to life in interviews quoted from Caribbean Poverty Assessment (CPA) Reports. Through the voices of the poor, this chapter demonstrates that the personal and very emotional experiences of the 'have nots' vary by age, gender, rural-urban life settings, and other socio-demographic characteristics. Equally important, the socio-psychological discourse illuminates the relational aspect of poverty that results in social exclusion and isolation.

Other methodological issues arising from the standard approaches used to study poverty are problematized in the next three chapters. They focus specifically on the interpretation and misinterpretations of women's experiences in resource-poor Caribbean households.

## Women Fighting Poverty

Chapters four, five and six build on the critiques of the earlier chapters and attempt to capture one of the least understood dimensions of poverty – the gender dimension. The chapters draw attention to what women from resource-poor households do every day to combat their dire living circumstances and those of their dependents. Women's coping mechanisms in their fight against poverty are seldom referenced in both poverty studies and women and gender studies. Generally, poverty studies highlight the high incidence of poverty in single-female-headed households with the underlying assumption that poverty results from the social practices of women who, by choice or *de facto*, engage in single-parent families. This trend of thought simultaneously speaks about the destitute living conditions in women-headed households, as well as demonizes women for their choices.

On the other hand, women and gender studies in the Caribbean continuously highlight women's roles in the public and private domains of society. While these studies speak to both the contributions that women make, as well as the gender barriers they face within and external to the household, they focus on women in general. Some studies centre on families and women from low-income households, and/or relational factors to poverty like health issues, HIV/AIDS in particular. As a result, while gender inequity in society and in families is drawn out, factors that contribute to the daily lived experiences and traumas of being poor with families to support are not well researched. The women and gender studies literature do, however, critique research for adhering to Western/Eurocentric stereotypes of women's roles, and failing to recognize that historically, and up to today, the economic roles of women in most developing societies, including those in the Caribbean, are different from the typical white middle-class housewife. Within this same context, they have also played a major role in shifting family studies away from a structural focus to a more relational approach and bring greater clarity on matrilineal and matriarchal understandings. It is within this framework that I build the chapters on women and poverty.

The main objective of these three chapters is, therefore, to link the two bodies of literature and interrogate how in the 'real world' women and men from resource-poor households negotiate their living conditions and develop strategies to survive. In each of the chapters, women's agency is central to the discussions. This approach does not depict women as victims of economic discrimination and patriarchy as others studies have. The book adopts a relational approach and, as such, women and men are treated as human agents capable of engaging in the process of change through negotiations and contestation of power, in both the public and private spheres of their lives.

Chapter four of the book centres on the conceptualization and application of the *feminization of poverty* perspective in the Caribbean. Here, it is argued that attempts to universally apply the logic and research tools used in poverty studies to examine women and female-headed households in developing societies, creates several methodological and theoretical challenges. In particular, the adoption of the *feminization of poverty* analytical frame developed from Eurocentric notions about the role and experiences of women, when applied to women with different social histories, result in wrong assumptions and conclusions. For example, the chapter challenges the explanation that *feminization of poverty* occurs in the Caribbean because of the absence of a male breadwinner. Moreover, the discussions and analyses in this chapter build on the works of Caribbean feminists and argue that the *feminization of poverty* model carries with it cultural biases that are not applicable to Caribbean women's experiences and identities. The chapter concludes that the broad use of the *feminization of poverty* poses a danger because it deflects attention away from issues of gender inequity in society, wage discrimination in the work force, and patriarchy and sexism in two-parent households.

Chapter five expands on arguments made in chapter four and highlights the work of Caribbean women scholars who have for years debunked the myth of the male as the primary income earner in Caribbean homes. The chapter interrogates the idea of the absence of a male breadwinner as a plausible cause for the *feminization of poverty* in single-female-headed households by highlighting female breadwinners in the Caribbean. The chapter unearths women's historical beginnings and reports on their contemporary contributions as income earners, supporting their household economies and building the economies of the societies in which they reside. Here again, the *feminization of poverty* perspective is critiqued for placing too much emphasis on women's reproductive roles in the household, particularly when, in the Caribbean, the concept of a stay-at-home housewife is shown to be alien for women who have always had to work. The chapter gives women agency by showing them consistently negotiating the economic climates of their societies and the living conditions of their families, whether or not a male income earner resides in their households.

Chapter six further develops how women negotiate change and power when economic shifts occur in the home and in society. It examines the internal workings of households and the how bargaining of resources puts a strain on social relations and changes the dynamics of gender power. This is particularly important in resource-poor homes where women's income (in cash or kind) is crucial to fighting off absolute poverty, in many cases, and where power relations are more stretched during financially difficult times. Discussions are grounded within the feminist critique of Foucault's idea of multiple sources of power and domination co-existing in different ways.

Case studies from a longitudinal study on women-managed subsistence sheep farms in the Caribbean are used to construct household models of co-operation and conflict. These models are used to show how gender power relations are complex and indeterminate, particularly in societies that are influenced by both patriarchy and other gender ideologies. In this chapter on women, power and change, women's agency is used to counter stereotypical beliefs that: poor people (women and men) simply respond to economic changes; women fear and/or are resistant to technology and technological interventions; when economic shifts occur women are subordinated and continue in supplementary economic roles; and that when technology is introduced women are marginalized. Instead, the chapter demonstrates how change is negotiated and power contested. What becomes glaring from the case studies is that households may be resource-poor, but women still desire their economic independence and autonomy. The negotiations, however, are different in form and intent from those in public spaces because they involve intimacy and familial relationships.

## Humanizing Poverty Research as We Move Forward

The last two chapters in the book, chapters seven and eight, offer some interesting insights into the role of agency in both research and development. Together they directly address why social inclusion can influence change and improve the living conditions of individual women and men, families and communities. Chapter seven shifts the level of analysis from individuals and households to the community. It introduces the concept of social capital, which is gaining importance in policy development, particularly those aimed at economic growth, social development and poverty reduction. Currently, there is a rejuvenation in the interest of social capital, partly due to the World Bank's endorsement of social capital as an important asset to social and economic development, as well as to sustainable development overall. The rationale behind interrogating social capital as a potential tool for poverty reduction is a response to the critique that physical and material forms of capital are not the only type of capital important for economic growth, but that 'capital' must now be broadened to include human elements. In other words, capital is about a person and not just a monetary indicator.

A case study of a small underdeveloped agrarian-based community in Trinidad shows how social capital works in the everyday survival of individuals and households in resource-poor communities. The chapter, however, cautions efforts to romanticize social capital, and points out that the less privileged do not have the social capital required to alleviate poverty. In fact, social capital simultaneously builds capital for some and isolates others from resources and social mobility. Issues of social inequality, social exclusion, social cohesion and social fragmentation are integral parts of the mechanisms of social capital. The chapter also points out that gender barriers and women's access to capital are not prominent in the social capital literature. Similar to other methodological and theoretical models, gender is treated as an 'add-on' and is not well integrated in the social capital discourse. As a result, we know very little about women's social capital or the role that social capital plays in women's access to resources and social mobility.

Chapter eight, the last chapter of the book, pulls together all the strands of arguments from the various chapters and presents the problem, the analysis and suggestions for alternate approaches in studying poverty, specifically women and female-headed households. It summarizes what works and identifies voids in the research process that leads to strategies with limited successes. The chapter highlights the need to not only capture the multidimensional nature of poverty, but also the multi-level impact, as well as the cognitive and the relational aspects. Within this context, understanding social exclusion, the role of agency, and women's roles in coping with their living conditions, are argued to be key elements to developing more effective and targeted poverty strategies, and to economic and social development overall. Suggestions are made for moving forward that include expanding the current approaches being used, adjusting the conceptual tools, and removing the Eurocentric cataract that continues to grow over the lens used to interpret local gender experiences. Suggestions for future research are made, and the missing elements of this book are identified.

# Abbreviations and Acronyms

| | |
|---|---|
| AIDS | Acquired Immune Deficiency Symptoms |
| BNTF | Basic Needs Trust Fund |
| CALC | Country Assessment of Living Conditions |
| CARDI | Caribbean Agriculture and Development Institute |
| CARICOM | Caribbean Community |
| CBO | Community Based Organisation |
| CDB | Caribbean Development Bank |
| CIDA | Canadian International Development Agency |
| CNIRD | Caribbean Network for Integrated Rural Development |
| CPA | Country Poverty Assessment |
| DIFID | Department for International Development |
| D-REP | Dominica Rural Enterprise Development Project |
| EAP | Economically Active Population |
| ECLAC | Economic Commission for Latin America and the Caribbean |
| EU | European Union |
| FAO | Food and Agriculture Organization |
| FDIs | Foreign Direct Investments |
| FTZ | Free Trade Zone |
| GDI | Gender Development Index |
| GDP | Gross Domestic Product |
| GEM | Gender Empowerment Measure |
| GEM | Gender Entrepreneurship Monitor |
| GII | Gender Inequality Index |
| GNP | Gross National Product |
| GSDRC | Governance and Social Development Resource Center |
| HD | Human Development |
| HDI | Human Development Index |
| HIPC | Highly Indebted Poor Countries |
| HIV | Human Immunodeficiency Virus |
| HPI | Human Poverty Index |

| | |
|---|---|
| IADB | Inter-American Development Bank |
| IDS | Institute for Development Studies |
| IFAD | International Fund for Agricultural Development |
| IFI | International Financial Institution |
| IICA | Inter-American Institute for Cooperation on Agriculture |
| ILO | International Labour Organization |
| IMF | International Monetary Fund |
| LAC | Latin America and the Caribbean |
| LDC | Less Developed Countries |
| MDC | More Developed Countries |
| MDG | Millennium Development Goals |
| NALC | National Assessment of Living Conditions |
| NGO | Non-Governmental Organisation |
| OECS | Organisation of Eastern Caribbean Countries |
| PA | Participatory Approach |
| PAR | Participatory Action Research |
| PPA | Participatory Poverty Assessment |
| PRSP | Poverty Reduction Strategy Papers |
| SAP | Structural Adjustment Policies |
| SLC | Survey of Living Conditions |
| TIC | Tumbasson Improvement Committee |
| UN | United Nations |
| UNDP | United Nations Development Programme |
| UNHRC | United Nations Human Rights Commission |
| UNICEF | United Nations Children Funds |
| UNU-IAS | United Nations University for the Advanced Study of Sustainability |
| UNESCO | United Nations Educational, Scientific and Cultural Organisation |
| USA | United States of America |
| WB | World Bank |
| WC | Washington Consensus |
| WICP | Women in the Caribbean Project |
| WHO | World Health Organization |

# 1. An Overview of Poverty in the Caribbean

This chapter gives an overview of poverty in the Caribbean; what it looks like at the individual, household, community and country levels. Issues of income inequality and gender equity are reported to identify the region's economic stratification by country and gender. Readers will gain a basic understanding of the issues and a socio-economic context for the following chapters, which discuss poverty research in the Caribbean. The statistics, descriptions and perspectives on the causes of poverty provide the backdrop in which the poor households discussed throughout the rest of the book, reside. They also afford the readers to place the case studies, the individual narratives and the community profiles described in later sections of the book. The objective of the chapter is, therefore, to create a bird's eye view of poverty in the region.

## Caribbean Poverty in a Global Context

The Caribbean consists of several small countries, some smaller in total size and population than a large US city, and with as few as 20,000 inhabitants. The Caribbean is a region that is surrounded by the Caribbean Sea, the North Atlantic Ocean, the Gulf of Mexico and the North American mainland. It is east of Central America and north of South America. Geopolitically, the Caribbean islands are usually regarded as a subregion of the Americas, and data on the Caribbean are often grouped with that of the Latin American countries and referred to as the LAC group of countries. The Caribbean region itself is organized into 30 territories, including sovereign states, overseas departments and dependencies.

The Caribbean has an interesting and diversified history with different colonial influences, including the British, French, Spanish, Portuguese and Dutch. As a result, the region has a very vibrant mix of people from different ethnic backgrounds and cultures. Because of the history of colonization and slavery (indentureship in only few of the countries), most of the region's nation states are highly populated by Afro-Caribbeans. The examples used in this book are taken mainly from the English-speaking or Anglophone countries sometimes referred to as the 'West Indies'. This includes: Anguilla, Antigua and Barbuda, The Bahamas, Barbados, Belize, British Virgin Islands,

Cayman Islands, Dominica, Grenada, Guyana, Jamaica, Montserrat, St Kitts and Nevis, St Lucia, St Vincent and the Grenadines, Trinidad and Tobago and the Turks and Caicos Islands.

World Bank estimates indicate that on a global level, extreme poverty rates have been almost halved in the last decade, moving from 43.1 per cent in 1990 to 20.6 per cent in 2010. While fewer people live in extreme poverty, measured as the proportion of the population living on less than US$1.25 a day, hunger and poverty still persist. Approximately, half of the world's population – three billion people – lives on less than US$2.50 a day. Moreover, 2010 estimates from the United Nations Food and Agriculture Organization (FAO) show that 925 million people were hungry, most of whom live in Asia, the Pacific, and in sub-Saharan Africa. In the Latin America and Caribbean region, poverty rates and people suffering from hunger are not as large as in other regions of the world (figure 1.1).

Hunger and poverty are not as high in the Caribbean mainly because the region continues to benefit from slow economic growth. Although each country has different populations and geographical land masses, with few exceptions, their economies rely on similar income generating activities (table 1.1).

*Figure 1.1: Number of People (in Millions) Hungry by Region*

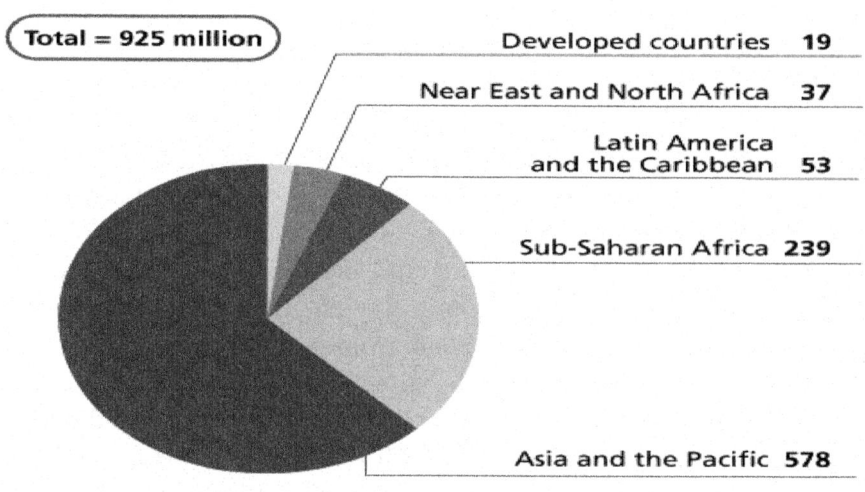

| Total = 925 million | |
| --- | --- |
| Developed countries | 19 |
| Near East and North Africa | 37 |
| Latin America and the Caribbean | 53 |
| Sub-Saharan Africa | 239 |
| Asia and the Pacific | 578 |

*Source:* FAO.

The Caribbean Centre for Money and Finance 2013 Report showed that the economies of Barbados, Jamaica, and Trinidad and Tobago grew between 0.1 and 1.2 per cent and in The Bahamas and Haiti between 2.5 and three per cent. The growth rate for Belize, Guyana and Suriname was even stronger as these countries experienced economic growth rates ranging from 4.5 to 5.3 per cent. Economic growth is also reflected in the countries' gross domestic product (GDP) shown in table 1.2. Although the Caribbean is experiencing slow but sustained economic growth, and reports of hunger are not as drastic as sub-Saharan Africa, Asia, and the Pacific, the Caribbean still has concerning levels of poverty and reports of high levels of crime and other social ills associated with poverty and social inequality.

*Table 1.1: Characteristics of Caribbean Countries: Population, Total Area and Type of Economy*

| Country | Population | Total Area (km2) | Type of Economy |
| --- | --- | --- | --- |
| Anguilla | 15,358 | 91 | Tourism |
| Antigua and Barbuda | 88,710 | 443 | Tourism |
| The Bahamas | 342,877 | 13,940 | Tourism |
| Barbados | 273,331 | 430 | Tourism |
| Belize | 307,000 | 22,966 | Agricultural Products, Oil |
| Dominica | 67,757 | 751 | Tourism |
| Grenada | 104,487 | 344 | Tourism |
| Guyana | 754,493 | 214,970 | Export Goods Export, Tourism |
| Jamaica | 2,741,052 | 10,991 | Export Goods, Tourism |
| Montserrat | 5,934 | 40 | Tourism |
| St Kitts and Nevis | 52,402 | 260 | Tourism |
| St Lucia | 174,267 | 617 | Tourism |
| St Vincent/ Grenadines | 109,333 | 389 | Tourism |
| Suriname | 524,636 | 163,270 | Energy, Bauxite/Alumina |
| Trinidad and Tobago | 1,341,465 | 5,130 | Energy |

*Source: ECLAC (2012, 8)*

Table 1.2: Percentage Real GDP Growth Projections (2015)

| Country | GDP % |
|---|---|
| Antigua and Barbuda | 1.7 |
| The Bahamas | 2.1 |
| Barbados | 0.5 |
| Belize | - |
| Dominica | 1.2 |
| Grenada | 1.2 |
| Guyana | 3.8 |
| Haiti | 3.7 |
| Jamaica | 1.8 |
| St Kitts and Nevis | 3.2 |
| St Lucia | 1.4 |
| St Vincent and the Grenadines | 2.6 |
| Suriname | - |
| Trinidad and Tobago | 2.1 |

Source: Western Hemisphere Dept. Table 1, Main Economic Report (2014)

## Poverty Rates and Indigence

For Latin America and the Caribbean region, the current poverty and indigence rates are the lowest they have been in the last three decades, but are still disturbing. The United Nations Economic Commission for Latin America and the Caribbean (ECLAC 2011) estimated that, by 2012, a little over 160 million people will be living under the poverty line, a million less than in 2011. However, no change is anticipated for the 66 million who were living in dire poverty. These figures are startling, although they are relatively lower when compared to some countries in the Far East and Africa.

As part of the Caribbean region's effort to strategize for poverty reduction, the Caribbean Development Bank (CDB) implemented a programme of support and contracted Country Poverty Assessments (CPA) for each Caribbean territory, beginning in 1995. These were organized in collaboration with the governments of the Caribbean and several international agencies, including the Canadian International Development Agency (CIDA), the Department for International Development (DFID) and the United Nations for Development Programme (UNDP). They serve as the main source of information on levels of poverty and indigence for the various countries (table 1.3).

Indigence rates represent the percentage of individuals who live below the indigence line[1] while the headcount index is the percentage of individuals who live below the poverty line.[2] The indigence rate is comparable over time as it is a measure of absolute poverty based solely on nutritional intake. However, although the headcount index (or poverty rate) cannot strictly be compared across time and across countries, it is often used to compare how countries are performing relative to their neighbours, and how they themselves are performing over time.

Overall, more than 20 per cent of the populations in most of the Caribbean countries live below the poverty line.[3] The Cayman Islands, Anguilla and Barbados have the lowest poverty rates, while countries such as Belize, Dominica, Grenada, Guyana, Montserrat, St Lucia and St Vincent and the Grenadines have poverty rates between 25 and 40 per cent. Despite the fact that poverty rates are high, levels of indigence are mostly low with the exception of Belize, Grenada and Guyana. Haiti is at the high end of the spectrum with 78 per cent of the population living below the poverty line, and 54 per cent in situations of extreme poverty.

*Table 1.3: Indigence Rate and Headcount Index of Selected Caribbean Countries*

| Country | Year Study Conducted | Indigence rate (% of poor) | Head Count Index (% population) |
|---|---|---|---|
| Antigua and Barbuda | 2005/06 | 3.7 | 18.3 |
| Barbados | 2010 | 3.2 | 19.3 |
| Belize | 2009/10 | 15.8 | 41.3 |
| Dominica | 2008/2009 | 3.1 | 28.8 |
| Grenada | 2007/08 | 12.4 | 37.7 |
| Guyana | 1999 | 19.0 | 35.0 |
| *Haiti | 2005 | 54.0 | 78.0 |
| *Jamaica | 2010 | --- | 17.6 |
| Montserrat | 2009/12 | 3.0 | 36.0 |
| Saint. Kitts and Nevis | 2007/08 | 1.0 | 21.8 |
| Saint. Lucia | 2005 | 1.6 | 28.8 |
| Saint. Vincent and the Grenadines | 2007/08 | 2.9 | 30.2 |
| **Trinidad and Tobago | 2005 | 1.2 | 16.7 |
| | 2011 | --- | 21.8 |

*Source: Country Poverty Assessments, published by the Caribbean Development Bank.*
*\*Worldbank.org/data.*
*\*\* Survey of Living Conditions (2005), conducted by the Kairi Consultants (2007)/CSO, Trinidad and Tobago and 2011 Household Budget Survey, CSO, Trinidad and Tobago.*

In some countries, poverty rates worsened because of severe, external economic shocks and natural hazard occurrences, but in many cases, poverty declined slightly in the last two decades. Usually, when poverty rates rise so too do the indigence levels; however, in some cases, such as in Grenada, the impact of natural disasters resulted in an increase in the poverty level from 32.1 per cent in 1999 to 37.7 per cent in 2007/08, but the indigence rates fell. Equally interesting is that Trinidad and Tobago, which is classified as a more developed country, has a relatively close comparative poverty rate to some of the less developed countries although, overall, its poverty rate and indigence is lower than many of its neighbours.

The fact that the number of people living below the poverty line in Trinidad and Tobago increased to 21.8 per cent in 2011 is clear evidence that economic progress does not always impact positively on poverty levels and the percentages of households living below the abject poverty level. But how does this translate to the realities of the people who live there? Why in spite of the progress and growing optimism, does poverty and extreme poverty persists? Of greater importance, the region is being noted as one of the most inequitable in the world, where economic turbulence and shortage of quality jobs make it difficult for working people to improve their standard of living or get out of poverty. For those who experience extreme poverty, pulling themselves up by the boot strap is not an option. Years of being trapped in a cycle have given rise to multi-generational poverty in families, households and communities who do not have boots or bootstraps to pull and lift them out of poverty.

With respect to the Anglophone Caribbean, estimates of income disparity are based on old data, with much variation in the years that the poverty studies were conducted. However, the data that does exist reveal that the degree of inequality based on income distribution is relatively high. The Gini coefficient ranges from 0.23 in the British Virgin Islands to 0.56 in St Vincent and the Grenadines. Table 1.4 highlights the income inequality in the region, with half of the listed countries having Gini Coefficients in excess of 0.40. These include Guyana, Trinidad and Tobago, Grenada, Belize and St Vincent and the Grenadines. In other words, while most Caribbean countries have economic growth and small reductions in poverty rates, the wealth and/ or income distribution between the rich and poor is wide. Similar patterns occur in both the more developed countries (MDC) and the less developed countries (LDC).

*Table 1.4: Estimates of Gini Coefficient by Selected Country and Year*

| Country | Year Conducted | Gini Coefficient |
|---|---|---|
| **MDCs*** | | |
| Guyana | 1999 | Not available |
| Barbados | 1997 | 0.39 |
| Jamaica | 2001 | 0.38 |
| Trinidad and Tobago | 1992 | 0.42 |
| **LDCs*** | | |
| Anguilla | 2002 | 0.31 |
| Belize | 1996 | 0.51 |
| British Virgin Islands | 2002 | 0.23 |
| Turks and Caicos Islands | 1999 | 0.37 |
| **OECS*** | | |
| Comm. of Dominica | 2002 | 0.35 |
| Grenada | 1999 | 0.45 |
| St Kitts | 2000 | 0.40 |
| Nevis | 2000 | 0.37 |
| St Lucia | 1995 | 0.50 |
| St Vincent and the Grenadines | 1995 | 0.56 |

*MDC refers to More Developed Countries

*LDC – Less Developed Country

*OECS – Organization of Eastern Caribbean States

Source: Thomas and Wint (2002)

The Gini coefficient or income inequality is better reflected in the living conditions of people rather than on a statistical number. For example, we see it in the housing conditions and settlement patterns throughout the Caribbean. Communities are often segregated by social class (and security walls and gates), but because of the small geographical space of most Caribbean countries, the housing settlements of the rich and the poor are often next to each other. Nevertheless, the services and infrastructures, including access to food, employment, water, schools, health and recreational facilities are glaringly disparate.

## What Does Poverty Look Like?

Most travellers to the Caribbean enjoy the many beautiful sceneries, blue skies, white sand and emerald-coloured seas. Some may even drive through the rustic neighbourhoods that border the grand hotels. In the larger territories like Jamaica, having a second airport on the north coast so that tourists and other visitors do not have to experience the capital city and other towns is convenient. The all inclusive packages ensure that foreigners are safe and warned not to leave the compound of the hotels and traverse among the 'locals'. They remain unaware that the picturesque Caribbean landscape is also scattered with a number of homeless people and food scavengers, including children. Domestic violence, child abuse, crime and violence, including gang activities and drug cartels, teenage pregnancies and HIV/AIDS are all on the rise. Many of these social ills are found within the growing length of unkempt, run-down, garbage-lined neighbourhoods that have become part of both the rural and urban Caribbean scenery – the other side of paradise.

People live in badly maintained housing, constructed with wood, or a combination of wood and concrete in *poor communities*. They may have access to electricity but lack sanitation, sewage systems and access to potable water. Roadways are filled with 'pot-holes' and have no sidewalks or farm roads. Rivers and drains are too small and badly kept, or are absent. Consequently, periodic torrential rains easily results in flash flooding, property loss, increased disposition to diseases and sometimes loss of life. Basic amenities, including public toilets and bathrooms, are in deplorable conditions or non-existent. Similarly, recreational facilities, including play grounds are unkempt or missing.

> Sliver Lake is a slum.
> The houses look like fowl cages.
> The galvanize when you look up you seeing heaven...
> The destitute, and the 'paros', drug users and abusers sleep on the side-walk.
> There are no public conveniences here and there are some families without toilets
>
> (CPA, Dominica 2008/09, 20–21).

Community Centres are dilapidated, if they exist. There is usually an elementary school but no public kindergarten or secondary school. Health facilities for families are not present, or offer very limiting services. In rural communities, the sick and injured cannot afford the transportation to access health amenities located in the small towns. Like many of the urban dwellers, they also do not have the income to pay for medical attention and/or supplies.

The incidence of extreme poverty in the region is more pronounced in the countryside than in urban locations. It remains a rural phenomenon although there is increasing migration of poor and unemployed rural residents to urban centres or overseas, in search of jobs. Those who stay continue to rely on farming mainly at subsistence production levels on small family farms. They suffer from the stress of not having access to land, credit, markets, affordable transportation, proper farm access roads, agricultural technology, and other support services that are important in moving their production from subsistence to commercial operations. They produce just enough to help feed their families and live on the cusp of poverty or indigence.

Over the last decade, the economies of rural communities and households have been devastated because of the decline in agriculture and the removal of protected markets for the two main export products, sugar and bananas. As a result, income generation from farming has diminished, families can no longer support their children's education, maintain or improve their homes, purchase vehicles or pay for health services and medicines.

What has occurred is abominable, as many of the women, men and families who were once independent and taking care of their families have become increasingly dependent on state assistance. The absence of alternative economic opportunities has resulted in the destitution of families and the withering away of many rural villages. The Windward Islands, St Kitts and Nevis, Belize, and Guyana were most affected by the new trade arrangements that eroded Caribbean agriculture. In many communities, entire families have 'pad-locked' their homes, left their villages and have gone elsewhere in search of work.

> The east of Dominica is now one of the poorest parts of the country. Residents report on the collapse of banana production and what this has accounted for poverty in large swathes of the rural communities... Poverty is reflected in decrepitude in rural communities and growing hopelessness (CPA, Dominica 2008/09, 140).

Rural and farming communities also face the wrath of the natural elements. Hurricanes, heavy rains, floods and mud slides have destroyed crops and livestock, and demolished homes and villages. Moreover, the poor are often allotted the worse lands because of skewed landownership policies and practices that favour government or private ownership. They have no insurance for their farms and are excluded from decisions on prevention strategies.

*Box 1.1: Case Study of Banana Farmers in Dominica (2009)*

The Windward Island Banana Industry for many years provided a direct income for thousands of small-scale producers and agricultural labourers. Up to 1992, the industry accounted for about 69 per cent of all exports and employed 60 per cent of agricultural workers. Rodriguez, Woolley and Lacher (2008) report that the Banana Trade accounted for about 50 per cent of all of the Windward Island Revenue, and 60 per cent of all Dominican exports. These figures indicate that the banana industry is critical to the economy of Dominica, where more than 30 per cent of the population lives below the poverty line.
*Source: CPA, Dominica (2008/09)*

The 1980s are identified both in the literature as well as by the farmers interviewed, as the period when income earned from the banana industry was at the highest. Monies earned sustained and educated families, improved housing and the standard of living for rural households. Many of the farmers interviewed spoke about the late '80s–'90s when income earned from banana sales was used to improve the dwellings of their families or build new ones. They described how they converted their wooden structured homes to brick exterior houses with galvanize roofs, added bedrooms, and moved from using pit latrines to indoor plumbing...'fig make them have what they have today.' Many also added basic amenities such as electricity and telephones. One male farmer happily reported that in addition to making similar improvements to his home he was also able to purchase a vehicle, his pride and joy in life, which he unfortunately had to sell in hard times. Years of a successful Banana Industry also supported the growth and development of small rural villages and towns.
*Source: Author's interviews with banana farmers, Dominica (2009)*

Further, there are few social investments in the small rural villages and towns. Thus, rural folk and their communities are vulnerable to both human and nature's interface, and life in rural spaces remains a challenge.

> Ivan mash up the whole house and everything in it. We rebuilding it piece by piece with help (CPA Grenada, Carriacou and Petit Martinique 2007/08, 16).

> The devastations of hurricanes Ivan (2004) and Emily (2005) on the agricultural sector further retarded in its contribution to livelihoods of large numbers (CPA Grenada, Carriacou and Petit Martinique 2007/08, xxxi).

The combined effect of natural disasters and market calamities has forced many villagers to move into temporary settlements in nearby towns and cities, resulting in the burgeoning of urban poverty. Approximately 55 per cent of the

Caribbean population can now be classified as urban, with an annual growth rate of 1.5 per cent. While rural poor communities are tucked away from the rest of the country, urban poverty is stark and noticeable. People live in concentrated and small spaces causing problems of overcrowding that stress the physical and social infrastructure. As a result, there is poor sanitation, housing shortages, and an overall corrosion of city neighbourhoods.

> There exists a network of narrow unpaved alleyways in which there are small and sometimes dilapidated one- or two- room houses with little space between them. Most of the houses do not have electricity or running water, and while a few may have outdoor toilets, several have no toilet at all. The public bathroom is therefore used by many of the residents (CPA, Antigua and Barbuda 2007, 11).

Most urban dwellers rely on wage employment for their livelihoods, as demand supersedes opportunities, unemployment increases, more youth are found 'rambling', young women are preyed upon and forced into prostitution, and juvenile delinquency, drug use, adult crime, and violence are augmented.

The same demographic trends in household and group poverty rates observed worldwide are also observed in the Caribbean region. At the *household level*, poverty is usually a multigenerational experience. Family sizes are larger than average.

> My family was always poor.
> My family was poor; there were ten children.
> The poverty pass down from the older generation (CPA, Antigua and Barbuda 2007, 45).

Many poor households are headed by single females with children, many of whom do not earn enough to support a decent standard of living for their families. Few receive adequate financial support from the fathers of their children.

At the *group level*, poverty rates tend to be highest among the indigenous people, particularly in Belize and Guyana, where roughly 70 per cent are classified as poor. There, these populations do not only suffer from higher rates of poverty but also experience landlessness, malnutrition, and internal displacement more than any other group in society. They have lower levels of literacy, less access to health care services, lower life expectancy and higher rates of infant mortality and deaths of women during childbirth than the average of the country in which they live. They are disproportionately found in rural communities, isolated, and socially excluded. Women and children are always the most affected among all groups of people.

## Women and Gender Inequality

In the Caribbean, the status of women at a glance looks much better than women in other parts of the world. They have higher participation rates in the economy, and enrollment rates for girls in secondary schools and universities are also superior to that of boys. Additionally, representation in parliament and other levels of government has slowly increased. Sadly, these developments have not, however, improved their status in the labour markets and society as a whole. They continue to suffer from a series of interlocking forms of discrimination that puts them at a disadvantage in accessing productive resources and making social progress at the same rate of men.

*Table 1.5: Gender and Human Development Index for Selected Caribbean Countries (2012)*

| Country | GII | HDI | Human Development Index Rank |
|---|---|---|---|
| Antigua & Barbuda | – | 0.76 | 67 |
| The Bahamas | 0.32 | 0.79 | 49 |
| Barbados | 0.34 | 0.83 | 38 |
| Belize | 0.44 | 0.70 | 96 |
| Dominica | – | 0.75 | 72 |
| Grenada | – | 0.77 | 63 |
| Guyana | 0.49 | 0.64 | 118 |
| Jamaica | 0.46 | 0.73 | 85 |
| Haiti | 0.59 | 0.46 | 161 |
| Saint Kitts & Nevis | – | 0.75 | 72 |
| Saint Lucia | – | 0.73 | 88 |
| Saint Vincent & the Grenadines | – | 0.73 | 83 |
| Trinidad & Tobago | 0.31 | 0.76 | 67 |

*Source: UNDP (2013)*

Comparative social progress is measured using a Gender Inequality Index (GII) that assesses differences in the distribution of achievements between women and men in three dimensions: (i) labour market participation; (ii) empowerment gauged by the share of parliamentary seats by sex and attainment of secondary school or higher; and (iii) reproductive health assessed by maternal mortality ratio and adolescent fertility rate. The GII for the Caribbean shows that gender inequality varies greatly across the different countries (see table 1.5).[4] It ranges from 0.3 to 0.6 with most of the territories having a score of over 0.4, which means that there is a high gender disparity in health factors, employment, and political representation in the Caribbean.

Women are almost half as likely to experience achievements in these areas, compared with men. Further, in three countries, Guyana, Jamaica and Haiti, the GIIs are higher than the world's average of 0.46. The data from table 1.5 also show that the better the Human Development Index, the more equitable the gender achievement, but not in all cases. For example, Jamaica has a higher HDI compared to Haiti and Guyana, but its GII (0.46) is very close to that of the two less developed countries (0.59 and 0.49 respectively).

Equally disappointing is the fact that for many of the smaller territories, there are no recent GII measures to assess the gaps between women and men, or the ramifications of such disparities. GIIs are good indicators of potential human development loss due to gender discrimination. The focus on gender disparity in labour market participation, higher education, politics and health are all important in understanding poverty in households of all types. A focus on gender inequality redirects the attention away from household composition and family structures, to gender discrimination in the formal labour market and at all levels of society. It also draws attention to the role that patriarchy still plays in Caribbean societies and homes. The data on the Caribbean suggests that despite the progress made by women there are still barriers that are contributing to why women are not making personal developmental progress that can remove their subordinate status when compared to men, and allow them to adequately support themselves and provide for their families.

## Human Development

As a whole, the region boasts of good human development standards particularly, in education and health. Most individuals have up to a primary school level education and literacy rates in the Caribbean are higher than the world's average of 84.1 per cent. It ranges from 98.5 per cent in Trinidad and Tobago to a low of 76.9 per cent in Belize, and 52.9 per cent in Haiti. Life expectancy has also improved immensely moving from age 57 in the 1960s to the '70s in the twenty-first century. Similar progress is observed where, for instance, infant mortality rates, maternal deaths at birth and fertility rates have all fallen (see table 1.6 below).

*Table 1.6: Human Development Indicators in Selected*
*Caribbean Countries (2010)*

| Country | GDP per capita (2005 PPP $) | Life Expectancy at birth (years) | Infant mortality Rate (per 1000 live births) | Maternal Mortality (deaths of women per 100,000 live births) |
|---|---|---|---|---|
| Antigua and Barbuda | 14,904 | 72.5 | 7.0 | – |
| The Bahamas | 28,135 | 75.4 | 14.0 | 47 |
| Barbados | – | 76.7 | 17.0 | 51 |
| Belize | 5,980 | 75.9 | 14.0 | 53 |
| Dominica | 10,989 | 77.4 | 11.0 | – |
| Grenada | 9,735 | 75.8 | 9.0 | 24 |
| Guyana | 3,104 | 69.6 | 25.0 | 280 |
| Jamaica | 7,001 | 72.9 | 20.0 | 110 |
| Haiti | 992 | 61.8 | 70.0 | 350 |
| St Kitts and Nevis | 13,468 | 72.9 | 7.0 | – |
| St Lucia | 8,268 | 74.5 | 14.0 | 35 |
| St Vincent and the Grenadines | 9,482 | 72.0 | 19.0 | 48 |
| Trinidad and Tobago | 23,168 | 69.9 | 24.0 | 46 |

*Source: UNDP (2013)*

The most recent statistics show that there are variations in health indicators within and among Caribbean countries. These differences are in some cases very glaringly gender oriented. For example, the life expectancy, infant mortality and maternal mortality rates at birth for Guyana and Belize are much graver than in most of the other Caribbean territories. On the other hand, Antigua and Barbuda, St Kitts and Nevis have high life expectancies, which are positive indicators of good health, but deaths of women at live birth are still unacceptably high.

One would expect that the higher a country's GDP per capita, often considered a good indicator of a country's standard of living, the better the human condition. However, while poverty rates have a strong effect on life expectancy and infant and maternal mortality, a country's GDP does not necessarily have the same effect. For instance, Trinidad and Tobago presents an intriguing case in that it has one of the highest GDP, but its maternal mortality and infant death at birth are higher than some of its neighbours. The life expectancy in Trinidad and Tobago is also lower than other less developed Caribbean territories, except for Haiti and Guyana. While a high GDP does not always translate into better human development or poverty rates, low GDPs usually render high rates of poverty and lower levels of well being.

## Theorizing on Causations

There are several perspectives and speculations as to why poverty exists and persists in the Caribbean. These explanations are not founded in the cultural discourse common in North America and are discussed in chapter four. Instead, they are located in the political economy debates of the region and other developing countries. Historically, poverty has been linked to colonization and/or global capitalism by theorists such as Andre Gunder Frank, from Latin America. Gunder Frank (1966, 1967), argued that characteristics of poverty and underdevelopment are direct outcomes of world capitalism. He further suggested that poverty will persist until the peoples of Latin America and other developing countries free themselves from world capitalism through radical means.

Later, Caribbean scholar George Beckford (1972) made a parallel argument. He employed historicity to examine the political economy of the plantation system in the Caribbean, Latin America, Asia, the southern US, and parts of West Africa. He observed that while the plantation system transformed underdeveloped countries to moneyed economies and introduced modern systems of transportation, amenities and facilities, at the same time, it kept the colonies undeveloped and on the margins of the world economy. Beckford noted that despite years of participating in a modern world, gaining independence and building modern infrastructure and services, the vast majority of people in plantation economies were still living in wretched conditions, while those in the North Atlantic enjoyed high levels of material comforts. This led him to deduce that the fortunes of people living in developed countries were directly linked to the misfortunes and poor welfare of those in underdeveloped countries.

The common thread in the arguments of Caribbean and anti-colonial scholars, such as George Beckford (1972), Walter Rodney (1974), and Andre Gunder Frank (1966, 1967), is the belief that the difficulties of the poor worldwide stems from having no control over the resources of their countries. This includes shaping their use to promote greater equity and food security. According to these critical thinkers, developed countries, by extracting raw materials and labour from undeveloped countries, create a dependency in which the economies of developing societies must rely on metropolitan countries for trade, banking, financial intermediation, processing of raw materials, technological innovation and policy formulation – all of which contribute to the further underdevelopment of undeveloped economies. Such relationships, Beckford thought, were dehumanizing and proposed that material advancement could only be satisfactory if it preserves the quality of life that people regard as important, and that 'all people wish to be independent' (xvii).

Similar analyses are found in the twenty-first century with more contemporary scholars on poverty. For example, Nobel Prize winner, Amartya Sen, in *Inequality Reexamined* (1992) addressed the issue of egalitarianism within societies and claimed that material resources cannot be treated in the same as freedom; poverty persists because of systematic patterns of intense inequality. Although Sen's analyses was at a different level from Beckford's, he too linked poverty to freedom and acknowledged that rigid patterns of social stratifications occur across race and skin colour (among other variables) that inhibit social mobility and limit participation in political economy decisions.

In 1995, a Caribbean symposium on Social Policy and Research Issues was organized by the region's governments as a concerted effort to once more interrogate issues of economic growth, social development and poverty. At the symposium, economist Norman Girvan presented an analysis and an assessment of Caribbean poverty and spoke about governments needing to focus on the capability of individuals and groups in society, as a way of addressing inequality and poverty similar to Amartya Sen's thesis. He also highlighted the need for governments to lobby for more equitable trade arrangements in the global market, as was argued before by protagonists such as Beckford (1972), Rodney (1974), and Gunder Frank (1966,1967). Girvan was critical of the structural adjustment policies (SAPs) of the World Bank and warned of the sacrifices that were made for what he calls 'short-term demands for economic stabilization'. He suggested that the problem lay in the development strategies and policies that separated social development from economic growth and poverty.

Girvan (1997) later explored his theses using poverty statistics on the Caribbean where he observed two consistent features of Caribbean poverty common to all the countries, but not reflected in the poverty statistics. That is, there was a steady increase of the 'working poor' in urban settings, and a rise in the number of landless rural poor. From these findings, Girvan further substantiated his claim that economic growth and social development cannot be accurately assessed by simply using data on employment figures. The premise of his argument was that, unlike the plantation labour needs, contemporary labour markets require skilled individuals who can earn the income necessary to keep a household above the poverty line. Instead, Caribbean societies today have layers of unskilled workers, who must engage in several different jobs simultaneously, because the income in any one job cannot support a family. Equally important, is that in many cases the collective incomes from several jobs cannot remove that household from indigence or improve the standard of living of the family so that they can subsist above the poverty line. This group of workers is usually employed in the informal economy as casual labour, and is not always part of the official labour market statistics. As such, they are recorded as being unemployed when in reality they are part of a 'working poor' group that continues to expand.

Interestingly, women have always had this same experience since their presence in Caribbean societies. The conditions created under more recent macroeconomic strategies have since broadened this pool to include more working men who now along with working women hold several consecutive jobs in both the informal and formal economies. Based on this state of affairs Girvan (1997) makes a similar recommendation to Sen (1992), that is, for governments to prioritize capacity building as part of poverty reduction and economic growth efforts. However, Girvan warns that economic growth may not necessarily translate to a drastic reduction of poverty and indigence, but to a burgeoning class of 'working poor' and identifies yet another emergent poverty stricken group – the 'new poor'.[5] This group is birthed from rising inflation, cutbacks in social assistance, and increased unemployment and underemployment, as a result of fiscal constraints and structural adjustments that highly indebted governments were forced to employ.

These observations and recommendations are made with the understanding that access and lack of access to resources and opportunities are based on the social stratification of society by race/ethnicity, social class, residency and gender. As such, gender development programmes should also aim at improving the capacity of women equal to that of men as part of gender equity and poverty reduction strategies. Indeed, the Caribbean has experienced increasing fiscal deficits, rising debt and debt servicing costs that have added to the economic problems faced by the region in the last decade (figure 1.2).

According to the International Monetary Fund (IMF), in 2011, five of the 13 most indebted countries in the world were located in the Caribbean. Moreover, the Caribbean debt problem is intensified by the persistence of unequal power in the global export markets which has given rise to the build-up of trade deficits and the consistent need to borrow externally to finance the importation of food and other consumer items. As a result, fiscal consolidation, in some cases under IMF's structural adjustment policies (SAPs), has aggravated the situation and made the burden even heavier for working families, particularly women and female-headed households.

*Figure 1.2: Economic Growth (GDP) and Public Debt of Selected Caribbean Countries*

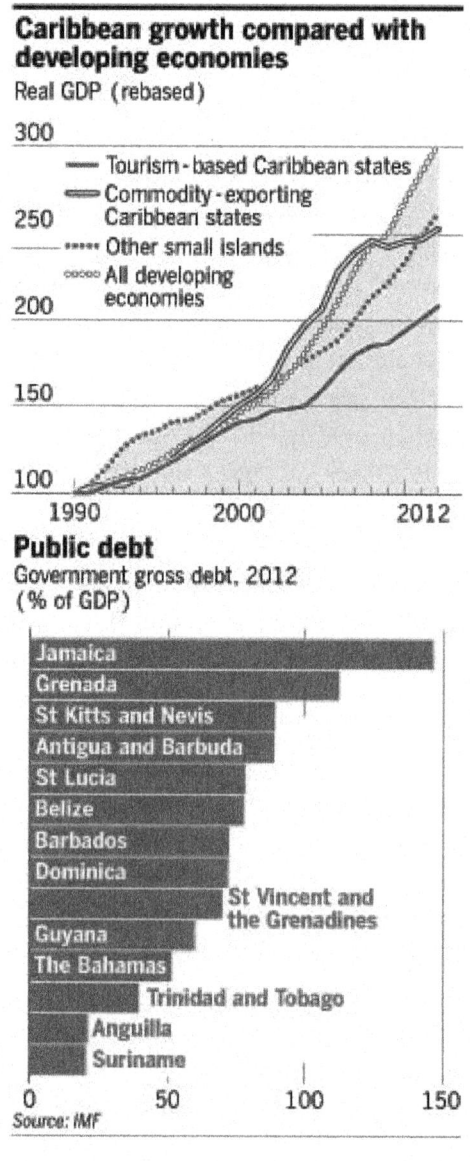

*Box 1.2: Grenada and the IMF*

In Grenada, aid from the World Bank resulted in high levels of unemployment when all government-owned enterprises were divested and social programmes discontinued. In addition, the removal of subsidies on basic food items and other goods and services combined with the devaluation of the Grenadian currency placed items in the food basket out of the price range of the poor. Overall, families who previously could afford basic food and social amenities now struggled and some were unable to survive above the poverty line falling.
Source: *(Payer 1975, 32–33)*

In general, SAPs and other initiatives of the IMF and World Bank have not reduced poverty, stabilized economies, or improved the standard of living anywhere as promised. The numerous multilateral Free Trade Agreements that parallel attempts to stabilize the economies of developing countries appear to have benefited others from the failures of the SAPs in these countries. One might even say that they have exploited the weak positions and state of dependency of these countries. The negative consequences of SAPs can be observed in all developing countries, including those in the Caribbean that were forced to go to the IMF.

As a whole, the Draconian domestic adjustments of SAPs and the disadvantages experienced in the open markets, resulted in a widening of the poverty net in many developing countries, including those in the Caribbean. In a sense, the structure and consequences of contemporary economic and trade policies, many of which emanate from the Washington Consensus (WC) of North America, closely resembles those of the Plantation Economy Model. According to Susan George (2007, 7):

> We seem to have come full circle...as in most developing countries the evidence shows that economic growth has slowed, inequalities have worsened and not only does poverty persist, but has deepened.

In 2002, at the Eastern Caribbean Central Bank's Seventh Annual Development Conference, Dr Juliet A. Melville, the Chief Research Economist with the CDB, presented a paper, 'The Impact of Structural Adjustment on the Poor'. Her presentation focused on the Eastern Caribbean territories and raised issues that mirror the conversation that Beckford introduced in the 1970s on the role of the Plantation System in underdevelopment and persistent poverty. Melville (2002) questioned whether current economic models linked to structural adjustment measures can lead to economic growth, and a reduction in poverty and inequality? Melville answered her own research question by using the evidence she found to show that structural adjustment resulted in slow growth, no growth, or growth rates below that of the pre-adjustment period for many Caribbean states.

Additionally, in some countries where there was economic growth, income inequality also grew as income was redistributed away from labour to capital, and the wage differential between skilled and unskilled workers widened. The analyses of the Caribbean data by Melville (2002) concurs with that of Girvan (1997), that is, economic growth that occurs under structural adjustment is not a good indicator of poverty reduction because it does not take into consideration social inequality and gender inequities, neither does it include the upsurge in the number of 'working poor' or 'new poor'.

## Poverty Reduction Strategies

Many scathing criticisms of the IMF and its SAPs eventually led the World Bank (WB) to respond by establishing Poverty Reduction Strategies along with SAPs. The fact that developing countries were still underperforming led the WB and the IMF to conclude that the SAPs were not 'bad policies', but that there was 'bad' implementation by the various countries. The WB also aligned itself with the UN Millennium Development Goals (MDGs), while maintaining its focus on balancing external debts and trade deficits. These two adjustments led to the development of Pro-Poor Policies by the Bank centred on: (i) good governance, democracy and human rights; (ii) gender equality; and (iii) sustainable development through supporting economic growth in rural sectors and improving environmental stability.[6]

It is doubtful whether the poverty reduction strategies once implemented along with the SAPs and other conditionalities of the International Financial Institutions (IFIs) will help, or continue to stunt domestic development. Furthermore, following in the perspectives of Beckford, Sen and others, it seems that the current macroeconomic policies and world trade systems ensure unequal terms of trade, unfavourable terms of foreign investment, and trade that is endemic to underdevelopment, hunger and poverty in developing countries. They put the economic sovereignty of nation states in the Caribbean and elsewhere at risk, and the freedom that Beckford (1972), Sen (1992) and others reference, in jeopardy.

> Debt is an efficient tool. It ensures access to other peoples' raw materials and infrastructure on the cheapest possible terms. Dozens of countries must compete for shrinking export markets and can export only a limited range of products because of Northern protectionism and their lack

of cash to invest in diversification. Market saturation ensues, reducing exporters' income to a bare minimum while the North enjoys huge savings (George 1990, 143).

It appears that the old plantation system and its modus operandi are now replaced by new forms, in which wealth and poverty continue to be determined by the relationship between the debtor (developing nations) and the creditor (the metropolis and the IFIs such as the World Bank). Consequently, the poor living conditions of so many households remain unabated, further removing the individual from adequate health care, education and access to quality employment. Thus, over time, intergenerational poverty in families, households and communities perseveres and is observed in many female-headed households.

**Poverty Across the Generations: Like Mother Like Daughter:**

Intergenerational poverty is sustained by structural inequality that excludes persons from accessing resources they need to develop their human potential. In the case of Gloria's family this is evident by the fact that she inherited her poverty from her mother (who in all likelihood inherited it from hers) (CPA, Dominica 2008/09, 212).

Caribbean governments have also responded to the economic and social situations in the region by developing national strategies for poverty reduction and meeting the UN Millennium Development Goals (MDGs). Some proposals are specific while others are unifying strategies across the countries in the region. The proposals and strategies can be grouped into two distinct categories: transformative and ameliorative. According to Ralph Henry and Alicia Mondesire (1997), the first category is long-term and involves social and economic transformation, some of which are listed in the MDGs. The second is aimed at temporary relief through safety-net measures and access to social services that are aimed at the physical survival of poor families. The two categories are not mutually exclusive, but work together so that the same clientele in need of ameliorative measures can later benefit from the more transformative strategies.

Although poverty alleviation strategies have been adopted by all the governments in the region, some leaders are more proactive and vociferous than others. For example, in 2009, the President of Guyana, Bharrat Jagdeo, was quoted in *Abeng Magazine* as saying that the region was declining into further poverty and called on leaders to:

Stem the slide of this social scourge in a region where upwards of 50 million people live in squalor, lack the basic social services, and suffer from hunger and access to food (Soares 2009).

*Box 1.3: The Millennium Development Goals (MDGs)*

In 2000, 147 heads of state and government together with 42 ministers and heads of delegations gathered at a UN meeting agreed to 8 Millennium Development Goals focused on (i) eradicating hunger, (ii) universal primary education, (iii) health (reduced child mortality, (iv) improved maternal health, (v) combat HIV AIDS and malaria), (vi) gender equality and empowerment, (vii) environment sustainability, and (viii) establish global partnership for development.
*Source: (ECLAC 2005)*

Moreover, the social problems that have ensued primarily because of the widening gap between the rich and poor and between women and men, have prompted Caribbean governments to be among the 147 countries which agreed that poverty reduction should be the first of the eight MDGs. Specifically, the goal is to *eradicate extreme poverty and hunger.* The two issues are related but because of their importance are treated as separate targets.

To eradicate hunger, ECLAC (2005) suggested that efforts be directed to three separate but integrated areas that collectively address issues of food availability, access, stability and utilization. With regards to eradicating indigence, the set target is to reduce by one-half the total number of people living on less than US$1 a day, by the year 2015.[7] However, to reach this goal, the rates at which per capita GDP will have to grow are approximately 2.9 per cent per annum for most countries and 4.4 per cent for poorer countries. Equity will also have to grow and will require institutional and policy changes. Additionally, efforts must be made to reduce poverty and hunger in the short run through social programmes (health, education, monetary transfers), especially for children and women and state resources must be used efficiently with transparency and accountability. Also, regional effort must be made to assist the poorest countries in the region and negotiations of the Doha Development Round[8] must be completed so that the region can gain better access to the developed-country markets, especially for agricultural products.

In order to achieve the MDG of eradicating poverty and hunger, governments have also partnered with several regional and international organizations, which have their own poverty reduction strategies. Some of the more active organizations in the Caribbean include: The European Union (EU) and its Poverty Reduction Programme; the International Fund for Agriculture Development (IFAD), whose 2011–2015 strategic framework enables the rural poor to improve their food security and nutrition, raise their incomes and strengthen their resilience; the United Nations Organization for Science and Culture (UNESCO) which advocates for the moral and political imperative to eradicate poverty with a focus on education, peace and security; the World Bank which works with governments to improve livelihoods and access to jobs, social services and infrastructure; the FAO which is focused on food security and sustainable environments; the UNDP which is involved in promoting inclusive and sustainable human development; and the ECLAC which provides estimates on the magnitude of poverty.

In addition, the regional governments continue to work closely with the Caribbean Development Bank (CDB) on several fronts. Earlier it was mentioned that the SLC and CPAs were and continue to be conducted in conjunction with the CDB. Additionally, since its inception in 1979, the CDB's Basic Needs Trust Fund (BNTF) Programme has been contributing to poverty reduction in targeted communities in the Caribbean by providing infrastructure and livelihood enhancement services nationally and regionally. The Programme supports a socially inclusive development process that empowers the poor and vulnerable, and supports institutional development. Community participation is expected for every sub-project to facilitate local ownership of BNTF investments and enhances social capital within each community. The participating countries are mainly from the Anglophone Caribbean (http://www.caribank.org/programmes/basic-needs-trust-fund).

Interestingly, many of the strategies listed above are based on economic well-being (income and market indicators) and social well-being (health, education, mortality, and other social variables). Gender equity and the role of women are stated as separate entities and are left up to chance of being included in the implementation of the other strategies. The BNTF Programme, through its Regional Gender Strategy, integrates gender equality into the project process. The CDB also adopts micro level analyses where it incorporates gender analysis at all levels of project cycles. This allows the conditions of specific groups of men, women, girls and boys to be highlighted and targeted for better development outcomes in programme or project planning.

## Summary and Conclusions

Currently, while economic growth and human development is improving in most of the Caribbean countries, food security, hunger and poverty are still being experienced by large sections of the population. The enjoyment of rich lifestyles is contained in air conditioned, high-end cars and behind gated communities. Just on the other side of the high walls that separate housing settlements, poverty and destitution are found beneath rusting zinc roofs, behind barb-wires fences, and/or tucked away by rural distance. But disparity in lifestyles, wealth and poverty are not just local; it is a worldwide phenomenon with far-reaching tentacles. Neither is the global nature of wealth and poverty new to the region.

The Caribbean has a history of colonial domination where much of its wealth, in the form of raw materials, was transported out to support the rich in metropolitan states. Decades later, the region is depleted and indebted. While it still has the capacity to feed its people and reduce hunger, the food importation bill soars higher every year. Several strategies to curb poverty in the region are in progress with local governments working in tandem with regional and international organizations. However, there is an urgent need to revisit the 'old' and 'new' theories and perspectives on why poverty exists and persists in the region.

The arguments presented in this chapter reaffirm that poverty is a historical legacy and a consequence of the continued greed of local and global capitalism. Currently, nation states are unable to manoeuvre in the open and free markets, and also cannot buy-in. Poverty and the undeveloped needs of women, men and children as human beings exist, not necessarily because of inadequate resources, but because local resources are exploited in the interests of multinational, transnational corporations and local elites. Beckford (1972) and others pointed this out a long time ago, namely that the forces that control the global economy and polity create underdevelopment and poverty through legitimized market forces.

As a result, economic growth is retarded, domestic economies never develop to the level of industrialized countries, loans are needed and structural adjustments recommended. After decades of foreign-designed mandates, there is nowhere in the region that these macroeconomic policies have worked in the interest of Caribbean people. Structural adjustments policies, by any name, have not had a positive economic effect, and the programmes recommended have not 'trickled down' to address poverty and income inequality. This political dimension of poverty, a running theme in this book, that links poverty to social exclusion and power relations of all kinds, is often lost in the study of poverty.

Neville Duncan (1994, 7–8) succinctly summed up the expectations on which these policies are based:

> People are to be passive recipients of 'universal satisfiers' from benevolent institutions rather than be given the structural opportunities to define what they want and how they want to do it...further these institutions were created and maintained/controlled by the (former) imperialist powers.

He further advocated that these economic policies and strategies from the outside constitute 'well-fare' rather than 'social reform' strategies. Their focus on GDP and economic growth is founded on the 'imperialist' assumption that 'well-having' is equivalent to 'well-being'. Duncan (1994) was adamant like Beckford (1972), Rodney (1974), and Girvan (1997) that governments have to take responsibility and be accountable, rather than being forced into the corner by the North. Moreover, national, regional, and international regimes should revisit the relationship between international competitiveness in trade, and the exclusion and marginalization of groups of countries, and poverty. The issue of sustained growth and poverty reduction in a region that is immersed in globalization and neo-liberalism is less about market competitiveness of regional products, and more about shifting control and responsibilities of development initiatives and macroeconomic policies back to governments, communities and civil society. If not, developing countries will remain caught in a vicious cycle of poverty.

To address the politics of poverty is, therefore, to argue for the rights of people to be able to regulate and protect the resources and domestic markets of their country and region. Trade should be managed in a way that restricts the dumping of products from the North and instead achieve self-sufficiency in food. Sustainable development, self-reliance and true independence and freedom requires agency. Capable agency is built on healthy, educated and skilled populations that can make informed decisions and put true citizenry in governance. Gender equity is of particular importance to breaking the cycle of poverty in the multitude of families that experience intergenerational poverty. Moreover, while measured indigence has declined disturbing levels of poverty are still present in many Caribbean households, particularly those that are female headed. The growing impact of global capitalism, neo-liberalism and trade is expected to have the greatest impact on this group. To this end, it is imperative that governments forcefully implement their social and gender policies in more efficient and effective ways (see also Thomas 2002).

Since the 1990s, governments have seen the need to include the poor in the development and implementation of poverty reduction strategies. The successes of this approach vary by country. But people also need to be included in macroeconomic policy formulation. This can be done through national dialogue, public debates, and in participatory approaches (PAs) to research, development and policymaking. On the other hand, policymakers need to participate in the PAs as they provide a better understanding of the conditions, experiences, priorities and recommendations of those most affected. Caroline M. Robb (2002) suggests that PAs can be linked closer to macroeconomic policy debates in three ways: improved access to information; strengthened analysis of the impact of macroeconomic policies and structural adjustment policies on poverty; and drawing civil society into the dialogue on these issues. She goes a step further and suggests that the IMF's poverty reduction and growth facility be modified to meet a country's poverty reduction strategies.

The overview of poverty described in this chapter, along with perspectives on causation and strategies for poverty reduction once again echoes the critiques on methodologies used to understand, measure and assess poverty in the Caribbean. That is, to pay closer attention to what development, freedom, and gender equality really means to the lived experience of people. For local, regional and international bodies to address issues of human capabilities and the role of agency, as well as respond to gender disparities in more direct and urgent ways. This requires social exclusion and gender analysis frameworks, not as separate objectives in strategic plans, but integrated in all national poverty reduction strategies aimed at eradicating hunger, reducing poverty, fostering human development and sustaining economic growth.

# 2. Measuring Human Poverty

> Poor and poverty is different, you can be poor but not living in poverty. Poverty is a state of mind.
> Poor is what I see on BBC/America TV, naked, malnourished people in Africa (CPA, Grenada 2007/08, 40).

Chapter one reported statistics on poverty in the Caribbean. Chapter two presents critiques of some of the more traditional approaches from which these statistics were generated. Many of these are heavily quantitatively oriented and data are collected and analysed at the macro level. These approaches are based on how poverty is conceptualized by scientists and policymakers who are predominantly males from higher socio-economic brackets. Needless to say, that how poverty is perceived by those outside the environment is very different from those who are actually living the reality. Perceptions give way to definitions, and definitions determine how poverty is measured. Consequently, there is an array of permutations used to measure and analyse poverty, some with and others without the involvement of the subjects of the studies.

Throughout the chapter, themes of human agency, social exclusion/inclusion and gender distinctions are intertwined. First, they are intertwined with the evaluation of the more traditional and empirical methodologies, then in the section on gender awareness and analysis and, finally, in the discussions on the participatory and social exclusion approaches used to understand poverty. The interrogation of the different approaches is an attempt to show the strengths and weakness of each in assessing the multidimensional features of the experience of those who live in poverty, as well as the power differentials that affect the life chances of women and men. Within this framework, more traditional ways of defining and measuring poverty are recognized for their usefulness, but come under criticism for ignoring human agency and being gender blind.

The objective of the chapter is, therefore, to show that poverty is not just about economic well-being and wealth, but about the social, political and gendered lives of people who are usually left out of the instruments that measure poverty. It examines the analytical lens that are used to define and understand what the experience of poverty really means.

## People's Definitions of Poverty and Human Development Measures

One of the most interesting aspects of conducting poverty studies is finding out how people define their situations, describe their living conditions, and measure themselves relative to others. What do they mean when they say 'we are not poor poor?' Equally interesting is hearing how the less fortunate explain their behaviour compared with how others interpret, define and measure people's behaviours and livelihoods. The value-laden lens used in research, policymaking, and in providing services to the poor becomes obvious and clouds the proper interrogation of the survival strategies adopted by many. The 'blaming the victim' tendency that emerged from the misuse and reinterpretations of the culture of poverty theory espoused by Oscar Lewis[1] immediately comes to mind. The idea that the poor are to be blamed for their demise because of unhealthy values and bad decision-making, and is passed from one generation to another, is deeply ingrained in all societies. However, those who live in the least desirable conditions see things differently and rarely think of themselves as 'poor'. Instead, they admit to lacking the resources that others are privileged to have. As such, there are vast differences in how living conditions are perceived.

*What does it mean to be poor?* Surprisingly, people are hesitant to call themselves poor. They prefer to describe their situation as well as others in their neighbourhood as:

> Struggling to meet basic needs and provide for the family...
> Living from pay check to pay check
> (CPA, Antigua and Barbuda 2007, 30).

> In between poor and getting by.
> Less fortunate but not poor.
> Poor but still ain't poor...not poor poor
> (NALC, Cayman Islands 2006/07, 53).

These comments illustrate that while individuals do not think that they are living in abject poverty they do recognize that they are resource-poor. To them, poverty means having difficulties meeting financial commitments at the end of the month, and so they explain that things are 'good sometimes' and other times 'not so good'. Similar patterns emerged in the findings of the global poverty study conducted by Deepa Narayan et al. (2000). The perception of oneself as poor is not popular among working and low-income groups the world over. In the US, an African American researcher tells of a black grandmother who became enraged when a teacher told her granddaughter that she wanted to help poor students like herself. The grandmother explained that:

> When someone labels you as poor that could mean poverty of the mind...we may be broke but we are not poor...and so do not ever tell my grandchild that she is poor.

There is no doubt that people who may be living in undesirable conditions do not always see themselves as being destitute. More commonly, people define their situations in multi-dimensional terms that include economic well-being as well as social, psychological and spiritual well-being. Lacking money and material necessities resounds in every group, as economic deprivation is a concrete phenomenon in people's lives. Nonetheless, the lack of social benefits and opportunities, particularly in health and education, is recognized as fundamental to their human existence. For example, residents complained that their community was:

> Too far from major health clinics or health services

> A lot of people here suffer with diabetes and hypertension but no health aid or anyone from the health department comes here (CPA, St Lucia 2005/06, 27).

The lack of facilities is further compounded by the inability to afford proper health care without some kind of government assistance.

> Many people cannot afford medication...if you don't have an exemption card you have to pay (CPA, St Lucia 2005/06, 27).

For some, being poor meant the inability to attend school regularly or get a high school diploma. Contrary to the misperception that low-resourced families do not value education, participants of the CPAs fully understood the dialectical relationship between poverty and education. In fact, some defined poverty as:

> Not able to finish school (CPA, Antigua and Barbuda 2006/07, 33).

From the Grenadian CPA, 1999, poverty looks like this:

> I wanted to go to New Life Organization to learn plumbing, but I could not go because we don't have money to pay bus every day.

> As for me, I missed out on school a lot because I am the first and had to stay home to take care of the others while my mother did odd jobs.

> I had to leave school at age fifteen to go and work in the (nutmeg) pool (116).

Unfortunately, these expressions are far too common and exist across the Atlantic. The author interviewed a young girl in a rural part of Kenya who explained that:

> I am in school on weekends because I believe that education is the only
> way out of poverty (Student at Kogelo Secondary School, Kenya 2009).

Those who live close to the poverty line consistently not only advocate for more jobs and better wages, but also for greater access to affordable social services, improved infrastructures, recreational facilities, and all other basic amenities. The same story is told over and over.

> There are no facilities here, no cable, no telephone, no library and no
> place to put one, and the preschool mash up....We do not have road,
> access to water is poor and the water quality is poor...We like sports, but
> there is no playing field or sporting facilities here (CPA, St Lucia 2005/06,
> 26).

> The roads are bad, they need fixing...We need street lights...Utilities
> are too high, low-income persons can't meet the expenses...Medical
> facilities are inadequate...and poor drainage is a problem (CPA, Antigua
> and Barbuda 2007, 31).

The commonality of human experiences of poverty is inescapable. Recurring themes such as poverty is pain, shame and humiliation, powerlessness, and social isolation surface alongside the obvious lack of money, food, jobs and social services. At the same time, signs of resilience, resourcefulness and solidarity emerge as survival strategies to harsh living conditions and inadequate resources and support from outside the communities. These strategies also help lift the spirits of residents. In each case, people expressed that, while material and social needs were of serious concerns, spiritual well-being ranks high among the people living in dilapidated communities. This, they explain, is because people in the Caribbean, particularly those with little money, have a tremendous amount of faith, and are God-fearing folks.

People's perception about their identities, hearing them describe their living conditions and the consequences and repercussions that they face daily, are important in understanding the nature and dynamics of poverty. Yet, researchers, administrators and policymakers rarely regard them. The participatory poverty studies in the Caribbean do an excellent job of capturing this aspect of poverty. Whether the information is being used to further poverty reduction strategies aimed at targeted groups, however, remains undetermined at this point.

## Self-Assessment of Living Conditions

The underprivileged also have certain vantage points which they use to assess their living conditions and that of others. These perceptions are heavily influenced by the stereotypical depictions of the global poor that are televised in the news and in fundraising advertisements. The image of the pot-bellied naked child with sad eyes and flies buzzing out in the open, homeless, dirty and with hands outstretched are tattooed in the minds of all people – rich and poor. As a result, what constitutes poverty for people, including those who live in low-income homes and neighbourhoods, is based on these images. Poverty is thus perceived relative to these stereotypical typecasts. This is observed in the following examples:

> While in our view some of us in the community could be classified as poor, by the international definition of poverty we know we are rich (NALC, Cayman Islands 2006/07, 111).

> We are affected by a different category of poverty. We cannot be compared with people in Africa...poverty here has to do with unemployment (CPA, St Lucia 2007, 28).

> While there may be some poverty, we are still better off, we can satisfy our basic needs...Everyone has a roof over their heads and most people eat two or three meals a day (CPA, Antigua and Barbuda 2007, 30).

The individuals in the poverty studies are, in fact, defining indigent poverty; living below the poverty line in conditions that constitute absolute poverty. Interestingly, relativity in understanding poverty at the international level is extended to the local environment. People measure their own living circumstances by also comparing themselves with those who are more fortunate and living in neighbouring spaces. In other words, people who are identified as living in poor households and/or communities define poverty in a social context, and they assess living conditions relative to international and local situations. This was found in the more developed Caribbean territories, as well as in the lesser developed countries.

> The community has both wealth and prominence and well-known persons who stand out...George Cooper Road is like Beverly Hills, the people own both house and land (CPA, St Lucia 2007, 29).

People also make distinctions between being in a temporary state of poverty due to natural disasters compared with a more sustained state of destitution often found in examples of multigenerational poverty. The comparison is not made relative to others, but to an accustomed standard of living that has suddenly changed. This categorization of poverty is found to be more prominent in countries that are at high risk of natural disasters such as hurricanes in the Caribbean, cyclones in Asia, periods of extended drought in Africa and earthquakes elsewhere. Victims believe that their situation is temporary, but feel somewhat abandoned and are afraid that their standard of living will not return to normal. Examples of this type of poverty are found in the Caribbean after some countries were devastated by Hurricane Ivan in 2004.

> I just want to move back into my original home so my children can have their own room. I was in the mist of Ivan...and I am still in the mist of Ivan...they have forgotten about us...nobody comes here (NALC, Cayman Islands 2006/07, 48).

This type of poverty is equivalent to the standard definition of transient poverty used in poverty studies and defined by the UNDP (1997). It can be short-term or seasonal.

Overall, three major categories of the poor emerge from the various definitions and assessments of what low-income and working people consider to be poverty. These include: (i) relative poverty or 'the not poor poor'; (ii) inter-generational or persistent poverty; and (iii) the new poor (victims of natural disasters, health disabilities and other unexpected situations). There is no doubt that the commonly used quantitative-oriented assessments of poverty capture absolute, relative, multigenerational, and transient poverty similar to the patterns identified by those being studied. However, investigations that focus on how resource-poor individuals, households and communities conceptualize their situations remain sparse in research and is absent in research methods and policy strategies. Some current poverty studies have attempted to address this gap by using triangulation data collection methodologies that involve both quantitative and qualitative data collection and analyses.

## Empirical Measures and Analysis

At the World Summit for Social Development in 1995, all nations agreed to develop anti-poverty strategies within a set time frame. This meant that every country had to adopt some kind of assessment tool to determine the extent to which poverty exists in their societies, the geographical locations and the demographic manifestations. In the Caribbean, country specific poverty lines were constructed for each country and used to determine poverty rates and indigence. Poverty lines are normally formulated in two distinct stages. First, the indigence line or food poverty line is estimated utilizing the local market cost of the selected items in a basket of basic food. Second, the indigence line is adjusted upwards to account for non-food basic needs. The poverty lines are established using local food items and the nutritional and caloric content of all foods generally consumed in the region. The selected food items in the basket amount to 2,400 kilocalories (kcal), across all the food groups, and at the minimum cost. The cost in each case is associated with a daily balanced diet and used as the indigence line for Caribbean poverty studies.[2]

Income thresholds and poverty lines are used to calculate (i) the extent to which *indigent poverty* is prevalent in populations, that is, the percentage of people living below the poverty line using a 'headcount index', and (ii) the 'poverty gap' or the average depth to which people are below the poverty lines. They are also used to assess how poverty in one location compares relative to another. The percentage of people who are indigent reveal the extent to which a country is impoverished, while relative poverty is used for international comparisons of the incidence of poverty,[3] and to discern local wealth disparities within a society.

The premise of this approach is based on the assumption that the income needed to purchase the most basic goods and services for consumption by an individual or a family, is calculable (Hagenaars 1991). The actual goods and services that people lack is not assessed, but the incomes needed to acquire these items are. In other words, poverty is measured by a 'lack of income' and is still the most dominant method used to determine economic well-being and levels of poverty. Plainly put, this approach answers the questions: How much money do people need to subsist? And how many people do not have this estimated income?

The idea that poverty is an objective, scientific phenomenon that can be determined by economic measures is continuously being challenged. Researchers note technical deficiencies in the use of the economic well-being approach as the only poverty measure (Iceland 2003; NRC 1995; Ruggles 1990), because they only capture one dimension of well-being. Income measures do not reveal how outcomes of poverty work nor give a holistic picture of causation. As a result, data collected using survey of living conditions has expanded to include human development measures and used alongside participatory poverty assessment methods.

## Human Development Measures

> People do not just want to be alive. They want to be knowledgeable; and they certainly may want a decent life, one that is not considerably undermined by extreme poverty and constant worry about sheer physical survival (UNDP 1991, 88).

The appearance of human development (non-income) measures of poverty has broadened the definition of standard of living to focus on both material and non-material well-being. Amartya Sen (1985, 1987), introduced the concept of *human capability* and argued that standard of living should include functioning (attainments of different attributes) and capability (ability to achieve). He suggested that emphasis should be placed on what a person can do and not what he/she can purchase as the ultimate metric of well-being. The human development (HD) model promoted by the United Nations Development Programmes (UNDP) is one example where attainment measures are used to assess standard of living. This model moves away from measuring human development solely in terms of income by including three additional dimensions of well-being: longevity, knowledge and a decent standard of living. These are assessed through a composite and multidimensional scale called the human development index (HDI).[4]

Human poverty is sometimes assessed by using a scheme, the human poverty index (HPI),[5] which is an extension of the human development model. These two models, the HDI and the HPI, are now considered alternatives to the use of a country's gross national product (GNP) as a measure of social and economic progress, and act as a complement to measures of economic well-being (UNDP Human Development Report 1997). They are also useful tools for planning policies aimed at poverty reduction and social development.

Overall, these standard models have many advantages, but there are also certain shortcomings. The two main areas in need of improvements are: (i) including qualitative data from the poor; and (ii) the development of more gender sensitive data.

## Human Capability

Sudhir Anand and Amartya Sen (1993) argued that the economic well-being as well as the human development and human poverty approaches are useful but restrictive; they exclude other types of human development, such as human rights issues. The main critique is that the standard approaches do not reflect how social inequality affects human capability. Sen (1987, 1992, 1999), delineated the poor based on whether or not an individual has a decent standard of living that allows him/her to achieve, make informed decisions and to live a long and healthy life. Rather than focusing exclusively on income and consumptive capacities, Sen (1999) identified five components that can be used to assess human capability. These are:

  i.   the importance of real freedoms in the assessment of a person's advantage;
  ii.  individual differences in the ability to transform resources into valuable activities;
  iii. the multi-variant nature of activities that give rise to happiness;

iv. a balance of materialistic and non-materialistic factors in evaluating human welfare; and

v. concern for the distribution of opportunities within society.

The capability approach suggests that access to a proper education and good health affect the capacity to earn an income appropriate to meeting basic consumption of goods and services. But having income or opulence does not lower mortality rates, undernourishment and improve other measures of human development. Sen argued that it is human capability which determines both income and other forms of deprivation. He introduces the idea of 'freedom' as a measure of poverty and human development, and suggests that having enough resources to choose out of desire rather than necessity should be treated as a measure of poverty and human development (1987, 1992, 1999). Within the capability approach, poverty refers to the extent to which an individual possesses the ability to exercise his choice freely.

Critiques of this approach argue that while it incorporates the capabilities of the individual as a poverty measure, it downplays the role of social stratification and the creation of hierarchical structures and relationships (Townsend 1970, 1979), including that of gender power relations and inequality. External and sometimes unseen social forces can determine human well-being; individual capacity is not independent of these factors. As such, all approaches used to understand poverty should include both structural and relational measures that affect access to resources, individual capability and human development, including the capability approach. It is within this same critique that we observe that while Sen explicitly acknowledges human diversity, the differences between women and men's capabilities are not fully developed and are left open to what Susan Moller Okin (1991) referred to as 'false gender neutrality'.

## Gender Awareness and Analysis

Gender awareness in poverty assessments is largely linked to the work done by feminists across the globe. According to Sylvia Chant (2003), previous studies that have had the most impact on the gender dimensions of poverty comprises:

i. research on women and development conducted during the UN-declared decade for women 1975–85;

ii. a later body of work focused on the impact of structural adjustment on women in the Caribbean by Moser (1989); Safa and Antrobus (1992), and others;

iii.  research focused on the growing number of single-female-headed
      households in the *feminization of poverty* perspectives.

The bodies of research (i) and (ii) indirectly link gender with poverty. On
the other hand, the *feminization of poverty* argument that originated in North
America directly focuses on the disproportionate number of women and
their families living under the poverty line (see chapter four). Influenced by
these perspectives as well as other feminist research, the conceptualization
and methodological approaches that examine women, gender and poverty
have improved. Traditional approaches to poverty assessment have since
sought to include gender-disaggregated data and the conduct of household-
level analyses. For example, in 1995, the Human Development Report
introduced a gender development index (GDI) that captures inequalities in
achievement between women and men. It is an adjusted version of the HDI to
measure gender inequality. The greater the gender disparity in basic human
development, the lower is a country's GDI relative to its HDI. There is also
a gender empowerment measure (GEM) that assesses the extent to which
women are actively engaged in economic and political life. It tracks the share
of seats in parliament held by women as well as female legislators, senior
officials and managers; professional and technical workers; and the gender
disparity in earned income, reflecting economic independence. Differing
from the GDI, the GEM exposes inequality in opportunities in selected areas.
      Nonetheless, feminist scholars (Chant 2003; Corner 2002; Kabeer 2003)
argued that the gender indices employed are compromised because of
inadequate data that can capture the full spectrum of gendered experiences
of deprivation, and the fact that stereotypes and biases still influence
how gendered poverty is defined and measured. In her book, on *Gender
Mainstreaming in Poverty Eradication and the Millennium Development Goals:
A Handbook for Policy Makers and Other Stakeholders*, Naila Kabeer (2003)
explained why gender equality merits specific attention both in policymaking
and in the research methods used to study poverty. On the whole, Kabeer
found that all of the common approaches used to assess poverty remain
'gender-blind' in a number of ways.
      First, the poverty line approach is critiqued for ignoring non-monetary
variables and the less tangible aspects of poverty, including understanding
the gender dynamics and differences in how poverty is experienced. The most
significant weakness of the poverty line approach, however, is that it employs
household-level analyses which do not take into account the differential
experiences, burdens, roles and responses of women and men. The focus is

on the 'means' and not on the 'ends'. Moreover, intra-household inequalities are not considered. Surveys that are used to collect and analyse quantitative data on income poverty simply do not explore the gender nuances and issues of equality within households (Chant 2003; Kabeer 2003; Razavi 2000).

Secondly, while the capability approach goes beyond poverty line measurements and captures some aspects of gender dimensions, it still falls short of information on gender equality in time use and work intensity. To its credit, it does employ gender development indices (GDI) and gender equality measures (GEM).

The third commonly used approach, participatory poverty assessments (PPAs), has made the most advanced improvements in understanding and measuring gendered poverty. However, not all PPAs include gender issues, primarily because the instrument, the process, and the analyses rely heavily on the gender awareness and sensitivity of the researcher and/or the facilitator conducting the assessments. In response to the limitations of the three approaches, Kabeer and others suggest that greater emphasis be placed on *gender analysis* regardless of the method of data collection (Chant 2003; Corner 2002; Kabeer 2003).

Only a gender analysis approach can provide a robust interrogation of the differences between women and men's lives. It reduces the possibility that poverty studies and policy development are constructed from incorrect assumptions and stereotypes. Gender analysis, in terms of research for development, is both a process and a tool. As a process, it assesses the differential impact of proposed and/or existing research on men and women of different ethnicities/races, classes or castes. As a tool, it enables research to be undertaken with an appreciation of gender differences that manifest different social realities, life expectations and economic circumstances.

The framework for conducting *gender analysis* contains four parts and is carried out in two main stages. First, information is collected and organized into a gender profile that describes roles and activities, as well as access to, and control of resources by gender. Secondly, the information is then analysed to decipher gender trends (Williams and Mwau 1994). In some instances, a gender analysis matrix is adopted as part of the analytical process. The *Gender Analysis Matrix* is an analytical tool that uses the participatory methodology to facilitate people's perspectives and analysis of the gender issues in their community (March and Mukhopadhyay 1999; Moser 1993). It provides a unique articulation of gender issues and, at the same time, enables people to conduct gender analysis from a grassroots' perspective. This framework is founded on the principle that all requisite knowledge for gender analysis exists among the people whose lives is the subject of analysis. It is, therefore, transformative because the analysis is done by the people being analysed.

Overall, gender analysis challenges the assumption that everyone is affected by research and development in the same way, regardless of their situation (Kabeer 1995, 1996; Moser 1993). There is no doubt that the lived experiences, needs, issues and priorities of men and women are different. Needless to say, all women's lives are not the same. Women's interests may be determined by their social position, their racial/ethnic identity, age, marital status, family size, culture, immigration status, as well as by other social demographics. Their life experiences, needs, issues, and priorities are therefore different. As a result, a variety of strategies are necessary to achieve equitable outcomes for women and men, and for different groups of women. Gender analysis aims to highlight the variations between the genders and to achieve gender equity. While Chant (2003), Kabeer (2003) and others suggest that greater emphasis should be placed on *gender analysis*, they do admit that among all the poverty research methodologies currently used, the participatory poverty assessments (PPAs) has made the most advanced improvements in understanding and measuring gendered poverty.

## Participatory Approaches (PAs)

> At last those above will hear us…before now; no one ever asked us what we think (Narayan et al. 2000, 13).

Many poverty studies that seek to understand poverty in its local, social, cultural, and political contexts undertake a form of participatory action research (PAR) called participatory poverty assessment or PPA. The participatory approaches arose primarily in response to an emerging advocacy for a more participative worldview. The PAR can be traced as far back as 1968 to the Brazilian activist, academic, and author of *Pedagogy of the Oppressed*, Paulo Freire.[6] Freire focused on the use of dialogue and participatory research to stimulate awareness and motivate people to take political action. The assumption here is that poor people are creative and capable, and should be empowered and facilitated (Pretty et al. 1995). Based on this viewpoint, practitioners began to adopt participatory approaches to establish dialogue with oppressed peoples and affect change.

The participatory approaches are the most widely practised 'bottom-up' approaches, and are significant to poverty studies because they emphasize the political aspects of knowledge production and knowledge use, including the value of indigenous knowledge. The methodology employs a wide range of data collection and analysis techniques, both quantitative and qualitative, such as surveys, field interviews, community workshops, focus group meetings and oral traditions. It varies from traditional research methodologies in that it places research design, data gathering and data analysis second to the process of collaboration, dialogue, empowerment and motivation.

Because participatory approaches are concerned with how relations of power impact poverty, they allow for the interrogation of gender relations and how it affects the living conditions of women and their families. PAs are centred on the powerless and question how certain elements of society are favoured, hold power and control knowledge. The voices and decisions of the least powerful and most affected by poor living conditions are given preferential treatment. Moreover, PAs focus on the lived experience of oppressed peoples and values their knowledge and experiences as important sources of research data. The partipartory approach is seen as 'rooted in the cultural traditions of people and is concerned with their welfare, as well as their co-operative and communal nature.'

Participatory approaches are genuinely socially inclusive rather than exclusive. The approach itself is conscience raising because it involves self-inquiry and reflection. The knowledge it produces can be used for research, education and sociopolitical action. Thus, it empowers people at a deeper level through the process of constructing and using their own knowledge. It assesses the capabilities of individuals, household members and groups, and highlights the impact of social exclusion, including gender discrimination in the society and in the home. The main concern with the use of PAs, with or without the more quantitative methodologies, is that to a large extent the level at which social exclusion and gender equity are addressed is dependent on the individuals who design and implement the research instruments. It also requires the appropriate gender perspectives to analyse the data collected.

## Social Exclusion and Women

Social exclusion in research approaches is important as barring access to resources, as well as preventing people from taking advantage of opportunities and resources, are directly linked to enjoying a decent standard of living. In other words, people's capability to earn an income and take advantage of social opportunities is dependent on the extent to which they are included or excluded from mainstream economic, political, civic and cultural activities (Atkinson 1998; Iceland 2005; Micklewright 2002). Women, in particular, are excluded from these activities because of their gender as well as their race/ethnicity, social location and other stratifying characteristics. Increased attention is being given to assessing women's poverty based on *social exclusion*. As a result of this attention, the question being asked is *why do women not have what they need to support themselves and their families?*

The concept of social exclusion is further dealt with in chapter seven that discusses how social capital works for the poor and the rich. The social exclusion approach to poverty assessment goes beyond economic, human development and capability explanations. The main supposition is that individuals as part of a group, with or without adequate income and capabilities, are socially excluded from mainstream activities that are important to their well-being as humans (Waggle 2002). They are denied access to the services necessary for them to participate fully in the society in which they reside (Taylor 1999). It is because of this type of alienation that women have low paying jobs, live in poor housing, lack access to proper health care and experience family stress and social isolation. Additionally, in developing societies where patriarchy thrives, women are tacitly prevented from equal participation in labour markets and entrepreneurial activities. Women form a large proportion of the low-income population who are kept out of the formal economy, and must survive in the informal economy. Some become entangled with illegal economic activities. In all these cases, women function in high risk situations and in uncertain environments (Waggle 2002).

> They are many persons in the community who cannot find employment in the formal sector; they work in the informal sector and at odd jobs (CPA, Antigua and Barbuda 2007, 33).

Studies show that social exclusion takes place at all levels, intersecting and causing a cyclic effect. In some instances, poverty and social exclusion are indistinguishable and one inevitably affects the other (International Institute for Labor Studies 1996). Moreover, socially excluded individuals are not only restricted from certain economic activities but are also excluded from exercising their rights as citizens. Robert Carr (2009) writes about social exclusion, citizenship and the rights of those who grapple with HIV and AIDs in the Caribbean. He draws out the interrelationship between vulnerability and social exclusion and observed that there is a tendency for the 'ghettoisation of the poor' whereby certain groups occupy the bottom of the social structure and are economically and politically dislocated from the mainstream (87). They are not included in electoral issues and are ostracized from political, civic and cultural organizations, networks and activities.

Consequently, women and men from poor households and communities lack a sense of social belongingness and do not benefit from political decisions, compared to those who are well off. They feel isolated, neglected and affronted. Hilary Silver (1994) suggested that solidarity, specialization, and monopoly are three paradigms that can be used to examine how disfavoured individuals and groups are excluded from membership and benefits from economic, social and political relationships. Social exclusion is, therefore, a highly political concept and approach to defining and assessing causes of poverty. But it is an experience that resource-poor women and men face on a daily basis. The social exclusion approach to understanding poverty tends to downplay blame on women's individual capacity, and looks more closely at the structural and ideological gender barriers of society. It focuses on the process and the players addressing relational factors; the dialectics between the 'haves' and the 'have nots', between women and men, and others caught in hierarchal power relationships. Eudine Barriteau (2003) writes about a theoretical framework within which social exclusion and gender analysis could be conducted in her book, *Confronting Power, Theorizing Gender*.

## Summary and Conclusions

In general, all the methodological approaches are important for assessing poverty. Those that are based on economic theories are focused primarily on resource-based paradigms and use quantitative formulae to measure disadvantage at the individual and household levels. These are deemed necessary for comparing poverty levels and policy development because they are viewed as objective, accurate and the data is easy to collect through household surveys. At the same time, emerging debates on how to define poverty and well-being have raised pointed scrutiny on the extent to which poverty assessments are grounded in quantitative measures and exclude how people themselves conceptualize and assess their living situations. Some current studies have attempted to address this gap by using both quantitative and qualitative methods of data collection and analysis that include participatory poverty assessment information and some gender analyses.

Using a triangulation of methods to research poverty is due to social deprivation gaining importance alongside physical deprivation in poverty studies. The mixed methods approach, therefore, include measures of human development, social relations of power and exclusion, as well as more gendered understandings of the process and impact of poverty, at all levels. Nevertheless, they remain embedded within an economic framework and, as a result, the human condition and lifestyles that differ according to demographic characteristics, especially gender, are only casually understood.

Research that is interested in giving voice and enabling disadvantaged women and men to engage in self-determination are turning more to the use of participatory methodologies, where social exclusion and gender awareness are centre to the analysis, regardless of the data collection methods. These methods challenge the embedded assumptions about the 'poor' and about gender roles and expectations. They are more inclusive in their analyses and transformative in practice. They embrace the idea of agency and people's freedom, or lack thereof, to make choices and take advantage of opportunities.

The participatory approaches are, however, not without weaknesses. Efforts to promote participatory approaches are based on the assumption that everyone who has a stake must also have a voice and a choice. However, choice is linked to social class status and the ability to accumulate wealth. According to Sen (1999), income alone does not affect people's ability to make choices, it is only important if it allows people to attain basic health care, a decent standard of living, and to participate in the social and political life of their communities. Additionally, community-driven participatory research that make claims of 'full participation' and 'empowerment' is largely influenced by facilitators and can be driven by particular gendered interests, leaving women without voice, or much in the way of choice.

In summary, the Caribbean is still heavily dependent on using quantifiable variables in assessing poverty and living conditions. This is primarily because the economic well-being and the human development/human poverty approaches are conceptually more advanced and adoptable, even though they may be methodologically incomplete. The participatory approaches are less used but can collect the qualitative data that assess gender inequities, people's capability and the extent to which social isolation from mainstream economic, social and political activities are linked to living conditions. When used along with the more quantitative approaches, the information gathered and analysed from the PAs give meaning to the income and human development data. The PAs can also be used to bridge the macro- and micro-levels of analyses by including subjects in the objectives of studies, and encouraging gender analyses as an integral part of poverty research. However, appropriate theoretical perspectives to guide the research design and data analyses are required.

# 3. The Socio-Psychological Pain of Poverty

> We believe that the person with a stigma is not quite human. On this assumption we exercise varieties of discrimination, through which we effectively, if often unthinkingly, reduce his life chances (Goffman 1963, 5).

While recommendations are made to include more human development, social exclusion and gendered factors in poverty studies, there is another less understood aspect – the socio-psychological dimension. The socio-psychological dimension refers to the psychological impact poverty has on the poor. This aspect of poverty is the most understudied aspect of poverty; yet, ironically, it is also the most human side of poverty, and the least talked about, including by those whose lives are most affected. When asked to describe their experiences, the material aspects are almost always the first thing that people report.

> The house in bad condition, it have holes everywhere – you could stay outside and see all inside...A family of 8 has to share 2 rooms (CPA, St Lucia 2005/06, 12).
>
> Things so bad the house leaking sun (CPA, Grenada 1999, 113).
>
> I ain't send them to school today 'cause I ain't have anything to give them to eat (CPA, Dominica 2008/09, 25).

But if you listen closely as individuals tell of their lack of basic human physical needs, you will hear pain, humiliation and shame in their voices. For many, the psychological impact is equally important to their well-being as the physical and material needs. Yet, over the years, poverty studies have not included socio-psychological factors and people rarely report on it. Consequently, projects and programmes aimed at poverty reduction have made no provisions for assisting women, men, youth, and the elderly with the psychological trauma of being poor. Nor is it common to analyse the socio-psychological implications to social mobility and equity in poverty research, or in poverty reduction efforts. People's emotions, lived experiences and treatment in society are not included simply because 'no one asked' or thought it was 'that important'.

For the poor, poverty is not a statistic or something measurable; it is personal and involves physical needs as well as emotions and social experiences. Being trapped in poverty also presents different challenges and responses based on age, gender, spatial location and other demographic features. However, common to all is a sense of powerlessness, humiliation, exclusion, and an overall lack of freedom.

According to Sabina Alkire (2007a), the exclusion or minimization of the socio-psychological dimension is a serious oversight that blocks or slows down poverty reduction efforts. The exposure of human suffering, both physical and psychological, while integral to poverty reduction, is also highly political.

This chapter of the book purposefully focuses on the socio-psychological dimension as an attempt to highlight this missing but important human component of poverty. It argues for poverty research to focus not just on access to resources and social services but also on the psyche of women, men and families from under-resourced communities. It uses direct quotes from the people being studied to communicate their experiences. In so doing, the chapter highlights aspects of poverty that are not normally recorded and analysed such as the effects of stigmatization, discrimination and humiliation on individual self-esteem and group progress. The narratives of these individuals help debunk popular notions and beliefs about women, men and the poor in general.

Contrary to the more used conceptual approaches, the socio-psychological issues discussed in this chapter provides an opportunity for individual agency to relay the nuances and intricacies of human actions and interactions in coping with poor living conditions. Through this process, many paradoxes emerge and are discussed. For example, evidence is presented to show how on one hand, the material pressures of poverty causes severe psychological pain, while on the other, the hope and faith of people are not expunged. Here, the positive experiences of self-worth, identity, spirituality and religiosity are described and linked to the survival and sustainability of people, who have very little material comforts in life.

Overall, the chapter helps us to understand how the poor who face marginalization, social fragmentation and powerlessness in the wider society develop coping mechanisms, maintain personal pride, uphold strong family ties and kinship as well as retain distinct cultural and community identities. Specific attention is paid to not make moral judgments about family structures and gender roles; instead, the focus is on practices, relations, responses and survival strategies. At the end, the chapter offers a brief synopsis of attempts by scholars to develop theoretical and methodological approaches to assess the socio-psychological dimensions of poverty.

## Poverty is a Painful Moral Dilemma

In describing their experiences, the poor often talk about the moral dilemmas they face when having to make decisions on how best to meet family needs. Deepa Narayan et al. (2000) reported the difficult choices that poor people worldwide make on a daily basis. Parents in the Caribbean make difficult choices when addressing the needs of all family members, especially those of hungry children. Sacrifices are almost always necessary and the psychological pain that goes with them is devastating for parents.

> The house have lights but I can only afford to burn one bulb at a time... Any little money I get is to buy food for dem children, it can't stretch to pay for lights (CPA, Grenada 1999, 111).

> When children are hungry they can't concentrate or learn...They can't learn on a hungry belly (CPA, Antigua and Barbuda 2007, 22).

> I could only send them (to school) when I have lunch to give them (CPA, St Kitts and Nevis 2007/08, 93).

> When children hungry they can't focus and concentrate (CPA, St Lucia 2005/06, 23).

For many, not having food becomes a norm. This researcher recalls during a household interview, two little boys ran into the kitchen and opened the refrigerator then softly sighed, 'nothing to eat or drink again', and then ran back into the streets to play. Even homes that are resourceful enough to own a refrigerator still struggle. At the end of the month, refrigerators and kitchen cupboards are empty, and the family has to wait until the next paycheck to restock. Watching their children do without food and other basic essentials is very painful for mothers.

The acute pain and anxiety of a mother are observed in another example, when in times of difficulty, she tells her children 'time for fasting'. The concept of having to 'fast' is a common practice of poor people around the world; for wage earners it is pay check to pay check and for farming populations it is seasonal. In West Africa, just before the rains come (and hopefully they do or there is mass starvation), the grain/cereal in the storage sheds gets close to the bottom. The local people refer to this period as the time of *fasting*. In other words, families must ration the food supplies until the next harvested crop. Similarly, in the sugar cane growing Caribbean villages, there is the crop or harvest season when paid work is regular, and families are able to buy enough food and other items. Then, there is the non-crop or growing season when paid work is scarce, and families depend on the grocery shops for credit or 'trust', and also have to 'fast'.

The pain of poverty is felt by every member of a family. Men agonize when they are unable to provide for their families, and are forced to tell their children that they do not have the money to get them things that other kids have. They constantly worry that they may lose their jobs and the ability to provide for their family. Mothers worry about their children's future if something were to happen to them.

> I see mi death is comin...and I must run away from it for the sake of my children (NALC, Cayman Islands 2006/07, 63).

Like most parents, the adults in the household try to shield the children from the woes of poverty. Nevertheless, children and youth are very aware of the 'hand to mouth' existence of their family. They are also conscious about the extent to which they are dependent on their mothers. Children feel insecure and talk about the fear of not knowing what might happen to them if a parent, especially a mother dies. They are aware that there are 'money problems' in the home, because they would hear their mothers crying.

> She would lock herself up in her bedroom and cry...but when mom cries...everybody cries, again and again (NALC, Cayman Islands 2006/07, 61).

Although every member of the family can tell of the moral dilemma and pain that they endure because of poverty, clear gender patterns emerge. The moral dilemma, shame and frustration felt by women are no more or less painful than those felt by men, but they are different and disproportionate.

## Gender Differentiated Pain

Qualitative data collected from poverty assessment reports indicate that women and men experience, perceive and respond to their living conditions in different ways. As a result, the socio-psychological ramifications vary, but both women and men believe that:

> Women try and cope and men pick up and go (NALC, Cayman Islands 2006/07, 114).

> Some of the men spend all their money in the rum shop (CPA Grenada 2007/08, 47).

These stereotypical beliefs are linked to socially defined roles in the Caribbean, particularly gender-assigned responsibilities for children and family. For example, because women assume the role of nurturer, it is believed that they are more stressed (than men) when they are unable to feed their families. According to the women:

> [A woman] has the load of the family...and that if woman is of poor condition then the children is poor (NALC, Cayman Islands 2006/07, 116).

These expectations are derived from a patriarchal ideology that promotes gender-specific expectations and do not always reflect reality as chapters four and five show. When these gender-specific expectations are not met, they give rise to gender patterns of psychological stresses and responses. These are sometimes interpreted as men not caring, or taking the easy route out when the family faces severe financial hardships. In reality, some men do run away from the domestic situation or engage in drug abuse and domestic violence. However, in many instances, these activities are responses to the psychological stresses of not being able to take care of the family's well-being. Their actions may not be appropriate, but they demonstrate the importance of looking at the manifestations of poverty through psychological lens.

Because of the patriarchal nature of gender-defined roles, women frequently associate poverty with feeding their families, and men with unemployment similar to the global findings in Narayan et al., *Voices of the Poor* (2000). But men's focus on employment and income is directly related to their role of providing for the family as part of their 'manhood'. Men talk about the shame, frustration and humiliation felt when unemployed or when they are unable to make enough money to comfortably support their children, girlfriend, wife and/or a family.

> You feel like a dog when you are poor (CPA, Grenada 1999, 124).

> I feel bad, really bad...I feel as if I am being deprived of putting my family through proper schooling (NALC, Cayman Islands 2006/07, 81).

> When you poor they (women) do not stay... Some women will not come if you do not have a dollar or piece of food (CPA, Dominica 2008/09, 82).

> I feel ashamed and embarrassed because my woman deserted me (CPA, Dominica 2008/09, 82).

On the other hand, women describe the shame, frustration, humiliation and strength they must endure to take care of their children. These experiences and expressions contribute to the common stigma of the emasculated male and the strong female matriarch.

Indeed, the defining quality of black womanhood globally is strength and the ability to head households in the absence of a male breadwinner. Scholars like Helen Safa (1995) and others have long challenged the analyses of gender roles in very stereotypical ways where men are portrayed as the breadwinner who are often 'absent' and 'irresponsible', and the Caribbean family as female-headed. From the 1960s to the 1990s, the matriarch emerged as one of the main stereotypes of black women, replacing the image of the 'mammy' found in literature on slavery. According to Christine Barrow (2010), Caribbean feminist joined this debate and, instead of focusing on 'matrifocality', began to look at the Afro-Caribbean 'matriarch', thus moving away from the more Eurocentric/Western orientations on family structure and function. Indeed, all families historically have benefited from having strong women, whether in nuclear families, in single-female-headed households, or in extended families with influential grandmothers and 'tanties'. This ideological shift also deepens our understanding of how these 'matriarchs' manage and support both female-headed and nuclear households as well as the extended family networks.

Poverty studies and women studies show that families, communities and societies around the world continue to benefit from women's contributions and strength. However, Tamara Beauboeuf-Lafontant (2009) in *Behind the Mask of the Strong Black Woman*, points out that this concept of the black woman can obscure her suffering and experiences of desperation. She describes the image as a restrictive myth because the assumption of strength can create a distraction from broader forces of discrimination and the imbalances of power in society and in the home. Moreover, the psychological trauma of women who bear the sole responsibility for poor families is masked.

Interviews with Caribbean women reveal that the matriarch is real; women do admirably bear the burden of the family, especially during hard times. At the same time, this does not preclude women's vulnerability to abuse and physical and emotional pain. These two characteristics of women are not mutually exclusive, but are simply not widely reported. This lack of information on women's 'human side' is due, in part, because their lives have rarely been explored from this perspective; the focal point has been on the matriarchal images and the 'super woman'. In fact, poor and working women often express bewilderment when others show interest in the emotional side of their lives. Consequently, interviews with women usually provide information that is congruent with the icon of the strong black matriarch. However, when this author probed from a humanistic angle, the façade of the matriarch cracked and women tearfully shared their pain. The most disheartening finding is that there are no support services to help women cope with their psychological ordeals. It was, therefore, not surprising to hear women say that they feel 'invisible' and confessed to, 'not having anyone to trust'...so they keep things 'bottled up inside'.

Women's strengths are further challenged when they are forced to remain in unfaithful and/or abusive relationships with husbands or partners because of their economic situation, and for their children. They admit to, 'turning a blind eye to men's indiscretions'. Although the social and financial stresses of the family are often unbearable, women 'keep up' an outward appearance of stability to persevere the family image. In so doing, their actions reinforce the image of the typical strong woman. She maintains this persona, so that her children can feel a sense of security as well as to uphold a level of family dignity in the public's eye. This is particularly important for impoverished households that are already stigmatized and looked down upon. But the conditions of life, and women's attempt to present a strong front and respectable persona, can create havoc on her psyche. One woman spoke about the grief she felt when her husband moved in with another woman right next door. Others in the Cayman Islands (NALC 2006/07, 59–60) shared some of their private thoughts:

> Once things got so bad that I wanted to do bad things to myself.

> I did not know what to do or where to turn...I don't know why but I just decided to cut my long beautiful hair off.

> When I feel sorry for myself, my heart get full and I go in the room, throw my head on the pillow and cry...eventually I turn to God and prayers.

The absence of psychological support and services for women were widely reported in the CPAs. For example, in Barbados, one woman revealed that she felt that:

> I ain't got no future. I feel as if I loss I does sit down and cry. I don't have nobody (CPA, Barbados 2010, 115).

The threat of violence on oneself also resonates in most of the Caribbean CPA Reports and was observed among men as well. Men indicated that during difficult circumstances they felt angry and wanted to 'lash out' at others.

> Make me feel like I want to kill...or I might end up killing myself, you understand (CPA, Dominica 2008/09, 82).

In all instances, the psychological stresses that women and men experience and respond to, often runs the risk of having harmful effects on self, family and society.

## Gender Tensions in Families

It is an established fact that the lack of money and poor living conditions have serious social ramifications on families and can result in break ups, child abuse, juvenile delinquency, alcoholism and domestic violence. In their own words, 'everybody gets angry'. Family members, in retrospect, become aware of their aggressive behaviour and associate this with the 'pressures of life and being poor'. The anger in stressed families is well known as some people reported:

> Family members are angry but do not know why (NALC, Cayman Islands 2006/7, 18).

> Men and women treat each other bad, there is much more jealousy now (CPA St Lucia 2005/06, 16).

> Alcohol is causing too much fighting and cutting up at the weekends... Too much alcohol is consumed in the village, especially among young men (CPA, Antigua and Barbuda 2007, 18).

> We quarrel, especially when the man drunk (CPA, Grenada 1999, 118).

> My boyfriend don't like me to say anything, he vex about everything (CPA, Anguilla 2007/09, 103).

Part of the family tension arises from the risks that some women take in trying to survive and provide for their children. This includes sometimes engaging in illegal activities or having peculiar relationships with men as boyfriends, husbands, partners, or fathers of her children.

> The house belong to he, when we vex and he put me out I does sleep in the plum tree (CPA, Grenada 1999, 113).

> Women know the heat of the iron (CPA, Grenada 1999, 122).

Tension between women and men also surfaces when men lose their jobs.

> When I go home and I have no money to buy things, my wife gets angry... or...Some women will not go with you unless you have a dollar or piece of food (CPA, Dominica 2008/09, 82).

> Men walk away when they cannot provide for the family and leave you alone in the situation...I am never comfortable when I have to depend more on my spouse (NALC, Cayman Islands 2006/07, 77).

Interesting gender identity emerges over what is considered a 'good woman' or a 'good man'. Infidelity is sometimes seen as a survival strategy practised and accepted by both women and men. The women in the Cayman Islands (NALC 2006/07, 77) echo the views of other women in the region living in similar circumstances.

> Poverty will make you do things out of the way...like have more than one man.
>
> If you nah find work, you have no money...you have fi go tek man.
>
> Sometimes when you become dependent on friends...they (men) will abuse you.

The women were concerned that people believed that these relationships were something they enjoyed, and would see them as promiscuous. They were sensitive to this and admitted that: 'The situation sometimes make you feel like a prostitute, as a woman you have no value.'

Overall, poor living conditions create relationships that are volatile and accommodating at the same time, with high levels of uncertainty and instability. Stress is felt by every member of the family, but responses vary from one household to the other, and by age and gender. The socio-psychological impact of poor living conditions on family and youth can be devastating and debilitating to efforts at making a better life.

## YOUTH AND CHILDREN

The youth also define poverty and assess their living conditions based on their life experiences. Some suggested that poverty was:

> Being deprived of love and affection (CPA, Antigua and Barbuda 2007, 63).
>
> Not having a mother or father (to take care of you) (NALC, Cayman Islands 2006/07, 116).

In an excruciating conversation with a young boy, he reported that, 'His parents consistently told him he would never amount to anything, and wished he was not there.'

As is expected, children are sometimes exposed to uncomfortable social relationships and violence in the home. They appear to have a very precarious understanding of the impact of financial hardship on family relations, including that between parents and between parents and children. They observe that parents sometimes stop communicating with each other and can get abusive. This behaviour is also duplicated with the children in the households. The youth confessed that although they sometimes 'act out', they are not really angry with their parents. They are aware that their parents are worrying about where the next meal is coming from and take this frustration out on the children. This understanding does not preclude that some children do feel anger towards their parents when they are unable to provide everything they request. As a result, parent-child relationships break down. This is more common with mother-child relationships because the mother is the parent who often has to say no when a child's basic need cannot be met.

> Kids just don't understand when their mother says that she don't have it...they see their mother go and buy food and believe that their mother lie to them (NALC, Cayman Islands 2006/07, 68).

Few women admitted that they are guilty of physically and/or verbally abusing their children when under stress. Faced with this moral dilemma, some women select to emotionally distance themselves from their children because they did not wish to, 'treat mi children bad because life hard...and families bicker and mash up.'

Tension in families also occurs when women and men are forced to work long hours in several jobs and/or in shift work. With these types of work schedule, adults rarely have enough time or energy for social interactions, proper communications and adequate supervision of children. Women from single-female-headed households often have to make the difficult choice of leaving their children at home alone, or to have them stay with relatives while they work. This is not an easy decision and sometimes leads to mothers feeling guilty of abandoning their children.

To a large extent, extended family members are important caretakers as women often leave their kids with their mothers, grandmothers, sisters and aunts. The pain felt by parents who separate from their children is shared by immigrants who leave their offspring with loved ones and migrate out of their villages, towns and country, in search of work. Research on the socio-psychological ramifications of migration on family life has reached two different conclusions. There are those who argue that it has a destructive effect (Larmer and Moses 1996; S. Mohammed 1998), and those who hail the resilience of the family in adapting to economic necessity of the absence of biological parents (Wiltshire-Brodber 1986). On the other hand, Christine Barrow (2010) suggests that research on families 'replaced the conventional preoccupations with family structures and family problems, focusing instead on parenting practices and family morality'(3).

Indeed, the data taken from CPAs did not only tease out parenting practices but also highlighted how both parent and child respond to separation and parenting by others. Sometimes, 'barrel children'[1] who grow up without their biological parents react positively and at other times negatively to later attempts of parenting by their biological mothers and fathers. Examples were also cited where adolescents and youth 'act out' on relatives under the aegis that 'you are not my real parents.'

Overall, youth admit that the lack of parental supervision, the poor living conditions in their homes, the absence of proper facilities and organized events for them in the communities can spur gang activities, drugs, sex and violence. This is further realized when young people drop out of school and/ or cannot get jobs. They simply lose hope and are vulnerable to the criminal elements in their environments.

> Because we are young and there is drugs in the neighbourhood we are influenced and want to do drugs like the big boys (NALC, Cayman Islands 2006/07, 67).

> The drug men entice the youth with money because they know that we don't have (CPA, Grenada 1999, 115).

> There were gangs during my school days we had to have gangs to protect ourselves. We had weapons, scissors and knives (CPA, St Lucia 2005/06, 22).

> That is why so many young boys drinking rum, ah don't blame them, we frustrated...When your parents can't give you the things you want you feel to kill yourself...I does think of committing suicide (CPA, Grenada 1999, 125).

The youth pointed out that there are some delinquent activities that are gender distinct. For example, young men get caught up in gang warfare and violence 'rambling and bullying' as 'fellas live on crime'. Young women either 'hook up' with the delinquent males or with older men for transactional sex that give rise to high levels of teenage pregnancy and prostitution.

> We go to the men for a little dollar to buy recess, to go to school, or to buy soap to wash clothes...you may end up having a child (CPA, Dominica 2008/9, 57).

> Girls are more vulnerable to the violence because they get raped (NALC, Cayman Islands 2006/07, 67).

> Young people have to go to Castries and sell their bodies to make money (CPA, St Lucia 2005/06, 17).

It was suggested that these gendered juvenile activities are, in part, coping strategies for poor living conditions as well as a result of the cultural impact of being exposed to sex and violence over time. Youth in the Cayman Islands (NALC 2006/07, 67 and 68) recalled that:

> As a young child when you witness domestic violence it affects you...and you become use to it.

> You feel guilty...shame...embarrassed...want to start doing bad things... some want to commit suicide, some go into prostitution, others hustle or sell drugs.

You have a different attitude towards your goals...like you trying but cannot get anywhere, so you quit...maybe sell drugs...

Whether it is the bigger people who bring it (drugs) in and give it to the smaller people.

Adults on the other hand, believe that young children and youth engaged in delinquent acts because they lacked supervision after school and are exposed to high levels of domestic and criminal violence in their neighbourhoods. According to one community leader:

There are no quiet spaces for the children.

The children are always on the go...in constant motion...rambling around. They also become angry and withdrawn (NALC, Cayman Islands 2006/07, 17).

Anger in response to hardships in the home spills out onto the streets and there are very few, if any, available interventions and/or preventive programmes for women, men, children and youth. In addition, programmes aimed at crime prevention, domestic violence, drug abuse and teenage pregnancy are not only under resourced, but are also not linked to poverty reduction and the psychological impact of living in depressed communities.

## Stigmatization, Humiliation and Discrimination

Poverty is almost always associated with criminality because poor living conditions can lead to high incidences of juvenile delinquency and adult criminal activities. Nonetheless, poor communities are also preyed upon by criminals and experience high police presence, more so than middle-class neighbourhoods. Thus, while individuals of all social classes may be drawn to a life of crime, individuals from poor homes and neighbourhoods are more likely to be arrested and incarcerated. It is also a common practice for crimes in poor communities to be highlighted in the media and in the public eye, so much so, that people are afraid of 'poor folks' and are fearful to go in their housing settlements. Outsiders are warned not to visit, invest, or reside in low-income communities because they are not safe. On the whole, deprived individuals are treated as if they are mentally deranged and physically violent. Consequently, all individuals who live in depressed communities are readily stigmatized, even though the vast majority of residents are hard-working, law-abiding citizens.

Poor communities are usually typecast as dirty with deplorable living conditions. The horrid sanitation and squalor found in these communities are blamed on 'bad' value systems or the personal failings of residents to adhere to proper hygiene, family practices and diligence. The inability to maintain and enhance one's property, combined with the lack of proper sanitation services to these communities, result in dilapidated and aesthetically unattractive housing settlements. While this is a result of structural failures, blame is pointed towards people's value and cultural systems. Poverty is thought to be self-inflicted and the result of a lack of effort by individuals in poor families and neighbourhoods (Chafel 1997).

These stereotypes exist despite the fact that resource-poor individuals work long hours in some of the most laborious jobs for little pay. For example, participants of poverty assessments reported that:

> I have no time, I hustle two jobs to make ends meet, construction in the day and security guard at night (CPA, St Kitts and Nevis 2007/08, 82).

> Lady, you got to help my mother...we have little money and food even though my mother works hard...she works so hard that her foot is swollen and painful...when she comes look at her foot. – Daughter of a domestic worker in a hotel (NALC, Cayman Islands 2006/07, 61).

> I go to the market and sell things...I pick up empty bottles and sell them.

> I make hats and sell but sale not good (CPA, Antigua and Barbuda 2007, 71).

> I does get a little washing sometimes for five dollars...Some of dem like slave drivers, and dey paying next to nothing...The money too little, it can't do...What is five dollars, that can't buy food, I rather don't work than work for that (CPA, Grenada 1999, 126).

Not only are the poor stigmatized as lazy, but they are also pigeonholed as preferring to be dependents of government assistance. Because of these negative stereotypes, people tend to despise the poor; women with children are particularly singled out for reprimand and scorn.

> They telling me stop putting dead people clothes (clothes from charity) on me. I don't care what they say nuh. So long as is not I ask them for their things and they giving it to me, I taking it well (CPA, St Lucia 2005/06, 24).

> People in the community taunt me they say go and look for a bed to sleep you don't have nothing. Before I live here, I used to live up there in a little room and on the floor there was no concrete. Some of them when they quarrel with me they say stop sleeping in stone like sardine in tin, because all of my children and me used to live together. They tell me stop sleeping on bed in cabin. I don't care with what they say. I saying someday God will give me something well (CPA, St Lucia 2005/06, 24).

In fact, single females with children all over the globe, including North America, are stigmatized and demonized (Rodgers 1990; Sidel 1966).

Traditional approaches to poverty assessments are not sensitive to the intense humiliation that people face because of stereotyping and stigmatization. Moreover, the discriminatory actions against individuals, families and communities because of these beliefs are rarely disclosed or addressed. Public servants and citizens along with researchers are usually ignorant of the shame that impoverished people feel and how they are perceived and treated by others.

> People look down on the children because they are poor (CPA, Antigua and Barbuda 2007, 58).
>
> I feel shame having to put back stuff on the shelf in Fosters because of not having enough money...feeling bad when you borrow money from someone and they throw it back in your face (NALC, Cayman Islands 2006/07, 86).
>
> I have to hide to buy a drink, or buy it and take it home because I can't afford to buy for the fellas (CPA, Grenada 1999, 124).

To admit to poverty can be taxing for people who spend most of their lives working and having to go through extreme measures to sustain their households, yet have little to show. As a result, some people try to mask their situations and are subsequently misunderstood and criticized because they 'look good', or because they have some 'nice things'. For the most part, the less fortunate tend to 'keep to themselves' and make a great effort to be seen 'poor but clean'. This 'covering up' is, in part, because the poor prefer to lead very private lives, but also because they want to avoid being humiliated by society. They are hesitant to let their economic status be known out of fear that they would be disrespected. On the other hand, there are those who are convinced that if others knew of their deplorable living conditions, they would more likely receive greater assistance and empathy.

## Shame and Blame

Regrettably, individuals face humiliation and shame on an everyday basis simply because they do not have sufficient income or assets to support individual and family needs. Often they encounter sadness and loneliness that prompt feelings of 'going crazy' and 'giving up'. Interestingly, two of the most damaging stereotypes of the deprived are that: (i) they are to blame for their poverty; and (ii) they enjoy being dependent on others, including the state. Depictions of the 'child mother' or the 'able-bodied man' who will not find work, the 'delinquent juvenile' who would rather sell drugs rather than finish school, are popular beliefs. In reality, most underprivileged people feel 'shame...because they have to ask for help'. For adults, there is no pride in being dependent, because this creates a certain lack of freedom and embarrassment.

For example, public welfare recipients in the Caribbean talk about the attitude and treatment meted out to them by the public and the people who work in social support offices and agencies:

> People treat us different because we are poor.
> They reject you.
> They see you as nobody.
> They watch you with scorn.
> Some people pull you down.
> I don't feel welcome at the Welfare Department (CPA, Anguilla 2007/09, 120).

People are humiliated when they have to ask for money and food; nevertheless, over time, they become despondent because no matter how hard they work, they are unable to make ends meet. These exacting experiences of humiliation and shame are sometimes reflected differently by women and men, although both find it difficult to accept being unable to support their families. Women are concerned about what others think about them as parents; while working men are humiliated, embarrassed and emasculated because:

> They see other children with things and want them, they say daddy not buy that for me (NALC, Cayman Islands 2006/07, 81).

> You feel like a dog when yuh poor, especially if you have to wait on people to give you something, you can't feel like a man (CPA, Grenada 1999, 124).

In the same vein, unemployed men feel disgraced because they are jobless, and single men feel hopeless about marriage prospects because they cannot make enough money to support a wife and family. Married men expressed frustration of not being able to afford to take their wives anywhere, and the elderly talked about 'not having sufficient funds to retire'. In all cases, the lack of income security, combined with the stereotypical gender expectations, leads to serious psychological pressures. Some react by bearing the pain, while others become aggressive and 'feel like turning on society'.

Young children and youth are also stigmatized and humiliated because of their living conditions. They respond to their circumstances in ways that are sometimes misunderstood and misjudged, and consequently face punitive actions. For example, if parents are unable to provide lunch or lunch money to their children, often children choose to stay away from school and become truants, rather than be labelled 'poor'. Similarly, if the parents cannot provide proper clothing, which for youth signifies a certain social status among their peers, then they will either 'act out' or 'drop out'. While poverty studies and reports focus on the health and well-being of children and youth, few address the psychological trauma and stigmatization that they face, and recommend programmatic support.

The emotional ordeal of being a poor child is heart-rending. It is common that kids tease each other, but for children of impoverished homes the teasing is painful and incessant.

> The kids tease me in school and refuse to play with me because they say that I smell...but miss we do not have enough money to buy deodorant or new underwear or clothes (NALC, Cayman Islands 2006/07, 62).

> When you need thing to put under your arm and your mother tell you it is not as important as food but your friends talking about you, you shame to move with them so you start to keep to yourself (CPA, Grenada 1999, 119).

In the Cayman Islands (NALC 2006/07, 62), the youth reported that:

> Because his house looks so poorish, he asked his mummy why don't we go and live somewhere else.

Some parents are aware of the humiliation their children face because of the conditions in which they live. Mothers are particularly pained when:

> Children from the neighbourhood play in each other yards...but none of them come into our yard.

The experience of poor living conditions and lifestyle take a toll on children and youth. Often, they feel and express anger, frustration and resentment.

> I look at the way other people are living and question my parents as to why we are poor (CPA, Antigua and Barbuda 2007, 63).

> Sometimes I get angry and go to my room and listen to music.

> When we go to some of our friends' houses and witness something we don't have...we feel like if we are at the bottom of the list. It is frustrating...really frustrating.

> I know that the kids on the east end think they better than us...because they live in a nicer community and go to better schools (NALC, Cayman Islands 2006/07, 66).

Not in all cases does the trauma of poverty lead to negative behaviour and values. Some youth are more hopeful and use their experiences to build character.

> You learn not to be selfish, or you learn new skills like when they say you can't (NALC, Cayman Islands 2006/07, 66).

More often than not, the comments from the youth reflect emotional stresses with nowhere to go for help. Parents and community leaders believe that it is this loss of hope that affects their life chances and sometimes leads to risky behaviours.

> Youth believe that this country is not going to let them get a piece of the pie...and so they are easily led into undesirable activities.

> When they see how I live then they think no sense doing well in school because they too will not get a job (NALC, Cayman Islands 2006/07, 86).

## Life Chances and Worthiness

Negative stereotyping and stigmatization of resource-poor individuals, groups and communities often lead to a lack of respect and exposure to discrimination in the wider society. This is because stigmas socially devalue and disgrace targeted individuals and groups. The impoverished people in the Caribbean relate well to Goffman's theory (1963, 5), which states that when a person is stigmatized it hampers their opportunities for advancement. They report numerous examples where stereotypes and beliefs about them often result in discriminatory behaviour and negative outcomes. The experiences vary based on demographic interests and concerns. Men, for example, speak about failed employment opportunities, unsuccessful financial transactions and exclusion from social life, because people's perceptions about their character were linked to where they live.

> When I tell them that I live in Faux-A-Chaux, he told me to get out of his office because he don't trust people who live here (CPA St Lucia 2005/06, 20).

> People look down on poor people as if they don't have any confidence in us; they think we can't do their high jobs (NALC, Cayman Islands 2006/07, 66).

> It difficult to get work once they know you from Haynesville...I lost my last job when the boss found out I from Haynesville.

> Fellas feel like outcasts, can't get jobs, have to change yuh address to get jobs.

Reputation of Deacons area makes it difficult for some to get work (CPA, Barbados 2010, 48).

In the same way, entire communities are sometimes ignored because:

They (the government) don't think we need much (NALC, Cayman Islands 2006/07, 66).

In societies where there are large groups of low-income immigrant workers, discrimination based on citizenship also occurs.

We are not here as parasites as a lot of people think.
We have the same surnames but they treat us like dirt, like beggars.
The locals and we are no different...we are from the same families.
Even though we are from the same blood lines, we are disliked, laughed at and cursed (CPA, Anguilla 2007/09, 89).

Immigrants believe that they are exploited because their employers pay them lower wages than the locals and make them work and live in substandard conditions. On the other hand, natives who are unemployed say that they are discriminated against because employers prefer to hire immigrant labourers who are more willing to accept lower wages and poor working conditions. In Caribbean countries with a thriving tourist industry, both locals and Caribbean immigrants agree that North American and European immigrants are favoured in the hotels and restaurants and are given better jobs, working conditions and promotions. Overall, people feel that there is discrimination in the work place based on socio-economic status, skin colour and nationality.

It's the same thing I telling you they (the people in the community who work in the hotels) choosing their friends...people that have already and they fighting you down. They complain about you. They don't like your head. If they don't like you, you don't bound to do them anything. They don't like your style. They don't like how you move...sometimes if they see you getting higher than them they make complaints about you (to hotel management) just to make them fire you. So I not sending applications, I not going to look for jobs. I don't like people like them (CPA, St Lucia 2005/6, 24).

While adults are preoccupied with discrimination in employment practices and social services, the youth believe that they are discriminated against in the school system because of family background and community residency. They compare the educational attainment of kids from poor communities with that of middle-class and rich neighbourhoods.

Our schools don't teach the good education like other schools...schools just want to suck the money out of poor people...People in Savannah high grade push their children, but people in the island downgrade East Enders (NALC, Cayman Islands 2006/07, 66).

Largely, the youth believe that rich children have a higher quality of education, and that sometimes it 'is not black versus white but rich versus poor'. The stigmatization and resulting humiliation experienced by young people from resource-poor communities and homes cause them to struggle with their self-esteem. They are often sad and miserable because:

> Being poor you can't have things that are popular....or a poor person feels left out because their friends have more things than them (CPA, Antigua and Barbuda 2007, 63).

The discernment that people young and old feel, because of discrimination against the least wealthy, creates an atmosphere of disappointment, uselessness and hopelessness.

> Poverty forces you to throw away your dreams (NALC, Cayman Islands 2006/07, 118).

## Hope in the Midst of Despair

Amidst all the negative practices and emotions there are positives because people believe that 'hope is inside of me'. Women, in particular, are firm believers that, 'although sometimes you feel to give up...you have to persist', and consistently defend their actions against all the derogatory stereotypes. They explain that although there are 'cries for help' underprivileged people 'do not want handouts'. In reality, most are afraid of becoming dependent on others, including the state. According to one woman, 'you feel better if you had your own, or can get it yourself.' Unemployed adult children and male spouses/partners think that they are a burden on their mothers, wives and partners.

In many instances, self-esteem is boosted when resource-poor families compare themselves with other less fortunate and are convinced that they are 'blessed'. A sense of pride in being able to help oneself is always present in conversations and reflections; most people in the Caribbean imagine that they can help themselves. Many see their situations as temporary and never give up hope that things will get better. Individuals, households, groups and communities may be resource-poor, but they exhibit resilience, resourcefulness, have strong social networks, and value their dignity, independence and honour.

> We are a proud people, we stick together, and they can't do anything to bring us down...I love my community, you can have confusion here, but when a house in flame everybody running, people forget they vex with you (CPA, St Lucia 2005/06, 27).

> We help ourselves; we don't depend on people from outside (CPA, St Lucia 2005/06, 27).

> Even though people in Grays Farm are poor they think very highly of themselves. They don't like people to look down on them and they don't like to get handouts from persons other than their family (CPA, Antigua and Barbuda 2007, 35).

> I now realize that the people see us (Community Development Officers) as only bringing gravel and sand to build road and community centre, but we need to spend more time on human resource development and on helping the people to develop themselves (CPA, Grenada 1999, 112).

Sharing a common history, culture and/or socio-economic living conditions creates a social bond that stabilizes communities of people (see chapter seven on social capital), and help individuals and families deal with the psychological stresses of life (Narayan et al. 2000). In the Caribbean, self-importance is found through the adherence to cultural traditions, rituals, festivals and ceremonies. For the poor, social solidarity, cultural identity and family life are often the only assets that they possess. For example, in a community assessment chart (CPA, Cayman Islands, Vol. II, 2006/7, 31), participants of a focus group assessed their physical and social well-being as average, their economic state as low, but judged the spiritual and psychological conditions of their community life as high.

Poor people rely heavily on their religious and spiritual beliefs to see them through difficult times. In fact, people tend to place a high moral value in believing that the people in their community are 'God-fearing' folks who despite hard times remain 'good people'. They often associate psychological and spiritual well-being with religious beliefs and practices.

> Extreme poverty does not exist here..., the community spirit makes up for what is lacking (CPA, Antigua and Barbuda 2007, 30).

> God will provide...a praying woman is a powerful woman (CPA, Grenada 1999, 123).

## Marginalization and Social Exclusion

Despite the hope, pride and desires to be financially independent and stable, the sustained and targeted discrimination that takes place in the wider society, eventually leads to marginalization and social exclusion of entire groups and communities. Assessment of the socio-psychological dimension of poverty exposes the deprivation of certain groups that arises from historical antecedents, and contemporary social and structural prejudices. It also divulges how the disenfranchised interpret their state of affairs and social exclusion.

Social exclusion usually refers to access to income and assets but it does also involve social and psychological factors (Sen 2000; Bourgignon and Chakravarty 2003). When poverty-stricken people talk about their exclusion they do not always refer to unequal distribution of money and material assets, but to the lack of voice and power in society, and group denial of access to opportunities relative to others. Within this context, social exclusion is associated with the concept of relative poverty rather than absolute poverty, and the social interactions of the powerful (rich) with the subordinate (not so rich) groups in society. It also includes both tangible and non-tangible benefits.

Narayan et al. (2000) identified at least five factors that contribute to social exclusion, namely isolation based on geography and nationality, bureaucracy, corruption, physical violence and psychological intimidation. The physical location of people who live in rural communities, as do approximately 70 per cent of the world poor, make it difficult for them to travel to towns and cities for services. Additionally, little resources, including infrastructure and social services are invested in these communities. Where services are available, they are often unaffordable as is the case for both the rural and urban poor.

> Belmont is not yet a place; Government refuse to build roads because this area is not in the project (CPA, St Lucia 2005/06, 26).

> Persons have died before the ambulance arrived. They could reach the hospital and it was not a major illness, if they had seen a doctor earlier they could have made it...When my mother was sick the ambulance stay so long to come that when we reach the hospital the doctor ask why we didn't bring her sooner (CPA, Antigua and Barbuda 2007, 24).

> We like sports but there is no playing field or sporting facilities here (CPA, St Lucia 2005/06, 26).

> There is nothing in place to access loans (CPA St Lucia 2005/06, 21).

Barriers to institutions and services are further compounded by bureaucracies that are inflexible in requirements, documentation and cost of transactions. Not only are the conditions necessary for services and resources out of the reach of the poor, but the process of applying is usually costly (financially and time wise), complicated and discouraging. Further, the treatment meted out to recipients by staff is hostile and intimidating. In the Caribbean, bureaucracy is a common hindrance for people who own family lands and cannot use it as collateral because it is difficult to get individual land titles and deeds. Similarly, application for work permits by migrants is always a daunting task, difficult to manoeuvre regardless of education. The imposition of the process and the detailed documentation required when applying for welfare is another way of socially excluding women, particularly single women, from much needed assistance. To a large extent, every aspect of bureaucracy handicaps and further stigmatizes, rather than facilitate those who require support as the examples below show.

> Before you had to present a birth certificate, now they ask for so many things, it is impossible to meet the requirements (CPA, St Lucia 2005/06, 19).

> The people who really need it can't benefit because they set some criteria that the common poor man cannot get in, those who already have are the ones who benefit (CPA, St Lucia 2005/06, 21).

Along with hostile public offices, corrupt officials also excludes certain groups from information, resources and opportunities. Too often we hear that 'it is not what you know but who you know.' For the poor, not having the 'right connections' or the finances to offer a bribe can have devastating and traumatic effects on their lives. Corruption can prevent families from getting jobs, health benefits, and access to educational assistance for children unless forms of monetary and sexual favours are met. Women and youth can be coerced into sexual relations, while men are forced to work free on personal jobs or offer money to officials. Whichever way it is taken:

> You going to be used by the big fellas (CPA, Dominica 2008/09, 98).

> All stupidness have to go on. You don't go to bed with dem, so they don't give you nothing...Government people who give work won't give work to women they can't touch up. They want to play with you first (CPA, Grenada 1999, 123).

> Years now I trying to get a licence and these guys refuse to give me (CPA, St Lucia 2005/06, 19).

> The house need repairs bad, is two years now since I put my name down in the house repair programme but I ent get call yet (CPA, Grenada 1999, 113).

> Politics cause a division and this cause further poverty. If you don't vote for them you can't get any work, if you not working, you will remain poor (CPA, Grenada 1999, 120).

The less powerful are afraid of responding to these atrocities as individuals or groups because they are physically and psychologically intimidated. It seems they are being held ransom because they are poor. In many instances, clients of public assistance accept abusive language and mannerisms and are pressed into silence and submissiveness.

> You feel different when you are unable to provide for yourself...you become unintelligent (NALC, Cayman Islands 2006/07, 86).

> Poverty is a disgrace not a sin (NALC, Cayman Islands 2006/07, 76).

One of the most damaging consequences of stigmatization is that the impoverished internalize the negative stereotypes. They sense that society sees them not just as different, but inferior and a disgrace (Eitzen and Eitzen Smith 2009). As a result, the underprivileged sometimes blame themselves for their failures and are insecure in trying to address their own problems. Many are uncomfortable speaking in public, including on matters directly linked to their well-being. Parents from poorer homes are hesitant to ask questions about their child's school performance and to engage in general discussions in parent-teacher meetings.

In general, the experiences and sentiments expressed vary by demographic characteristics whereby women feel obscure, the disabled speak of being excluded from knowledge, the elderly feel abandoned by society, and youth think they must throw their dreams away. These examples illustrate that social exclusion is not an inevitable condition, but results from certain social and structural antecedents. In many instances, social exclusion is not just happening, but is being made to happen.

> Because Grays Farm is known as the ghetto, political leaders don't pay much attention, only when it is election time...We are being used as political pawns (CPA, Antigua and Barbuda 2007, 29).

> Note the community map did not include clustered areas of "tenement yards"; instead they made reference to "condos and apartments" (NALC, Cayman Islands 2006/07, 119).

> We do not have a voice.

> We need a voice and someone to listen to us.

> Government make decisions they think we need but they need to ask us (CPA, Anguilla 2007/09, 46).

## Why Socio-Psychological Methodological Approaches and Theoretical Perspectives are Missing in Poverty Studies

Although poverty is widely recognized as a multidimensional phenomenon, the material or physical characteristics still dominate poverty studies. The popularity of this focus is directly linked to three main factors. First, statistical data drive policy, and policies are based on quantifiable variables such as income and expenditure. The extent to which poverty exists in any population is determined by where these measures place individuals and households  relative to a predetermined poverty line. While people's experiences and feelings are essential to our understanding of poverty, these variables are not easy to measure and, as a result, there are no comparable data locally, regionally or internationally. Attempts have been made to identify indicators that can be used to assess psychological dimensions, specifically that of shame and humiliation (Tangney and Dearing 2002; Zavaleta 2007).

Consideration has also been given to develop intrinsic measures of psychological well-being that can appraise human experiences and values. For example, Emma Samman (2007) suggested a two-pronged approach based on: (i) people's perceptions of the meaning of life, and (ii) one's ability to strive towards achieving this idea. Despite these efforts, there are still only few gauges that measure the psychological effects of human poverty, and fewer yet that can be used at a comparative level.

 Second, the measurable physical characteristics of poverty, such as hunger and mortality, are too severe to not be the centre of attention. It is difficult to ignore the nearly 800 million people who suffer from chronic undernourishment every year. We cannot turn a blind eye to the 900 million people who remain hungry every day (FAO 2010), particularly, in developing countries. Worse still, eight million children die each year from hunger, that is, 22, 000 every day (UNICEF 2012).

 Third, poverty is usually defined and measured based on the discipline of the researcher, or the purpose of the study. For example, the economist is concerned with monetary measures and looks at income and consumption patterns. The sociologist focuses on how economic status affects social inequality and assesses poverty based on access to resources and human services as well as the motivational and social capabilities of people. The psychological perspectives centre on the humiliation and shame that individuals, groups and communities experience because they lack resources and are stigmatized. To a large extent, political economists drive poverty assessments and are frequently used by policymakers to measure economic well-being. On the other hand, research that includes the sociological and psychological dimensions reinforces the more visible and quantifiable material and economic aspects of people's lives, but because they also link poverty to social relations of power and wealth they are not necessarily politically palatable.

Traditional sociological research has always been interested in the opportunities that people from different socio-economic strata were availed of, and the resulting consequences. According to this school of thought, high status and powerful people exude dominance, self-confidence and pride, while the poor are expected to exhibit embarrassment, vulnerability, powerlessness and shame. These arguments are found in the discourse emanating from the classic works of sociologists such as Emile Durkheim, Max Weber, Karl Marx, Georg Simmel and others, who theorized on the life chances of individuals in stratified societies. Unfortunately, less attention has been given to this aspect of poverty over the years. Instead, debates ensue on the extent to which poverty persists because of the retrogressive cultures of subgroups in society.

The culture of poverty arguments originate from a line of reasoning made popular by protagonist Oscar Lewis who sought to explain the social responses of people to economic deprivation, from an anthropological standpoint. In his seminal work on five families in Mexico, Lewis (1959) introduced the idea of a 'culture of poverty' in which he suggested that the living conditions of poor people forces them to adopt certain behavioural strategies, relevant to their marginal environment. Since these strategies are passed from one generation to another, they are sometimes perceived as a cultural phenomenon. Lewis's theory has since been misinterpreted and used to blame the impoverished for their inability to break a cycle of poverty. The assumption is made that certain negative values and practices are embedded in the culture of specific subgroups which hampers them from progress, because they are unable to pull themselves up by the proverbial boot straps.

Such thinking is still current among policymakers, service workers and members of the community in the Caribbean and elsewhere.

> The people's minds are closed to up-liftment, they do not have an open mind, if you try to start something to develop them you practically have to beg them to participate...poor attitudes (CPA, Antigua and Barbuda 2007, 31).

The ability of less fortunate groups to advance has less to do with culture and is more likely based on access to resources, including intellectual and motivational opportunities. Moreover, access to resources is dependent on one's socio-economic position in a stratified society. Getting ahead requires having the 'right' interpersonal relationships with resourceful individuals and groups who tend to be far removed from the reach of certain subgroups. Thus, devoid of the social capital and the economic resources, as will be discussed in chapter seven, the marginalized must seek 'adoption strategies or a culture' that helps them survive, but not escape intergenerational poverty.

Apart from Lewis's work and other research related to his propositions, the concept of shame and humiliation experienced by the poor and the impact of this on well-being remain under researched. The few contemporaries who have done some research on the subject conclude that people from lower social classes are not treated as equals, and that shame and shaming can contribute to their deficiency and failure (Clark 1990; Lehtinen 1998; Neckel 1996; Retzinger 1991; Scheff 1990, 2003). There is no doubt that material poverty does have psychological consequences that are far-reaching and prevent persons from participating in social and political life (Narayan et al. 2000; Sen 1987). This understanding was ratified in a UN 2006 declaration where poverty was defined as *the lack of participation in decision making in civil, social, and cultural life*. This new way of thinking about poverty is an extension of the argument of Sen (1999) that poverty not only robs people of the freedom to access basic needs for living, but also denies them of their political and civil liberties to participate in the political, social and economic life of their communities (see also Carr 2009).

## Summary and Conclusions

The voices in this chapter tell the stories of the powerless. By focusing on the socio-psychological dimension of poverty, human agency was placed at the heart of poverty, and the subjects of poverty were made both visible and audible. This is important because rarely do we read about what a man feels when he is unable to financially support his family, or to hear the 'matriarch' cry as she bears the family's burden and maintains a strong persona. What do financially stable children, tell children from impoverished homes? The socio-psychological examples in the chapter exposed the realities of people who experience pain, humiliation and discrimination daily. It also helped to illustrate how people think and behave under harsh living conditions, and how strategies of survival could easily be interpreted as a debilitating *culture of poverty.*

A careful examination of the various factors that affect people's lives can for heuristic purposes be divided into material well-being, social well-being, and psychological well-being. However, for the poor, the various dimensions cannot be separated because they are experienced simultaneously. Furthermore, each dimension reinforces the others. For the poor, not being able to feed and clothe their families brings physical pain as well as emotional pain. Economists, sociologists, politicians and others have all attempted to count, classify and analyse populations by income, race/ethnicity, gender, households and geographical communities. Some have concluded that social class and other forms of discrimination, impact the physical and mental health of the poor. But what does this mean? How does it work? The various stories and analyses in this chapter gave very colourful descriptions to help us understand the reality of discrimination and the impact it has on individual women and men, children, families and entire communities.

But poverty research and assessment studies are not focused on capturing the socio-psychological aspects of people who live below the poverty line, and whose life chances are directly linked to their socio-psychological experiences. Maybe it is felt that this is not important in understanding poverty and developing strategies, or maybe poverty is just a statistic and not a person? Nevertheless, poverty research remains stuck in economic well-being and structural approaches, the social, psychological and gender dimensions are merely 'add ons'. As a result, the processes and interactions of those who are being studied, that is, the relational aspects that involve power hierarchies and social exclusion are ignored. Consequently, summations and analyses from current approaches are restrictive in understanding social behaviour and how social exclusion and forced social isolation act as barriers to social capital, socio-economic opportunities, and social mobility for women and men, households and communities.

Further, the lack of information and understanding of how people respond and cope with economic hardships is unfortunate as it has direct impact on strategies aimed at poverty reduction and the enhancement of people's lives. It also leaves people vulnerable to policymakers, service providers and public opinion to individualize the problem of poverty, making it look like some kind of human defect, family deficiency, or a cultural flaw among some groups. Women are particularly singled out for and are morally judged. Officials and others working with the less fortunate are often heard commenting on the amount of money that women with low incomes and families spend on their physical appearance, such as their clothes, manicured nails and expensive hair styles. Without a proper understanding of the psychological aspects of poverty, we would never understand why:

> Every woman must want fi look good...just put yourself together, even if your clothes cheap (NALC, Cayman Islands 2006/07, 76).

The socio-psychological aspect of poverty is sometimes referred to as the missing or hidden dimension. When included, it puts a human face back into poverty studies. Moreover, it directly challenges the complexity of social injustice and helps us understand what people feel and do in response to their living conditions, as well as to each other. Without a deeper understanding of this dimension of poverty, not only will it persist, but so too will the stereotyping and stigmatization of the impoverished. Stanley Eitzen and Kelly Eitzen Smith (2009) pose the following interesting questions: 'Are the poor deserving of their fate? Is it their fault? Should solutions be aimed at changing the poor rather than society?' In other words, not only is poverty continuously seen as a matter of personal causation, but poverty alleviation is linked to self-improvement.

Excluding the socio-psychological dimension of poverty is to deny people their agency and make humanity invisible. Without including the voices of the impoverished, we cannot completely understand their lives. Moreover, the value of knowing how people manage their social and economic circumstances and how they relate to each other is underestimated. Research and analyses remain a 'top-down' exercise and the possibility for human agency to create change from the bottom up is left unknown. Additionally, by keeping the focus on 'top-down' macro-level analyses, the social behaviours by women and men are least understood and, as a result, gender-related stigmatization are not addressed.

Alternatively, the inclusion of the socio-psychological dimension in poverty studies brings the analyses down to the micro levels of the home, family and community and deconstructs the Eurocentric-based stereotypes and gender role expectations. The socio-psychological dimension of poverty helps us to understand the conflicts and resolutions associated with the 'strong matriarch', the 'emasculated man' and the social fragmentation of families and communities.

Moreover, the incorporation of the voices of stigmatized individuals exemplifies the extent to which poverty continues to be treated as a structural fix and/or a moral condition. Without the inclusion of the human side of poverty what we know about the impoverished is simply data, a category, a percentile and, more importantly, a stereotype. Thus, the socio-psychological dimension of poverty provides a human presence, a personality and a voice to those who are left out of decision-making processes, including plans that directly affect them. Most importantly, while the poor are depicted as dependents, the examples and discussions confirm that marginalized individuals and groups desire individual freedom, self-determination and full participation in civil society. Also important, the scenarios presented in this chapter show how these facets and desires are negotiated every day in the home, the community and society at large.

# 4. Are More Families Poor Because of the Increase in Female-Headed Households?

## A Critical Review of the Feminization of Poverty Perspective

This chapter is a continuation of the interrogation of the methodological and theoretical perspectives used to understand and assess poverty in the region. Too often we see statements such as *'Poverty in Jamaica is increasingly feminized'* (UNDP 2009, 5). But what meaning is being conveyed by this descriptive? Is poverty linked to prevalence of female-headed households? Indeed, female-headed households have always been a feature of the Caribbean landscape and, in some countries, it is a growing phenomenon (tables 4.1 and 4.2). Moreover, surveys of living conditions in Caribbean countries show that there is a higher incidence of female-headed households falling below the poverty line. For example, the Barbados Country Assessment of Living Conditions (CALC) 2010 Report indicated that 62.2 per cent of all poor households were headed by women and that the poverty rate for female-headed households (19.4 per cent) was higher than that for male-headed single-parent households (11.5 per cent). Similarly, the Jamaica Survey of Living Conditions (2005) noted that almost half of all Jamaican households (46.3 per cent) are headed by women and many of these are in the poorest quintile of the population.

That female heads of households are more likely to be in the poorest quintile appears to be typical for the Caribbean. Even in the more developed countries such as Trinidad and Tobago, an Analysis of the Survey of Living Conditions (SLC) for Trinidad and Tobago, conducted in 2005, found that almost 37.7 per cent of the poorest households in that country were headed by women (Kairi 2007). Similarly, the United Nations Caribbean Women's Office website reports that women head 96 per cent of poor households in St Vincent and the Grenadines communities, and that, in Belize, 30.5 per cent of all households are headed by single women and are defined as poor, compared to 23.6 per cent of the other types of households

But what do these statistics mean? Do they suggest that female-headed households are the 'poorest of the poor' as the *feminization of poverty* concept, imported from North America, is often taken to mean? Should the attention be placed on family structures or on why women who head households are more likely to be living and supporting families in impoverished conditions? These questions challenge the universal applicability of the ideas of the *feminization of poverty* model and whether the incidence of female-headed households is a useful measure or indicator of women's poverty in the Caribbean? Equally important is to ask, what does this tell us about the lived experiences of the women, men and youth in resource-poor Caribbean households, including why a large number of female-headed households are yet to break the cycle of poverty, despite the many advances made by Caribbean women.

This chapter attempts to bring some clarity to these issues by examining the ideological and methodological challenges in the universal adoption of the *feminization of poverty* perspective. It critiques the focus, the underlying assumptions and the implications of the *feminization of poverty* model in its applicability as a heuristic device to understand poverty in the region and globally. It does this by interrogating the structural factors and cultural arguments that link Caribbean female-headed households to poverty. The ensuing discussions highlight the Eurocentric gender biases embedded in the ideological manifestation of the concept. The chapter argues that preconceived notions can affect measures of poverty in essentialist and limiting ways that defy a thorough understanding of the nature of gendered poverty in the Caribbean and elsewhere. In its totality, the chapter offers discussions that are important to understand the various economic, social and cultural dimensions of gendered poverty in the Caribbean and the role of women's agency in negotiating these interrelated aspects of their lives. It redirects the *feminization of poverty* focus from dis-proportionality and family structures to discussions on why female-headed households and women in general are more likely to experience poverty.

## What is the Feminization of Poverty?

The term *feminization of poverty* dates back to a US study on the gender trends in poverty between the 1950s and mid-1970s. The findings showed that women over the age of 16 were increasingly falling below the poverty line and that larger percentages of the American poor were in female-headed households. Diane Pearce (1978) used the term *feminization of poverty* to refer to her findings and linked women's poverty to the lack of government support for divorced and single women. Other researchers looked at similar trends using the US Census data and agreed with Pearce's findings, but explained that this pattern was based on *relative* and *not absolute* decline in women's economic status. In fact, they observed that poverty rates for women and men were on the decline (McLanahan and Kelly 1999; McLanahan, Sorenson and Watson 1989). Nevertheless, by the mid-1980s, it was believed that almost half of all the poor in the US were living in families headed by women in various stages of their life-cycle, and that intergenerational poverty existed in homes headed by women who had early child-bearing experiences and low levels of education.

Following the US studies and observations, various definitions and measures of the *feminization of poverty* developed. In Latin America, Marcelo Medeiros and Joana Costa (2006, 2008), looked at different scenarios of what constitutes a *feminization of poverty* and proposed that a fair definition would be that the *feminization of poverty* assesses the change in poverty levels for women and female-headed households. More distinctively, it represents an increase in poverty levels between women and men or between households headed by either of the sexes or couples. For them the *feminization of poverty* measures *changes* and *not prevalence* and, as such, does not imply a worsening of women's poverty or that of female-headed households. Instead, the *feminization of poverty* is treated as a relative concept and refers to an increase in the share of women or female-headed households among the poor. Despite these distinctions, there are those who interpret the *feminization of poverty* as a measure of the incidence of poverty among female-headed households (Fukuda-Parr 1999).

Sylvia Chant (2003) approached the concept in a different way. She believed that the growing burden of poverty on women was encapsulated in the *feminization of poverty* discourse. Rather than trying to give a precise definition of the concept, Chant looked at the *factors responsible* for the *feminization of poverty*, and the link to gender disparities across a wide range of factors, including the rising occurrence of women who are heads of poor households. Like others, Chant was not so much focused on a precise definition of the concept but was concerned that despite social and economic efforts to reduce gender inequality, women continue to comprise the majority of the world's poor. In this regard, the *feminization of poverty* hypothesis, by drawing attention to women's poverty, has been a powerful tool of gender advocacy. It ignited debates and discourses on possible causes of women's poverty and that the number of female-headed households was forming an increasingly larger percentage of the poor, even though more women were entering the work force. In fact, as more women attempted to become economically independent by entering the job market, the more they were being drawn to 'pauperization and dependence on welfare' (McLanahan and Kelly 1999, 127–45).

As a result, the *feminization of poverty* rhetoric, by emphasizing women's poverty, has resulted in a proliferation of policies, programmes and projects directed towards improving women's literacy, education, health services, skills building, access to micro-credit, and overall social, economic, and infrastructural support to female-headed households (Chant 2003, 1999; Kabeer 1997; Marcoux 1998; Pankhurst 2002). Gender issues are also now an integral part of poverty reduction strategy policies and have moved from being gender-sensitive to being a vital part of the process. According to Medeiros and Costa (2008, 1), the *feminization of poverty* centres attention on two 'morally unacceptable phenomenon' – poverty, and gender inequalities. It, therefore, makes policymakers aware of the need for pro-gender equity and anti-poverty measures. In this regard, the *feminization of poverty* has helped advance the 'engendering' of poverty analysis since the 1970s (Chant 2003), and illuminate gendered dimensions of poverty beyond a focus purely on household incomes (Razavi 1999).

The concept does carry with it controversies and ambiguities, both in its meaning and applicability for different groups. The use of the term *feminization of poverty* has been widely adopted in the Caribbean to describe the prevalence of poverty in female-headed households. This is not surprising because for decades, research on Caribbean family and poverty studies have been preoccupied with explaining the origins, structures and economic functioning of the family, primarily that of the lower social class, Afro-Caribbean people (Clarke 1957; Henriques 1953; Frazier 1966; Rodman 1971; Rubenstein 1980; Simey 1946; R.T. Smith 1988). Some of the early value-laden studies also implied that the social ills in black communities were a result of family structures and the practice of single-female-headed households. Fortunately, this has since changed primarily because of the research and epistemologies of feminist and women scholars in the region. The *feminization of poverty* model, therefore, offers a mix-bag of interpretations when used in the region.

## Caribbean Families and Female-Headed Households

Caribbean households are highly complex with many patterns of family and kinship arrangements co-existing side by side. Among these forms are legal marriages with nuclear families; common-law unions consisting of a man and woman living together as husband and wife but without legal sanction; and stable visiting relationships. In some Caribbean societies, common-law relationships are recognized by the laws of that country and in most Caribbean societies, common-law unions are socially accepted. Many children are born to couples who are not legally married, and there are single parent homes where a single woman or man lives with their children. Then, there is the widely practised extended family system in which women play a central role in the social, cultural and economic life of a wide range of familial individuals. Extended families consist of grandmothers, aunts, siblings and other relatives and may also be a result of migrant parents and are, therefore, transnational in scope.

Although it is commonly believed that female-headed households dominate in the Caribbean, the limited data that exists show otherwise. Compared to North America and Europe, the percentage of female-headed households in the region is relatively high and ranges for most countries between one-third to a little below one-half of all households (table 4.1). The diverse family forms emerged from historical, economic and social forces and are characterized by many forms of conjugal relationships. The literature on the Caribbean family centre on Afro-Caribbean and show variation over time in theoretical perspectives and how these perspectives are linked to Eurocentrism (Rajack-Talley and Talley 2005; Barrow 1996).

In the past, family studies were preoccupied with the structural and functional explanations, where the focal point was on the impact of slavery and colonization, and later on economic adaptations to harsh living conditions. These structural functionalist approaches were used to explain the comparatively high levels of female-headed households and single-parent families in Caribbean societies. They were moralistic in their orientation and viewed non-nuclear families as deviant and dysfunctional (Frazier 1966; Simey 1946), a result of the conditions of slavery and/or economic marginalization (Blake 1961; Clarke 1957; Frazier 1966; Goveia 1965; Matthews 1953; Patterson 1967; Simey 1946; R.T. Smith 1956).

Others explained the non-nuclear Afro-Caribbean family in relation to the nature of a Caribbean plural society (L. Braithwaite 1959; Henriques 1953; M.G. Smith 1957), while the more empirical research that emerged in the early 1970s explained how different forms of Afro-Caribbean family and kinship practices were adaptations to economic circumstances (Rodman 1971; Rubenstein 1980; R.T. Smith 1988). This literature implicitly used the European family norms as the standard, but viewed the differences as functional adaptations to economic and social marginalization.

Another trend that emerged in the literature of the late 1970s studied the Caribbean family through understanding how gender dynamics and relations are linked to family and kinship practices (Barrow 1997, 1998; Black 1995; Chevannes 1993a; 1993b; Morrissey 1998). This research orientation is not concerned with structural or functional-centred analyses but adopts a more interpretative perspective. According to Christine Barrow (2010, 35) it is a 'more phenomenological approach that centres the meanings of lived experiences of Caribbean family life as expressed by informants, reflections and interpretations.' The focus is on the relational processes involved in parenting and other types of familial interactions. Household sites are treated as spaces where conflicts and cooperation are continuously negotiated (see chapter six), and where families are created through actions and interactions.

Women are viewed as social actors who make rational decisions about their various conjugal arrangements. For example, Sheila Stuart (1996) found that the formation of single-parent headed households was a deliberate choice made by women and men. Women, in particular, value legal marriage, children born in wedlock and permanent family arrangements, but did not hastily enter into permanent or semi-permanent unions with men for several reasons. The findings of her study explained that single women found that they: (i) were better off financially if they remained on their own; (ii) could maintain their independence and not become subordinated to men; and (iii) have greater custody of their children. In other words, <u>women elected to be single parents because of social and economic benefits that can be accrued from being single (L</u>eo-Rhynie 1993). For many Caribbean women, contemplation of marriage has measures of economic stability such as a steady job, house and/or land, as well as sentimental values (Dreher and Hudgins 2010).

Single-parent households, male-headed and female-headed households were also formed due to men and women who migrated in search of work and a better way to support their children and families.[1] In such instances, the extended family, particularly that of grandmothers, sisters and other female relatives, is important in assisting with child care, in the absence of a parent. As a whole, while single-female-headed households are quite common in the region, the population census statistics reveal that there are more male-headed households in the Caribbean, with wide disparities among the different countries (table 4.1). Using the data from 18 Caribbean countries, Leith L. Dunn and Alicia Mondesire (2009) identified three groupings based on percentage of female-headed households. These included seven of the 18 countries with averages of 40 per cent, nine with 30 per cent, and only two with less than 30 per cent of female-headed households. The researchers alluded that the wide variations in heads of households may be due to differences in the cultural make up of the populations with non-African ethnic groupings. For example, in countries with low levels of female-headed households like Belize and Guyana, there are large populations of Amerindians and East Indians who practise more traditional male-headed household arrangements. Interestingly, there is little variation based on the level of development or economic base of the different countries.

When the 2000 data is compared with the 1990 census data, they show that in the previous decade the number of households headed by women slightly increased (see table 4.2). The shift to more female-headed households, albeit small, has implications for family arrangements, the economic status of women and men, and poverty trends in households (Dunn and Mondesire 2009; St Bernard 2003).

*Table 4.1: Percentage Household Heads by Country and Sex (2000)*

| Countries | % Male | % Female |
|---|---|---|
| Anguilla | 64.5 | 35.5 |
| Antigua and Barbuda | 56.5 | 43.5 |
| The Bahamas | 63.6 | 36.4 |
| Barbados | 55.5 | 44.5 |
| Belize | 76.1 | 23.9 |
| Bermuda | 53.1 | 46.9 |
| British Virgin Islands | 66.7 | 33.3 |
| Dominica | 63.2 | 36.8 |
| Grenada | 59.1 | 40.9 |
| Guyana | 70.9 | 29.1 |
| Jamaica | 58.7 | 41.3 |
| Montserrat | 66.8 | 33.2 |
| St Lucia | 57.5 | 42.5 |
| St Kitts and Nevis | 57.4 | 42.6 |
| St Vincent and the Grenadines | 60.1 | 39.9 |
| Suriname | 69.0 | 31.0 |
| Trinidad and Tobago | 69.9 | 30.1 |
| Turks and Caicos Islands | 69.2 | 30.8 |
| **TOTAL** | 63.2 | 36.8 |

*Source: Dunn and Mondesire (2009)*

*Table 4.2: Percentage Change in Sex of Household Heads 1990 and 2000*

| Heads of Households | % Male | % Female | % Difference Male/ Female |
|---|---|---|---|
| TOTAL 2000 Census | 63.2 | 36.8 | 26.36 |
| TOTAL 1990 Census | 65.1 | 34.9 | 30.25 |

*Source: Dunn and Mondesire (2009)*

The continued existence of female-headed households, over time, and their transcendence across social classes have posed serious challenges to the assumptions and explanations of Caribbean family structures and their relations to socio-economic lifestyles. Poverty assessments continue to look more at quantitative data that are disaggregated by gender and household headship to measure incidence and levels of poverty in the region. They are limiting in their explanations of why material changes have not reached female-headed households. Neither can these studies be used to explain why there is also the predominance of non-poor female-headed households.

On the other hand, there are feminists and gender scholars in the Caribbean like Eudine Barriteau who are interrogating why despite the material gains made by women in the region, socio-economic, cultural, and political gender equality remain elusive. Others are making tremendous progress in understanding women's economic roles, family processes and relations, matriarchy and matrifocality, parenting, sexuality, social exclusion and human rights, and issues of health and labour (Barrow 2010; Barrow, de Brunn and Carr 2009; Kempadoo 2004; Leo-Rhynie, Bailey and Barrow 1997; P. Mohammed 1998, 1999; Reddock 1994, Safa 1995 and others). Few (Ellis 1986, 1988, 2003; Safa 1995; Momsen 1991, 1993, 1998 and others) have examined women and development, and some researched women in agriculture (Momsen 1988; Rajack-Talley 2015; Rajack-Talley and Talley 2000; Reddock and Huggings 1988, 1997). Many of these studies are either focused on women from low-income families or address how the social issues are affected by and/or affect women's poverty. However, there is no single group of literature centred on women's poverty, and single-female-headed households. As a result, aside from the CPAs, the region is still poor in research that examines factors that contribute to why female-headed households continue to be a fair share of the region's poor, and how women cope with the various dimensions of their lives, including poor living conditions.

## Feminization of Poverty in the Caribbean

The data being collected in the Caribbean through surveys of living conditions and country poverty studies reveal that female-headed households are among the poorest in many Caribbean societies, though not in all countries. The poverty studies make clear, that in spite of this trend, there is not a strong association between poverty and single-female-headed households as alluded to in the North American model of the *feminization of poverty*. In some instances, like in the case of Belize, female-headed households fell below the poverty line only by a small margin. Overall, the findings of the studies reveal that the association between household headship and poverty is uncertain and, instead, several other factors are more directly linked to poverty in households, such as family sizes, income, structural barriers, social exclusion, gender, social class discrimination and others.

## Structural Factors

Specific to single-female-headed households, there is a range of social and structural factors that contribute to the likelihood of them falling in the poorest quintile in many countries. These factors are all interrelated and cyclic in their overall impact. For example, all the studies conducted in the region suggest a strong correlation between labour force participation and levels of education with poverty. As a whole, individuals with little or no education are either unemployed or in low-wage jobs and living in resource-poor households. For example, in Barbados, approximately 56 per cent of those in the lowest poverty quintile had no qualifications, although education is free and compulsory to age 16. In Trinidad and Tobago, it was suggested that close to 40 per cent of all the unemployed were vulnerable to poverty and most likely have low levels of education (Kairi 2007). Here again, gender disparities are glaring, where for example, the Trinidad and Tobago data showed that there were less unemployed males (19.8 per cent) with no education compared to unemployed females (26.7 per cent) with no education.

Overall, women from single-female-headed households tend to possess low levels of education and job skills and are unable to get jobs with higher wages. This is in spite of the fact that in countries like Barbados, Trinidad and Tobago and others, the labour market witnessed an increase in the educational attainment of workers and a growth in the number of professional females in employment. It is apparent that the achievements by women in education and professional employment do not impact all women, as there are still high numbers of women employed in low-skill, low-paying jobs.

The gender disaggregated statistics in the region show that women's employment in the formal market is lesser in proportion and in earnings compared to men. Women are found mainly in the lower-level service jobs and in sales. Additionally, women's unemployment rates are almost twice as high compared to men.[2] Further, gender discrimination in the workplace continues where women with the same qualifications are paid less than men in the same job (see study by Dunn and Dunn on off-shore data centres in Barbados and Jamaica, 1998). This information on labour force participation and education helps in understanding why impoverished households are more likely to be female-headed (Kairi 2007). It does not, however, explain why women from certain households are still not getting the education or skills and training needed for higher paying jobs or why wage discrimination persists.

Young women, in particular, lack training even for some of the more traditional 'women's work' in health, education and the service industry. They are also not employable in emergent contemporary jobs because as both Girvan (1997) and Sen (1992) explained, the changing workforce due to globalization and technological advances, demand new skills and the 're-tooling' of labour (see chapters one and two). Women from resource-poor households are unable to take advantage of such opportunities because: (i) they are socially excluded from the information; (ii) they do not have the funds or qualifications to apply; and (iii) they do not have the freedom due to the disproportionate burden they bear in taking care of others in the household (Barbados, CALC 2010).

Female-headed households are also identified as having early child-bearing practices, large family sizes, and greater numbers of non-income earning household dependents (Barriteau 2001b; Dreher and Hudgins 2010; Henry-Lee and Le Franc 2002; Prendergast and Grace 2006). These patterns were also observed in the SLC and CPAs database. Additionally, because of slow economic growth and structural adjustment policies, the region has witnessed a decrease in public assistance and social services, forcing women to take up the slack through increased childcare responsibilities as well as care of the elderly, the sick and the unemployed. As a result, many women from low-income households are unable to take on supplemental jobs or have the time to pursue job training and improve their level of education. Economic downturn and structural adjustment policies have also further causualized women's labour. As a result, most working-class women who have full or part-time jobs, still do not earn sufficient incomes to support a family, and are more likely to head poor households.

The high number of non-wage earners in these homes translates to lower per capita income and expenditure, including available funds to 'better' oneself. All these factors limit the capability of women from low-income households, single or two-parent, to improve themselves and the standard of living of their families. Moreover, findings from the survey of living conditions and the country poverty studies reveal that little difference exists between poor women and non-poor women, in terms of labour force participation rates. But, there is evidence of labour market segmentation between the genders that could lead to differential life chances for poor women vis-à-vis men (Kairi 2007).

While nuclear families with two working adults fare better than single female headed households, only in some cases does marriage prevent extreme poverty (Henry-Lee and Le Franc 2002). In the Caribbean, neither education nor employment in itself determines an individual's position relative to the poverty line. Instead, opportunities in the formal sector and wage differentials are greater determinants of income, social status and poverty. Patricia Ellis (2003) also observed that in families that are headed by men, women in these households still give financial support to the home and manage the household budget.

The low level of education and employment status of this group of women is, however, not reflective of the advancements made by other Caribbean women. Barriteau's (2001b) assessment of the political economy of gender in twenty-first century showed that women in the region did make important material gains in education and politics. Expanded educational opportunities have put Caribbean women ahead of men where even at the tertiary level the ratio between males and females are 1:2 in university enrolment. The University of the West Indies Statistical Review for the academic year 2009/2010 showed across the region 69 per cent of the students enrolled at the university were female and 31 per cent males.

Similarly, Godfrey St Bernard (2003) in his assessment of the labour markets found that, with the exception of Haiti, there has been a persistent increase in female labour in the formal sector. He found that the increases were a function of women's educational achievements over the past three decades as well as to the vibrant social movements that stimulated greater social and economic gender equity. Further, increase in employment possibilities has resulted in higher percentages of women employed in professional jobs (Prendergast and Grace 2006). For example, at a Caribbean Human Resources Forum, in 2008, women in professional positions was estimated to be between 73 and 78 per cent of the total labour employed in two private organizations (Guardian Holdings and Scotia Bank) in Trinidad and Tobago.

These developments did contribute to an increase in the employment of single women with families in higher paying jobs. However, Barriteau (2001b) argued that these advancements have not disrupted gender systems of power and structural discrimination against women, but has resulted in a disconnect between material gains and gender ideological shifts. Similarly, the advancements in women's education, employment and political rights have not benefited all women equally. The benefits were not expansive and have not trickled down to Caribbean women who remain concentrated in low-paying 'female occupations' (Ellis 2003). Accordingly, women in resource-poor families and many single-female-headed households remain trapped in a series of interlocking forces, like a fly caught in a spider's web.

Caribbean households, both single-female-headed and nuclear arrangements, serve as an impetus to query the wide-scale adoption of the *feminization of poverty* explanations of gender inequality and poverty. Certainly, the evidence points more in the direction of structural antecedents specific to the various countries. The data and the analyses support the proverbial 'glass ceiling' claim that women make less money than men, even within the same job category. Since female-headed households which are often also single-headed have larger families, take care of bigger numbers of dependents, earn less than men, and get little assistance from fathers of children and the state, it is more likely that their households would fall near or below the poverty lines.

Conditions of women's material poverty therefore arise because of a series of interrelated structural barriers that are economic, social and gendered. These conditions affect working and unemployed women and men, but the negative impacts are heightened in single-female-headed households. While gender inequality lies at the centre of poverty, *feminization of poverty* suppositions make it appear that women's poverty and that of their children, can be better in a different type of family. Change, in this view, is a cultural shift in family structures towards a nuclear two-parent model (Ezeala-Harrison 2010) and a male breadwinner, although the economic well-being of female-headed households are due to women's disadvantages, particularly in education, job training, skills enhancement and labour market participation.

Thus, on a broader scale, concerns about the idea and use of the *feminization of poverty* perspective centre on the history of its origins, the tendency to treat women as a homogenous group, and for assuming that all households function as altruistic units (Ezeala-Harrison 2010; Elmelecha and Lub 2004; Lin Chin and Harris 2008; Rodgers 1987, 1990). It is argued that the *feminization of poverty* perspective fails to recognize that women have different histories, live in different circumstances and have different social experiences and relations (Rajack-Talley and Best 2015; Palmer 1983). Therefore, one of the most important misgivings about the use of the concept is that causations of women's poverty, as a group and in single-female-headed households, are implied but not well explained. More dangerously, causation hinges on assumptions that are culturally biased.

## Cultural Assumptions and Biases

The *feminization of poverty* perspective carries culturally biased assumptions that are pathological in nature and poses problems in its broad application (Rajack-Talley and Best 2015). This includes the underlying assumptions that single-female-headed households are the 'poorest of the poor' and that poverty in these households is the result of 'unfortunate' domestic circumstances that are symptomatic of family breakdown, and places children in worse off living conditions compared to 'complete' families. The implicit danger of this idea is that gender inequality and poverty are both reduced to cultural practices rather than economic and social forms of discrimination (Moore 1994, 1996). This school of thought is observed in the literature that focuses on the structure and practices of black families and which portrays single women in female-headed households as welfare dependents (Brenner 1987; Rodgers 1987, 1990). Similarly, in the Caribbean there are those who believe that women deliberately choose to have children so that men can support them (Stewart 1996). The statistics on the number of children born out of wedlock, and women on public assistance, are used to support these popular stereotypes. However, these arguments are inconclusive, misleading and value-laden in their premise.

Theresa Ann Rajack-Talley and Clarence Talley (2005) found that value orientations that influence beliefs about the black family are contained in the literature on African American and Afro-Caribbean households. Moreover, some of these value-laden assumptions are similar to those in the *feminization of poverty* perspective. First, it is assumed that the middle-class, nuclear-family model is the norm and that non-nuclear families are caused by an inability to conform to Eurocentric family values, are dysfunctional, and lead to high levels of poverty in African American and Afro-Caribbean societies (Dubois 1909; Frazier 1966; Moynihan 1965). This school of thought associates poverty with the predominance of single-female-headed households, child poverty, and the social behaviours of youth.

These perspectives have now been highly critiqued and refuted by contemporary research. For example, Melanie Dreher and Rebekah Hudgins (2010) study of 59 Jamaican families found that marriage, nuclear family structures and even a father's presence does not constitute a cure-all for child development, if living under impoverished conditions. In fact, their findings revealed that the developmental outcomes of children are more closely related to the capacity of the mother and care givers (grandmothers, siblings, aunts) to create a safe and effective child-rearing environment, typical in many extended family situations. Ironically, the women in their study suggested that being married and/or having a common-law husband can detract from child rearing because of 'man-keeping' demands.

Sylvia Chant (2006) also questioned some of the (mis)conceptions about children's poverty and single-female-headed households. Grounded in the *feminization of poverty* rhetoric that female-headed households are the 'poorest of the poor', the assumption is made that children suffer more compared to the ideal two-parent, male-headed household. This line of thinking conjures the idea that not only are children and youth's material well-being compromised in single-female-headed households, but also their emotional, psychological, and social well-being. However, Chant reports that mounting evidence show that household headship is not a good predictor of children's well-being and life trajectory. Instead, the gender dynamics and social relations in any household have more weight. In light of this, it was suggested that policies should focus more on ensuring that children in female-headed households can afford equality in all their basic needs and human rights requirements.

The findings and analyses of these studies challenge the simplistic correlation made with the wrong application of the *feminization of poverty* logic, which links poverty and dysfunctional family practices with single unmarried parents. Without first situating the household in a social, economic and cultural context, and examining the human interactions that take place, these analyses are more likely to be biased and incomplete. In other words, the use and meaning of the *feminization of poverty* must always be contextualized and given agency.

. Women's experience of poverty is quite different from men's, but there are also variations from one culture to another. As such, what is required are indigenous interpretations that do not employ value orientations, are non-comparative (Rajack-Talley and Talley 2005), and which moves away from structural-functionalist approaches in understanding families and households (Barrow 2010). The more interpretive approaches that centre on looking at gendered scripts, relations of power, social exclusion and the role of ideology will facilitate a better understanding of the problem, the cause, the consequences and the gendered differences in the experiences, responses and actions of humans in resource-poor single-female-headed households and in all family types. It gives women and men agency and examines the complex decision-making processes that take place in family decisions and which practices, including coping mechanisms, have maintained families in single-female-headed households for generations.

The second assumption of the *feminization of poverty* that is challenged when used in the Caribbean is that families are poor because of the absence of a male breadwinner. The myth of the male breadwinner in Caribbean households has long since been challenged. For example, Helen Safa (1995) argued that the idea that Caribbean households depend solely on a male breadwinner is false. In fact, black women, women of colour, and women in many developing societies, have always worked and continue to do so to support families in two-parent households and in single-female-headed households. They play central roles in their household economies and the economic development of their countries. Some women work because they are the sole supporter of their families or because the money earned from a male partner in a two-parent household are inadequate to support the family (this discussion is expanded in chapter five). Today, it is increasingly more difficult for working women to make enough to buy adequate food, pay rent, utilities, and educational and medical bills. Despite their brave attempts, especially in single-parent households, to provide for their families, they are continuously negatively stereotyped and humiliated as described in chapter three.

The moral judgments and value orientations that are Eurocentric, cut across both traditional Caribbean family studies and the North American theoretical model of the *feminization of poverty.* They strongly affect how statistics and causations of poverty are interpreted. Furthermore, approaches that employ these cultural arguments cannot explain the nuances and persistence of poverty in two-parent households. Most importantly, cultural biases ignore the role of women's agency and, as a result, cannot embrace the idea that women negotiate gender discrimination and inequality, in the home and in the workplace, because they must feed, clothe, educate and provide shelter for hundreds of families globally.

It is, therefore, important to look at the relationship between gender and poverty minus the Eurocentric lens, recognizing that we cannot simply import concepts and measures from the North to understand poverty in developing countries, and among non-traditional groups in developed societies (Rajack-Talley and Best 2015; Rajack-Talley and Talley 2005). Their social histories, experiences and gender ideologies are usually quite different and are negotiated in unique and nuanced ways that are empowering, on one hand, and also very difficult and disheartening on the other (see article by Agarwal 2012).

Caribbean women of all social classes and households exercise choice and preferences for different marital relationships. The nuclear family is not always considered a practical financial solution or a socially desirable arrangement for women. Consequently, Caribbean women adopt other types of social relationships and conjugal unions that, in their view, are more appropriate for their economic and social well-being and that of their dependents (Dreher and Hudgins 2010). In none of the poverty studies did women suggest a change in their conjugal relationship and family composition as a possible solution to their economic situations. Instead, they advocated for structural antidotes such as greater opportunities for women in education and employment, improved wages and working conditions, court action against men who are not supporting their children, getting back to growing food, and more skills building programmes as needed strategies. These same strategies were also recommended in the CPAs as important to poverty reduction in female-headed households, as well as for all types of impoverished households.

Assumptions and cultural biases have constructed socially the female-headed households as the 'poorest of the poor' (Chant 2003). They are also used to depict women as either being without agency and therefore victims of poverty or, where agency is given to women, to blame women for their poor living conditions and that of their children. Women's narratives, however, provide evidence that contradicts these depictions and show, instead, ways in which Caribbean women fight every day to prevent abject poverty in their homes, with or without a male breadwinner. This does not suggest that a high incidence of poverty in single-female-headed households does not exist, but that poverty is not caused by women's choices in the public and private spheres of their lives. For women, poverty and harsh living conditions in their households result from gender inequality and discrimination that prevents them from improving their education, health, wage earning capacity, and the ability to take better care of their families. It is not a result of weak personal characteristics or failed cultural and familial practices. Regardless of family structure, this is believed of a woman:

> She has the load of the family...and that if woman is of poor condition
> then the children is poor (NALC, Cayman Islands 2006/07, 16).

## Methodological Challenges

While the *feminization of poverty* model and rhetoric is widely used in the Caribbean and elsewhere, its global adoption has also been met with certain logistic research issues, including finding a consistent definition and measure for the *feminization of poverty* that allows for comparisons at an international level. In addition, some studies conclude that the relationship between poverty and women's headship varies from one country to another and is, therefore, inconclusive (Buvinic and Gupta 1994). Moreover, micro-level studies show that female headship is not necessarily a poverty-specific phenomenon (Gonzalez de la Rocha 2001; Moser 1996; Willis 2003). As a result, in Africa, Asia, Latin America and the Caribbean, the orientations and findings of poverty studies often differ from the *feminization of poverty* conjectures of North America.

Similar to the Caribbean, few studies conducted in Brazil and urban areas in India found that female-headed households were more likely to experience poverty (Barros, Fox and Mendonca 1994), others found weak evidence of a higher incidence of poverty among female-headed households in some sub-Saharan African countries,[3] in Asia,[4] as well as in 13 Latin American countries (Buvinic and Gupta 1994; Fuwa 2000; Marcoux 1998; Moghadam 2005). Parallel to the Caribbean, some researchers query the extent to which poverty in households results from a single-female-headed household, or because women have higher numbers of dependent children, heavier work burdens, lower wages, lack of access to resources from the state, and the overall lack of mobility in society (Beneria 1991; Chant 1985, 1997a, 2003, 2006; Dwyer and Bruce 1988; England and Folbre 2002; Kabeer 2003).

In addition to the problem of finding adequate evidence to prove that female-headed households are the 'poorest of the poor', there are also several methodological problems associated with the concept. Many of these are linked to: (i) the focus on female-headed households more willingly than gendered poverty; (ii) a heavy reliance on quantitative data and macro level analyses of households particularly female-headed households; and (iii) the attempt to universally apply the suppositions about female-headed households, including that they are the poorest of the poor (Rajack-Talley and Best 2015). These methodological challenges have been pointed out by Chant (2003, 62) as they pertain to developing countries and by Aldrie Henry-Lee and Elsie Le Franc (2002) with regards to the Caribbean. These scholars identified several factors that illustrate how problems arise when measuring poverty and socially constructing female-headed households.

 First, the conceptual tools used to assess poverty in female-headed households are out of sync with the data and experiences of many women and households in developing societies, including those in the Caribbean as well as minority groups in developed societies. This is primarily because the origin of the term influenced the focus of *feminization of poverty* studies everywhere it was applied. Medeiros and Costa (2006, 3) explain that when Pearce coined the term *feminization of poverty* she was looking at *a group among the poor* and *not poverty inside a group*. Similarly, Sarah Bradshaw (1996) and Steven Pressman (2002) observed that, in the 1980s and 1990s, poverty studies in developed countries focused on the gender of the poor and the feminization of households, while in developing countries the focus was on poverty in female-headed households. The difference in focus affects what is measured and results in two distinct analyses.

In the first approach, the measure of female-headed poverty will not change even if the number of poor female-headed households decreased because of a decline in the number of female-headed households in the population at large. Thus, regardless of the criteria used to look at poverty, female-headed households would be the poorest (Sen 1999). The other approach examines whether there is an over-representation of female-headed households in poverty. When applied to most developing countries it was found that like in the Caribbean, there is no clear pattern that links poverty and household headship (Buvinic and Gupta 1994; Medeiros and Costa 2006). Both approaches have empirical and definitional issues associated with the *feminization of poverty*, and these in return, pose methodological challenges in the level of analysis and conclusions.

Secondly, the empirical problems associated with the feminization of poverty studies stem from the dominant use of quantitative data collected from household surveys, which in many countries in the Caribbean and elsewhere is the primary and/or only source of data on poverty. Survey data do not always provide adequate gender disaggregated information that allows for cross-national or time series comparisons. In addition, survey analysis does not always look within groups to take into consideration the significant effect that race/ethnicity, social class, immigration status, and rural/urban locations can have on women's poverty. Additionally, the heterogeneity of female-headed households based on status, composition, stage in life course and other social demographics are not recognized and treated accordingly (Chant 2003). Equally important, surveys are not designed to capture quantitative or qualitative data on the survival strategies adopted by female-headed households to compensate for gender disadvantages. This includes financial and social assistance from relatives, friends, churches and community members as well as the sacrifices and ethical choices that women must make when living conditions deteriorate (see, for example, the participatory approach findings in the CPAs).

Further, the adoption of quantitative measures showcases female-headed households because female-headed households are visible, easily identifiable in statistics, and can be used to fulfil a range of political agendas, including poverty reduction programmes for targeted groups (Chant 1997a and 1997b, 2003, 2006). For example, the measures used in the *feminization of poverty* provide convenient information to be incorporated in welfare or poverty reduction projects under the aegis of efficient programming, rather than address the larger issues of structural and systemic gender inequity and its relation to poverty (Jackson 1996; Kabeer 1997; Molyneux 2001; Pankhurst 2002; Razavi 1999; World Bank 1994, 2002). This is not to say that in some developing countries, there is a de jure or de facto,[5] proliferation of female-headed households, and that high numbers of female-headed households dominate poverty statistics (Chant 2003).

The most controversial empirical challenge to the *feminization of poverty* conclusions, however, remains that female-headed households are the poorest. Statistical reports and poverty studies are unable to conclusively say whether there is an over-representation of female-headed households among poor households. For example, while Buvinic and Gupta (1994) concluded that in Latin America and the Caribbean, female-headed households are over-represented among the poor, Medeiros and Costa (2006) found that this was only true in households with children. On the other hand, reports by the World Bank showed that, in Indonesia and Vietnam, female-headed households are not worse off than men, and Chant (1997a and 1997b) found that 'life' for members of female-headed households in Mexico, Costa Rica and the Philippines compared favourably with those in male-headed households. These findings further substantiate the argument that for many developing populations not only is there inadequate empirical evidence to support the presence of a *feminization of poverty* but also that female-headed households on average are not poorer than male-headed households.[6]

Medeiros and Costa (2006) recommended the adoption of other measures that can more succinctly capture gender characteristics and biases. In this way, data may reflect an over-representation of women among the poor, but not necessarily a *feminization of poverty* empirically defined. Moreover, in some countries, Jamaica for example, using female headship as a criterion for social programmes for the poor will only reach 50 per cent of the poor compared to targeting rural households that will reach 87 per cent of the poor (Louat et al. 1993). Using female-headed household as a strong indicator of poverty is, therefore, not always methodologically sound and not always the most appropriate unit of analysis for every society, including those in the Caribbean.

Thirdly, one of the main reasons why it is difficult to substantiate that female-headed households are the poorest in some developing countries is due, in part, to the wide variation in definitions of what constitutes a female-headed household. The *definitional ambiguities* include not having a standard definition of single-female-headed household (Chant 1997; Kabeer 1999; Pearce 1983; Razvi 1999), and not being able to capture the needs and gender biases of different types of households. For example, the category of household that is labelled female-headed can represent an array of different scenarios such as lone-female units, households of single wage earners with young dependents, households in which women earners receive significant remittances from absent males, and so on (Razvi 1999). Each category of household is generated by a different process, life cycle, and/or socio-economic circumstances and opportunities.

Furthermore, in the Caribbean, not only are the definitions of what constitutes a female-headed household different, but categories of households are different from that of North America. Caribbean household categories are complex and include the nuclear, extended, single-female, common-law and visiting family structures, each with a different set of gender relations. Based on the various categories identified in the Caribbean, it is difficult for the traditional *feminization of poverty* to include the different arrangements and nuances found in this wide variety of household types.

The fourth major methodological challenge, both with the universal adoption of the feminization of poverty concept and its assumption that female-headed households are the poorest, has to do with the way poverty is measured and analysed. Specific to gender and poverty measures, there is a heavy reliance on the material elements of human deprivation such as income-expenditure indicators. Researchers (Kabeer 1994; Chant 2003, 2006) believe that this approach negates the importance of social indicators, including gendered power relations, livelihood strategies and socio-economic inequalities to incidences of poverty. Hence, the income-expenditure measures of household well-being are equated to the economic status of the head (Chant 2003). Moreover, gender and other forms of discrimination are not considered, although they have direct effects on the income and economic opportunities of women and female-headed households. The multidimensional characteristics of well-being and poverty, which extend beyond income, expenditure and material assets, are not integral to the analyses.

The income and consumption approach adopted by many *feminization of poverty* studies captures the incidence or size of the problem for women as a group among the poor. It also measures the occurrence of poverty in single-female-headed households and concludes that they are the poorest of the poor. However, the problem with its use, apart from not capturing the social dimensions of poverty, has to do with its focus on macro-level analyses. Critics have warned that a focus on macro-level analyses does not adequately reveal gender specific forms of deprivation that are observed in micro-level research (Chant 1997a and 1997b; Kabeer 1996). For example, household-level analysis in *feminization of poverty* research rarely captures intra-household dynamics and gender inequalities in the distribution of resources that exist in nuclear families. Instead, its macro-level focus is critiqued for the homogenizing tendencies that ignore patriarchal family structures, where the distribution of household resources is highly dependent on gender hierarchies (Chant 1997a; Muthwa 1993; Rajack 1996; Rajack-Talley and Best 2015). On the other hand, research that specifically looks at intra-household resource distribution and household bargaining provides empirical evidence and qualitative understandings of the modus operandi of household economies in ways that the *feminization of poverty* research cannot (see chapters five and six).

There are variations in the way in which household resources are distributed and negotiated in female-headed households and male-headed households. Research shows that income, nutritional intake, healthcare and education are more equitably distributed in female-headed households (Blumberg 1995; Chant 1997a; Engle 1995; Kabeer 1996, 2003). This gender pattern in distribution of resources occurs primarily because women are more likely to use a greater share of their earnings on family welfare and needs (Rajack 1996). On the other hand, studies conducted in Latin America found that men sometimes withhold one third to a half of their earnings from the household expenditure to use on discretionary personal items (Bradshaw 1996, 2002; Gonzalez de la Rocha 2001).

In many instances, men's discretionary spending is linked to activities socially defined as masculine and linked to their gender identities. These patterns become problematic in resource-poor households, particularly where men have limited employment opportunities. In these situations, there is often a great deal of social, psychological and economic pressure that is different for women and men (Chant 1997b; Muthwa 1993; Rajack 1996). These important findings could only be observed through intra-household analysis that moves away from poor female-headed households as the unit of analysis. They challenge the assumptions of the *feminization of poverty* perspective that bases its analyses on the Western model of an altruistic nuclear family with a male breadwinner, as the only economically and socially functional unit.

Intra-household inequalities are inextricably linked with extra-household social factors that shape or hinder opportunities for women and young girls at the societal level. As a result, while there is little doubt that female-headed households face a unique set of constraints; these represent only a fraction of the issues which affects women as a whole. Gender-related laws and entitlements, family rights, access to literacy, health care opportunities, labour laws, social welfare resources, and the overall economic and social policies of a country affect gender status and expected roles (Moghadam 2005). Moreover, the trajectories leading to women's poverty are divergent and the category of household labelled 'female-headed' is a highly heterogeneous one that differs across cultures and regions. As such, attempts to universally apply the *feminization of poverty* approach has serious methodological limitations, including arriving at the conclusion that female-headed households are the poorest of the poor. Many of these challenges stem from the way poor households are defined and understood. A shift in the ideological realm is, therefore, essential if a different methodological approach is to be adopted to understand gendered poverty, and poverty in female-headed households (Rajack-Talley and Best 2015).

Overall, the *feminization of poverty* framework is not well developed conceptually or methodologically. It lacks compelling data and, as a result, despite years of research, available evidence to link causes of poverty to households headed by single females is inconclusive. Similarly, the claim that female-headed households are the poorest cannot be fully substantiated even though gender discrimination and the disadvantaged status of women in most countries are incontestable. A more plausible explanation is that single-female-headed households are poor because the women who head these households experience simultaneous gender, class, race/ethnicity, immigration status, and other forms of discrimination. Vulnerability within this context is more closely associated with social forces of discrimination rather than family traits and cultural values. As a result, it is important to move beyond the blind adoption of universal paradigms that insert cultural explanations with Eurocentric bias, and instead try to separately capture the extent, plethora of determinants, and nature of poverty, for specific groups of women.

At the same time, the discourse on the *feminization of poverty* highlights that women and single-female-headed households are more vulnerable to transitory and chronic poverty. However, the use of more conventional measures of income and well-being by the *feminization of poverty* approach are premised on the notion of the male experience as head of household and major income earner, and are therefore not good measures of women's experiences of poverty. As Naila Kabeer (1996) noted, 'the form in which women's poverty manifests itself depends on cultural contexts far more than it does for men, suggesting that it cannot be understood through the same conceptual lens'(11). In order to get a preliminary handle on the gender dimensions of poverty, it is necessary to understand how discrimination looks in the context of scarcity in different societies as well the interrelatedness of other forms of prejudices. Women are generally poorer than some men and other women because their race/ethnicity, caste, social class and immigration status limit their range of endowments and exchange entitlements as well as their ability to translate labour into proper wages and income into choice, thus affecting their personal and family well-being (Rajack-Talley and Best 2015). Capturing the lived experiences of women is important in understanding the gendered impact of poverty on women, on single-female-headed households, and on poor households of all types.

Any meaningful analysis of the causes, consequences and attempts to alleviate and eradicate poverty should, therefore, consider which women and their families are being impoverished, in what ways, and why. The *feminization of poverty* as a concept and a measure of women's poverty is not adequate for understanding the interrelated and cumulative effect of various forms of discrimination and incidences of poverty. Further, intra-household inequality remains hidden and poverty among men and children unexplored. In most instances, the conceptualization of the term *feminization of poverty* is dependent on the political agenda, in any particular society, tackling women's poverty. It is also influenced by existing ideologies and stereotypes on gender and poverty. These variables, in turn, shape the perceived determinants of, and measures used, in poverty studies. As a result, there is a divergence in the analyses and summations of the *feminization of poverty* arguments, including that female-headed households are the poorest.

## Summary and Conclusions

Overall, within the Caribbean context, the *feminization of poverty* model in itself does not provide a satisfactory and succinct measure or explanation for gendered and household poverty for three main reasons. First, there is insufficient data and the data that exist do not show a direct correlation between single-female-headed households and poverty. Moreover, the perception of an economically functional family as nuclear-structured is not largely applicable in the Caribbean where 30–40 per cent of households in many countries are female-headed but do not have the highest poverty or indigence levels. For example, Antigua and Barbuda, Barbados and Jamaica have over 40 per cent female-headed households, but poverty levels are under 20 per cent compared to Belize, Guyana, and St Vincent and the Grenadines that have high percentages of male-headed households and over 30 per cent poverty levels.

Second, the *feminization of poverty* arguments, by focusing on family structures, remain constrained like the earlier family studies. They do not give adequate credence to women's agency and, therefore, the understanding of family practices, interactions, and rationale. Consequently, there are several misunderstandings and misdiagnoses of the problem, the causes and the solutions. Furthermore, only the negative outcomes of women's experiences are highlighted and women and men's contributions to Caribbean household economies and family well-being are ignored or misconstrued. *Feminization of poverty* blinds us to the important role of single mothers and grandmothers, who are in many households responsible for providing for their children and grandchildren, despite their low economic circumstances. Nor are we cognizant of the challenges they face and their needs. Instead, it is assumed that the advancement of women in certain areas trickles down to low-income households and poor and working women.

Third, there are inherent cultural biases in applying the *feminization of poverty* model. Consequently, the model cannot uncover the complexity of gender roles and ideologies in the region and, instead, supports the traditional perceptions about manhood and womanhood that are Eurocentric and andocentric, even when actual roles and thinking are not (Barrow 1998; Ellis 2003). Earlier in this chapter, I discussed how cultural biases demonize single women in female-headed households. In the same vein, men are commonly viewed as irresponsible, absent, or playing a marginal role in the family. It is true, in the Caribbean, some men 'pick up and go', abandoning their partners and their children. But the generalization of this image has been challenged and the central roles that husbands and fathers play in their children's lives are slowly emerging (Chevannes 1993; Stuart 1996; UNICEF 1994). More frequently, men's roles have been reduced to providing finance and discipline to their offspring, and most men do provide for their children and are usually assisted by their parents (Brown and Chevannes 2001). However, other aspects of men's roles are being explored, including that of fathers, stepfathers, grandfathers, uncles and other male relatives (ECLAC 2000; Reddock 2004; Roopnarine 2013).

The data, examples, and discussions presented show how cultural biases inherent in theoretical perspectives can lead to wrong assumptions and interpretations of statistics. Research should always consider the socio-historical backgrounds of people who do not just respond to their environment but make rationale choices based on their circumstances. Biases lead to value-laden concepts that, when applied, ignore the reality and the meanings that people give to their experiences. As such, any attempt to posit *the feminization of poverty* will result in a quagmire for indigenous research.

Are more households poor because of an increase in single-female-headed households in the Caribbean? We still do not know due to inadequate research data in this area. The Caribbean case study where female-headed households have historically existed in statistically significant numbers, point to the fact that these households play important roles in the sustenance and well-being of families. Nonetheless, they experience severe challenges in trying to improve their living conditions, and not simply 'get by' but to 'get ahead'. The region is a good example where material gains and the advancement of women do not necessarily reflect a change in gender power relations and discrimination in the public and private spheres of women's lives. Also, it highlights that benefits seldom reach those who are in the poorest quintile and who remain trapped in socio-economic and gender-enclosed cages.

The *feminization of poverty* rhetoric continues to be used loosely in the region, although it is not yet adequately conceptualized, defined and theorized within a local context. As a result, it is difficult to decipher its use whether it is in reference to measures of prevalence, incidence, relative or absolute occurrences, or to change and factors responsible for women's poverty and poverty in female-headed households. The broad use of the term in the region, therefore, needs to be properly examined and analysed. Currently, its applicability leaves open for poverty studies and assessments to have the wrong focus on family structures, to base descriptions, discussions and analyses on Eurocentric social constructs, and to give a false impression of the impact and setbacks of gender advancement and continued discrimination.

Equally important, the *feminization of poverty* perspective fails to look at the relational aspect of poverty and the role of human agency. As a result, not only is there a need for clarification on its definition and measures, but also for the adoption of new modes of inquiry where the narratives of gender relations practices in the Caribbean are incorporated in the research and analyses of poverty among women and female-headed households. The interactive approach that is now being used in family and gender studies is a useful start. If a similar approach is applied in poverty studies, it will highlight that poverty is a person. Also, it will show that people are social actors who exercise agency in dealing with the many dimensions of poverty and inequality. In the Caribbean, women are exceedingly good subjects to observe agency at work in the family and in negotiating poverty as well as give new meanings to the concept *feminization of poverty*.

# 5. Female Breadwinners

Although I make most of the decisions on the farm I say he is the head of household...because the Bible says so.

— Female farmer, Jamaica, 2006.

This chapter is a continuation of the interrogation of the *feminization of poverty* perspective that assumes that female-headed households are the 'poorest of the poor' because of the absence of a male breadwinner. Where this argument is made, women's financial contributions to the household budget are considered marginal or supplementary. Moreover, women's economic roles in the wider society remain invisible and undervalued. Conversely, males are stereotyped as the primary income earners.

Ironically, Caribbean women have always been single female workers in a brutal labour market. We see this from history. Yet, women have been stereotyped as economic dependents rather than economic contributors. They are increasingly cast as stay-at-home or part-time working mothers and housewives; their actual responsibilities and tasks are mystified and redefined based on Eurocentric constructs of gender roles.

The concept of a stay-at-home housewife is, however, alien for Caribbean women who historically worked as enslaved and indentured sugar cane workers. Later they became employed as farm labourers, factory workers, small traders and business operators in the informal market as well as service workers in the tourist industry and in government jobs. Over the years, economic circumstances pushed others to migrate for work to support their immediate and extended families. Improved educational opportunities have resulted in more women working in the public and private services, at all levels. However, as the last chapter pointed out, although Caribbean women are making tremendous advancements, not all women benefit equally and women's overall status in society has not changed to commensurate economic and educational gains. Nonetheless, women continue to be breadwinners in their households, with or without a male partner.

The discussions and examples in this chapter challenge the stereotypical and patriarchal ways of thinking about the male breadwinner and female homemaker in the Caribbean and elsewhere. It specifically focuses on certain areas of employment – agriculture, manufacturing, entrepreneurship and working as a migrant, where women from low-income families are found. The argument made is that in resource-poor households women must work because it is necessary to financially support themselves, their households and their extended families. In these homes, women's economic contributions, regardless of the sum, are not supplementary but central to the family's sustenance. Moreover, as women work they are consistently negotiating the economic climate of society and in their households, while simultaneously coping with the challenges of gender barriers and patriarchal stereotyping. The examples and discussions in this chapter argue that it is important to be *au fait* with women's agency, the economic roles that they continue to play in staving off poverty, and the difficulties of doing so because of lack of support and discrimination based on their gender and social class. The information and analyses in this chapter highlight the paradox between what is perpetuated as women's role and the lived experiences of working women in low-income families.

## The Household Economy and Women's Work

To understand why and how women and men earn incomes in the Caribbean requires an analysis of the relationship of the household economy with the formal and informal sectors. These relationships are both complex and fluid. Moreover, attempts to understand the concept of the informal economy and its relationship to the formal or regulated economy, though not new, are still unclear. What is known is that the informal economy is a central part of the economic and social dynamics of all developing societies (Catells and Portes 1989; Chen 2007). Although, many of the characteristics of the structure and function of the informal economy remain elusive, there are some common identifiable characteristics. For example, economic activities operate on a small scale, they avoid state regulations, are located at flexible sites, and use primarily family labour.

Further, a common feature of the informal economy is that it is universal, existing in both developed and developing societies, even though the boundaries of the informal economy vary in different socio-economic and historical contexts (Minigione 1991; Rajack 1996). The informal economy is sometimes referred to as the underground, submerged or secondary economy. While there is no comprehensive theory of the informal economy, it has been defined as a process of income-generation that is unregulated by the legal and social institutions in society (Catells and Portes 1989). While many poor people participate in the informal sector as a survival strategy, there are others who participate in ways that are linked to successful businesses. Women predominantly work in the subsistence sector of the informal economy, and depend on it to make a living.

The formal economy, on the other hand, is defined as an institutional framework of economic activities that are regulated by the legal and social institutions of a society (Castells and Portes 1989). One basic distinction between economic activities in the formal and informal economy is not what is produced, but the manner in which items are produced and exchanged. The formal economy is transparent both in its structure and function and operates within a formal regulatory environment of government laws, policies, and regulations (Chen 2007). The tenets of the formal economy include an organized system of employees with clearly written guidelines for recruitment and job responsibilities, and a standardized relationship between employee and employer maintained through a formal contract. In the formal economy, employees are expected to work fixed hours for wages and fringe benefits. Men are more likely to be employed in the formal economy, but in certain sectors designated as 'women's work', large numbers of women are hired (Ellis 2003).

Research has shown that there is a strong link between the formal and informal economies, but this relationship varies and remains fluid. For example, changes in the institutional boundaries of economic activities in the formal economy can produce a realignment of this relationship, the movement of individuals between the two sectors (Castells and Portes 1989; Chen 2007; Mingione 1991), and a shift in gender employment and social relationships (Rajack 1996). A common assumption is that if the formal economy grows and develops, the informal economy will shrink. However, if the formal economy expands but income and assets are not equitably distributed, economic growth will not lead to increase in formal sector employment but a steady growth of the informal sector. Over the past few decades, this is what has occurred in most developing countries, so much so, that the informal economy is no longer seen as a temporary phenomenon and accounts for approximately 50–75 per cent of all labour employment (Chen 2007). Consequently, households rely more on income earned in the informal sector and on women's wage employment and entrepreneurial activities.

In reality, members of low-income households engage in a spectrum of activities, moving between the two sectors, sometimes during the same work-day (Catells and Portes 1989; Minigione 1991; Rajack 1996). This arrangement arises because income earned by women and/or men in either sector is insufficient to meet household needs. Consequently, household members frequently engage in a range of income earning activities, including wage employment in the public services and private sectors, and as casual labourers, petty traders buying and selling food items and haberdashery, or proprietors of small businesses in the informal sector. Also, while most Caribbean countries are now regarded as service-driven, there are still those like Belize, Guyana, and even Jamaica that maintain an agrarian base where a large part of informal sector work is in agriculture. Women and men work as farm labourers or as small family farm operators. In many instances, women and men in peasant households engage in a combination of subsistence agricultural production and part-time wage employment in the formal economy (Best 1968; Beckford 1972; Gomes 1984, 1985). For example, women from farm households grow some of their food for domestic consumption and sell the excess for small amounts of cash.

Women also make certain consumer goods at home so that they do not have to purchase these items from their limited budgets. For example, women sew family clothes and household linens, bake goods, make preservatives, cure meats, and make domestic and consumption items for the home. They do, however, depend upon their own wage earnings and/or that of their spouses for non-food necessities, to pay their rent or mortgage, utilities, transportation and the school needs of children. Thus, rural and farming women and men often combine subsistence activities with other economic activities, and shift between a modern capitalist economy and a non-capitalist system of production. T.A. Rajack (1996) described these individuals as 'neither peasant nor proletariat'. Interestingly, while these households, like most poor households, operate under heavy risk and uncertainty, their economic activities support the formal economy because it subsidizes wage labour. A substantial part of the reproduction cost of formal sector labour is borne by the household economy because peasant labour, and more specifically peasant women's labour, can be employed at low wages (FAO 2010–11; Smith, Wallerstein and Hans-Dieter 1984).

In general, resource-poor Caribbean households are not static entities as family members act and react to changes in the wider economy. The household, as a unit, is an intermediary between the individual and larger social institutions. Members of resource-poor households are often caught between the exigencies of two modes of production: subsistence activities based on a collective consciousness in a moral economy; and participation in the formal market sector as the rational choice-making individual in a political economy. Consequently, household members are constantly changing their work and social relations within the household economy and in the wider economy (Mingione 1991; Poats et al. 1984; Tickamyer and Talley 1994; Wilk 1989). Typically, national statistics on income do not take into account the nuances that occur between the informal and formal sectors. As such, there is a wide range of social, economic and gender factors that go un-noticed and undocumented in resource-poor households. Economic activities in the informal sector are also usually underestimated or not included in national-income measures. Since women engage in a lot of domestic work and subsistence production, much of what they do is therefore not accounted for, and their contribution to the national economy is grossly underestimated.

This failure was first noted, in 1970, in Esther Boserup's argument that women's contribution to the agricultural sectors as well as in domestic work, such as caring for the elderly, administrating medical services to the sick, collecting food, water and fuel, along with other activities, were traditionally not given an economic value. Similarly, women's innovative production of some of their household basic needs is usually not given an intrinsic monetary value (Beneria 1998; Deere, Safa and Antrobus 1997). Overall, activities linked to use value are not part of statistical data on labour or wages. The impetus of the women's movement has made some strides in accounting for and analysing all aspects of women's work, including subsistence production and domestic production. The issue was given further recognition at the 1985 Nairobi Conference at the end of the UN Decade for Women. A report from that meeting, *Forward Looking Strategies for the Advancement of Women,* strongly recommended that there be concerted efforts to measure the contribution of women's paid and unpaid work in all sectors.

A close examination of the relationship between the informal and formal economy, as well as accounting for women's work in the informal and formal sectors, are both important in understanding how low-income households meet their family needs. Economic decline and the introduction of structural adjustment policies in the 1980s have resulted in the further informalization of the Caribbean economy, and a greater movement of men and women between the formal and informal economies. The economic situation has highlighted the central roles that women play in the household economy because as men lost their wage employment or faced wage reductions, women increasingly entered formal sector wage employment, particularly in small processing factories and in the service industries. More Caribbean women also began to migrate to the US and elsewhere in search of work, sending remittances back home to support their nuclear and extended families (Deere, Safa and Antrobus 1997; Momsen 1993; Rajack 1996). These developments give rise to interesting gender dynamics as household incomes increasingly become dependent on the economic activities of women across a wide spectrum.

## All Women Work and Women Always Worked

All women work, and women of all ages and marital status work. According to Joycelin Massiah (1986), Caribbean women have always worked in their homes, in all sectors of the economy and in every stratum of society. Women encounter high rates of work in the Caribbean due to a combination of historical, social and structural factors (Rajack-Talley and Talley 2000). The history of Caribbean women who were brought to the islands as slaves and indentured servants is founded on work on the sugar-cane plantations and on small family farms. Their first roles in the region were as workers and not wives or mothers (Rajack 1991; Reddock 1985; Reddock and Huggins 1988). In fact, even before the institution of slavery, Amerindian women made major contributions to the Caribbean's agriculture (Momsen 1993), so did pre-colonial Mayan women who enjoyed economic equality with their men (Nash 1978; Safa 1995). As the Caribbean shifted from agrarian economies to urban industrialization, women's labour and wages also migrated, and some women took advantage of early employment opportunities in urban centres.[1]

Today, women dominate in some segments of the informal and formal sectors: in agriculture and in the manufacturing and textile industries. They are also found in abundance in certain public service jobs such as teaching and nursing, as well as in the service sectors including tourism. Women comprise the vast majority of the labour on small family-owned farms, in small family businesses and as self-employed individuals in marketing, petty trading, and vending of a wide variety of goods and services. For many Caribbean women who work, marriage is not seen as an alternative to wage labour; and for working-class women, paid employment is often about meeting family needs rather than their personal or professional fulfilment (Safa 1995). These practices of Caribbean women are also observed in other women across the globe. For example, the centrality of women's economic activities to families of poor and working-class black families is observed in Britain (Bryan et al. 1985; Lewis 1993), and in the US (Davis 1981; Harley 1997).

Overall, in all distinctive historical movements, women of colour on a global scale were forced to work, irrespective of their mothering and other reproductive roles (Reynolds 2001). At the same time, women's work is often excluded from official labour market statistics. According to Massiah (1986, 230), it is not surprising that census data reports show that more than half of the adult female population in the Caribbean are 'not economically active'.

As a result, Helen Safa (1995, 84) argued that the myth of a male breadwinner is a 'powerful Western norm' that continues to persist over time.

The information and perspectives discussed in the following sections of this chapter illustrate that women's economic contributions in all types of households prevent abject poverty, although there is room for much improvement in their living conditions. Such understandings are necessary in illustrating how women's agency is effective in negotiating gendered relations, at home and in the workplace. For many resource-poor households, the issue of poverty is not one of the presence or absence of a male breadwinner, but the extent to which wages for women (and men) from working families can sustain a family. This chapter presents a succinct depiction of women's economic contributions to the household economy through work in the agricultural and non-agricultural sectors. These synopses build on Theresa Ann Rajack-Talley and Clarence Talley's (2000) research on farming women, and on the works of Patricia Ellis, Safa, Janet Momsen, Rhoda Reddock, Eudine Barriteau and others, whose research since the 1980s centre on women and industrialization, entrepreneurship and migrant work. Although Caribbean households are used as a case study, parallel arguments can be made for poor and working women globally.

## Women in Agriculture

In most developing countries, agriculture continues to play an important role in export earnings as well as a source of employment and livelihood. Although not well statistically documented, women provide an important share of the agriculture labour force as individual food producers, marketers, or as farm workers among other agriculture related activities. A 2006 report by the Food and Agriculture Organization (FAO) showed that the overall proportion of the economically active population (EAP) working in agriculture declined during the 1990s, but the percentage of economically active women working in agriculture at the global level, remained at nearly 50 per cent through 2000 (see figure 5.1). Based on the most recent internationally comparable data, the figure remained relatively high with women comprising 43 per cent of the agricultural labour force in most developing countries. These averages are higher for Eastern and Southeastern Asia and sub-Saharan Africa, but lower for the Caribbean and Latin America countries (FAO 2012). The statistics for the Caribbean, however, are generally limited to data collected on the formal agricultural sector involved with the production and exportation of sugar, banana and other plantation crops. The data does not reflect the important roles that Caribbean women play in providing food for the home and the local markets (Rajack-Talley 2015).

*Figure 5.1: Percentage of Economically Active Women Working in Agriculture,*
*1980–2010 (projected)*

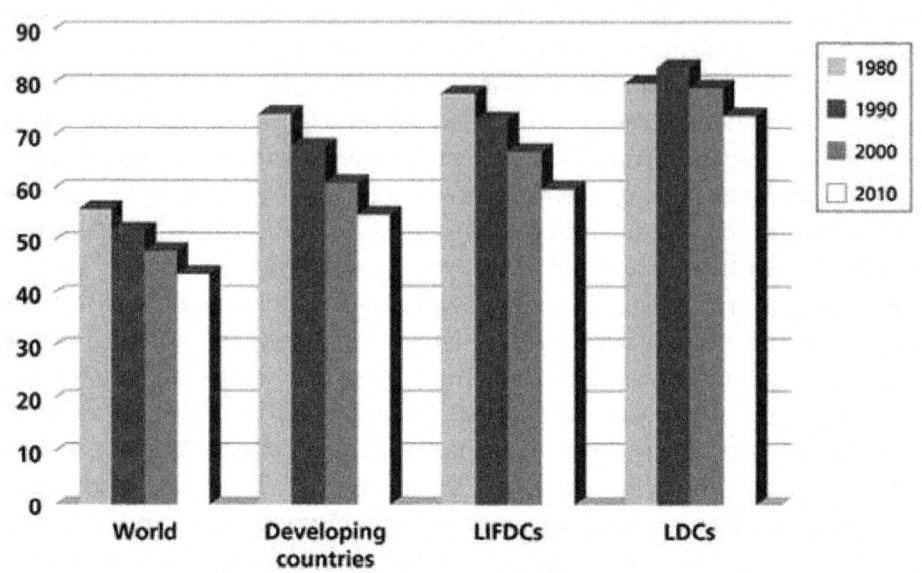

Source: FAO Report on Agriculture, Trade Negotiations and Gender (2006)

Neither do quantitative reports reveal that women are the primary nurturers and managers of biodiversity and the environment.

In this section, the role of Caribbean women in agriculture will be examined to show that Caribbean women have always worked in the agriculture sector, whether or not a male spouse is present in the household. Over the years, they have been pushed more into domestic food production while men are now more typically active in the traditional export market of agricultural commodities. As such, an analysis of the domestic food sector in the Caribbean is essentially an analysis of women's roles in the small family farming system (Rajack-Talley 2015; Rajack-Talley and Talley 2000). The dichotomy, however, has led to socio-economic barriers that limit women's success and rate of employment in agriculture, with discernible gender patterns.

## History of the Female Breadwinner

Caribbean women's economic participation in agriculture is not recent and can be traced to the period of colonization in the seventeenth and eighteenth centuries (Rajack 1991; Rajack-Talley and Talley 2000; Reddock 1985, 1988; Reddock and Huggins 1988, 1997). Then, the economy was propelled by imported slave labour of both women and men from West Africa. Sugar was one of the most valuable commodities on the market and slave labour the cheapest. The commonly held image of enslaved African women on the plantation is that of her in the stereotypical role of the 'mammie', the house servant, and/or the 'slave breeder'.[2] Enslaved African women, however, played several roles that contributed to the economic life of the sugar-cane plantations. Massiah (1986) refers to a three-tiered status system in which enslaved women were used as labourers in the cane fields, domestics in the plantation houses and as primary food producers and marketers in the slave communities (see also Mathurin 1974; Patterson 1967; Reddock and Huggins 1988, 1997).

The European planters used the knowledge that African women raised much of their own food to justify using them as field workers on the plantations. Slave labour then, was, of course, unpaid and exploited without any moral or ethical restrictions. Both enslaved women and men performed the same tasks in the cane fields. There was no economic or social benefit to the planters to have a sexual division of field labour (Reddock and Huggins 1988, 1997). It was more profitable for the plantation owners to have the enslaved women and men produce much of their own food. As such, slaves were allowed to engage in peasant-like activities, cultivating subsistence food crops to feed themselves (see also Mintz 1974). Interestingly, women slaves were perceived to be less of a threat than the enslaved men, and so were given permission to buy and sell any extra food grown for home consumption at a common public market on Sunday mornings (Mair 1986; Mintz 1974; Reddock and Huggins 1988, 1997). These roles were characteristic (in varying degrees) of many of the Caribbean islands, including Montserrat, Tobago, St Vincent, Dominica, Grenada, Barbados and St Christopher (Edwards 1980). The prevalence of women in the local market and as hucksters/higglers in the municipal markets today, is a continuance of the historical dominance of the local food market by women, throughout the region.

When slavery ended, many of the enslaved African women retired from agricultural fieldwork with the intent of becoming housewives and homemakers. What is not made clear in history texts is that this did not mean women were giving up earning incomes, but that they no longer selected work on a plantation. However, very soon after, the pressures of declining wages and rising food prices encouraged large-scale migration of former enslaved male workers in search of work in other countries. Consequently, the women returned to work on the plantations (Momsen 1991, 1993). At this juncture, freed African women now had to be employed for wages and a stringent gender division of labour was implemented so that women could be paid lower wages than men. The wages received by women were so low that this had to be supplemented by other income-earning activities.

Women drew on their marketing experiences selling produce in the open public Sunday markets during slavery, and established themselves as the primary marketers in the domestic food market networks (Mintz 1974). Some sought multiple wage employment while others embarked on setting up their own businesses, such as retail food shops, in the urban centres. Regardless of whether they lived in rural or urban communities, the freed African woman worked because the idea of a male breadwinner was unrealistic and unattainable, within the economic environment of that time. They also had to continue growing food to feed their families. The gender stratification of labour that enforced differential pay for women and men emerged alongside the system of indentured labour (Rajack 1990, 1999; Rajack-Talley 2015; Reddock and Huggins 1988, 1997).

## Indo-Caribbean Women

In Trinidad and Tobago, Guyana, and to a lesser extent other Caribbean countries, the abolition of slave labour led to the demand for another source of cheap labour. Since India was also under British colonization, it was both practical and profitable to establish an indentured system of labour using the men and women from this colony. Hence, after slavery, and between 1845 and 1917, an Indian indenture labour system was introduced to the plantations of some Caribbean countries, in particular, Trinidad, Guyana, Jamaica and Suriname. Under this system, human labour was perceived as a variable that was to be manipulated for profit maximization (Parmasad 1983; Rajack 1996). The women who were brought to the Caribbean from India as indentured labourers had to renegotiate their gender identity within a stratification system that was different from India. The women did not migrate as part of a family within traditional Indian family systems, nor were they under the control of male husbands and relatives.

It is argued that, to some extent, Indian women who migrated to the Caribbean were freer of the social sanctions imposed on them in India. Bridget Brereton (1979) explained that the disparity between the sexes of indenture servants that settled in the Caribbean may have resulted in greater value of the migrant Indian woman's labour and her reproductive role, compared to what she may have experienced in her homeland. The sex ratio and women's economic roles also produced interesting gender dynamics that was alien to the traditional East Indian cultures but persisted in Caribbean gender ideologies (further discussed in chapter six).

Within the indentured labour regime, women often carried out the same tasks as men – planting, weeding, hauling cane trash, applying fertilizers, cutting, bundling and loading sugar cane (Rajack 1990, 1999). In many ways, the social experiences and standpoints of East Indian indentured women were parallel to that of Afro-Caribbean women's history. They operated not as wives but as female workers for independent wages on the plantations. For individual free women, this offered them economic autonomy from male counterparts; however, all women worked, even the married ones, as women's wages were essential to the indentured labourers' family incomes and expenses. However, women and men indentured labourers were not paid the same wages. Planters discriminated against female labour by rationalizing and formalizing a division of labour system in which work was categorized as heavy and light; light work was assigned to women and paid less. The indentured East Indian women, on average earned two-thirds of the wages earned by men. By the early twentieth century, the average weekly wage was one dollar per week for men, and women were paid one half to two-thirds the wages of men (Brereton 1985; Rajack 1991, 1999; Reddock and Huggins 1988, 1997). Women also performed domestic work that fetched very low wages.

The plantation owners rationalized paying women lower wages by asserting that all women had extra support from men (Rajack 1991, 1999; Reddock 1985, 1988). The gender stratification of labour with wage differentials was carried over into the twenty-first century and adopted by the government-owned sugar companies of the Caribbean (Rajack 1991). As a result, Indo-Caribbean women who did manual work on the sugar plantations were paid lower wages than the men for the same job. They continued to work because wages earned solely by the men could not support a family, and also because they were used to having an independent source of income. At the end of indentureship, the Indo-Caribbean women who did not retain employment on the larger sugar cane estates supplemented the household income by working on small family farms, or as casual labourers on small privately owned sugar cane plots. In some islands, like Trinidad, at the peak of the sugar industry, female sugar-cane workers were more likely to be of East Indian ethnicity. Their role as independent wage earners, however, runs counter to the stereotypical personification of the docile and domesticated East Indian woman walking three steps behind the man (Rajack 1999).

## Current Trends

Since colonization the plantation system of production has sprouted two distinct but related agricultural sectors in the Caribbean, with different ownership and labour structures (Beckford 1972, 1984; Best 1968; Gomes 1984; Rajack-Talley and Talley 2000; Rajack-Talley 2015). On the one hand, there is the plantation sector centred on commercial production of cash crops and then there is the subsistence sector consisting of small family farms producing food items for the home and for the domestic market. In the Caribbean, data for the involvement of women and men in agriculture are generally confined to transactions in commercial cash crop production of the formal market sector. Statistics relating to the production and marketing of agricultural produce focus on export crops in which men predominate. As a result, official estimates for the Caribbean indicate low percentages for women who are economically active in the agricultural sectors. Women are also less likely to declare themselves as employed in agriculture, even though they often work longer hours than men (Beneria and Sen 1981). Consequently, although over the last decade the collection of gender disaggregated data has improved, the definition of employment has not been made clear (UN, Department of Economic and Social Affairs 2010) and, as a result, labour force statistics still do not reflect an accurate account of women's participation in the formal and informal agricultural sectors. As a result, statistical reports are more likely to underestimate women's work in agriculture.

The most recent FAO report on the State of Food and Agriculture divulge that the labour force in agriculture was low and had decreased over the last 20 years moving from 24.5 per cent to 12.2 per cent, with wide variations across the region (table 5.2). The lowering of the percentages of women and men's employment in the agricultural sector (except for Haiti) reflect the overall decline in the export crop industries, including sugar, bananas, citrus, coffee, cocoa, and other plantation crops. These industries were historically a major source of employment for rural populations and their decline has seriously impacted farming families and their villages. Women were particularly affected by the downturn of the agricultural sector, as more women participate in agricultural wage employment when men find jobs in other areas of employment, including as migrant workers in urban areas. Statistical data that show low figures for women's employment in the agricultural sector is, therefore, not an accurate representation of the number of women in agriculture. It also does not include women in other agricultural sectors such as in marketing and agro-processing.

*Table 5.2: Agricultural Share of Economically Active Women by Country in 1980, 1995 and 2010*

| Country | 1980 | 1995 | 2010 |
|---|---|---|---|
| | % | % | % |
| Anguilla | 0.0 | 0.0 | 0.0 |
| Antigua and Barbuda | 22.2 | 10.0 | 12.5 |
| Aruba | 25.0 | 18.2 | 10.0 |
| The Bahamas | 2.6 | 1.6 | 0.0 |
| Barbados | 8.2 | 4.3 | 2.7 |
| British Virgin Island | 0.0 | 0.0 | 25.0 |
| Cayman Islands | 50.0 | 20.0 | 10.0 |
| Cuba | 10.4 | 7.4 | 5.0 |
| Dominica | 20.0 | 20.0 | 8.3 |
| Dominican Republic | 11.1 | 8.8 | 7.3 |
| Grenada | 25.0 | 14.3 | 11.1 |
| Guadeloupe | 10.7 | 2.3 | 0.0 |
| Haiti | 61.0 | 53.9 | 44.0 |
| Jamaica | 18.1 | 13.5 | 10.9 |
| Martinique | 6.9 | 3.6 | 1.0 |
| Montserrat | 0.0 | 0.0 | 0.0 |
| Netherlands Antilles | 0.0 | 0.0 | 0.0 |
| Puerto Rico | 0.4 | 0.4 | 0.2 |
| St Kitts and Nevis | 16.7 | 16.7 | 11.1 |
| St Lucia | 25.0 | 16.0 | 11.4 |
| St Vincent and the Grenadines | 20.0 | 13.3 | 13.6 |
| Trinidad and Tobago | 8.6 | 4.5 | 2.5 |
| Turks & Caicos Islands | 0.0 | 0.0 | 16.7 |
| United States Virgin Islands | 25.0 | 16.0 | 11.5 |
| **Caribbean** | **24.5** | **15.5** | **12.2** |

*Source: FAO (2010–2011).*

## Women Marketers: Huckstering and Higglering

There is very little information on the regional food trade in which women hucksters and higglers buy directly at the farm gate in one country, export and sell in neighbouring islands (e.g., from Grenada and St Vincent to Trinidad/ Tobago and Barbados). These marketing activities, however, have always been an income earning source for Caribbean families and especially single female-headed households (Rajack-Talley 2015). Historically they were performed largely by Caribbean women (Lagro and Plotkin 1990; Mintz 1974) and were developed out of the custom of enslaved women selling the extra food that they were allowed to produce for themselves on the plantation in Sunday markets. It rapidly expanded immediately after emancipation (Besson 2003). As independent small producers and family farms were established, the common market outlets for small producers also expanded to now include sales at the farm-gate to hucksters or higglers, agents and middle men. Hence, contemporary patterns of marketing at local sites, huckstering or inter-island trading within and between the islands, haggling or sidewalk tray or 'fruit stand' selling, are not new income-earning practices for Caribbean women. Currently, women are responsible for producing and selling between 12 and 50 per cent of local foods, mainly fresh fruit and vegetables, root crops, some export crops such as bananas and rice as well as a range of other non-traditional export crops (Mantz 2007).

The level of trade and capital exchange is unfortunately often not recorded and thus undervalued, alongside the entrepreneurial abilities of women. In the Caribbean, there are three distinct forms of market vendors in which women predominate, namely marketers, higglers and hucksters. Men also participate in all three forms, but historically women dominate in each category of the marketing operations. In each case, women are self-employed individuals engaged in economic activities, encompassing bargaining, bartering, and selling of produce that requires high levels of financial competence as well as negotiation and business skills. The economic roles of these women have never been captured, although they serve as important forms of providing food and generating economic activities. Jeffrey Mantz (2007), for example, found that 'huckstering' by the predominantly Dominican women accounts for the second largest foreign exchange earnings for that country.

These trading patterns continue to be under the aegis of women and are sustained with little or no capital from governments or the private sector, but from women traders, small producers and family farms. Little research has been done on women traders but what is known suggests that it is a longstanding matrilineal vocation, in which marketing skills are passed from mother to daughter and other female members in the same family. It is not unusual to find, aunts, nieces, sisters and others plying the same trade. Mantz (2007) described this occurrence as 'women for women' and a most vibrant and self-sustaining economic activity. Although several hundred women remain committed to the trade, their numbers are shrinking for a myriad of reasons. Labour shortages, contracting market users and competition from big supermarkets as well as higher levels of educational attainment by young female family members are all factors. However, there is still an active intra-island movement between the islands of Dominica, Guadeloupe, Antigua, St Kitts, St Martin, and the Virgin Islands, St Vincent, St Lucia, Grenada, Guyana and Trinidad and Tobago, among others. The socio-economic importance of the three categories of marketing activities at the local and regional levels, have been seriously undervalued and unrecognized as a key link in the food security chain of the region, in addition to supporting many resource-poor households (Rajack-Talley 2015).

## On the Small Family Farm

On the small family farm women participate in all aspects, as farm managers, farming partners, farm family labourers, or as farm wage labourers. Gender distinct farm management practices on small farm holdings can be observed. Rajack-Talley (1996, 2015) observed these various arrangements and has identified four gender distinct models of farm management. First, there are separately managed enterprises where women and men are responsible for separate crops or livestock production. It is common for women's agricultural projects to be located near to, or at home. Decisions on each enterprise are made separately, although the couple usually discuss farming issues and help each other with the work. Another pattern is where women and men are involved in the same crop and/or livestock production but participate in distinct tasks – shared but in stereotypically female and male jobs. Under this arrangement, men are the major decision-makers and farm managers, while women are considered farm family labour. Discussions on farming issues are at a minimum level.

The third farm management model is based on the understanding that both women and men can do the same tasks – not set gender distinct work. The responsibility for all the farm enterprises is also shared. However, the male is considered the head-of-the-household and, as such, is treated as the major decision-maker and farm manager while the woman farmer is not documented as being economically active in agriculture. Lastly, in this fourth model, the division of labour, decision-making and farm management are simple. They are all done by one or the other where one partner in the couple has very little to do with farming. The person identified as the farmer (male or female) makes the agricultural decisions, performs the lion's share of work and manages the farm. Rajack (1996) suggested that these models are not exclusive or exhaustive and each gives rise to a different set of gender dynamics and relations of power (see chapter six).

Although there are no recent studies on women farm managers in the Caribbean, what is known is that all four models exist within the region. Past studies showed that although there were wide variations from one country to another, women as major farm decision-makers could be as high as 47 per cent, and 42 per cent as joint managers with men. Gender specificity could also be observed in the types of farming decisions made by women. For example, women participated more in decisions about what type of crop to grow, or livestock to rear, how farm labour is to be organized, and where produce is to be sold (Kleysen 1996; Rajack-Talley and Talley 2000; Rajack-Talley 2015).

These gender patterns also permeated the division of labour for specific crop or livestock production activities (CARDI 1997; IICA 1996; Henshall 1986; Overholt et al. 1985; Rajack 1996; Rajack and Hosein 1993). In livestock production, more women engaged in small animal production (e.g., sheep, goats, and poultry); while men tended to be involved in large livestock production (e.g., cattle). Even when women participate in large livestock production, such as raising dairy and beef cattle, they were found mainly in certain activities such as feeding, grazing, milking, and taking care of young and sick animals (Kleysen 1996). A gender division of labour was also found in crop production, where although women participated in all aspects of crop production, tasks were gender disaggregated and women primarily undertook planting, weeding, harvesting and post-harvest crop activities. On the other hand, men tended to engage mainly in land preparation, application of agro-chemicals, and in the operation of farm equipment and machinery (CARDI 1997; Kleysen 1996; Rajack and Hosein 1993; Rajack 1996; Rajack-Talley 2015).

Overall, within the agricultural sectors of the Caribbean, women are more likely to hold low-wage, part-time, and seasonal jobs that make them easily employable. They are wage employees on the more commercial farms and estates, and in agricultural processing, marketing, and other agribusiness activities. FAO (2011) predicted that new jobs in the export-oriented agro industries will offer better opportunities for women compared to the traditional tasks they perform. Regardless of the type of farming and level of production, agriculture remains the most important source of employment for women, especially in rural areas. Studies have shown that the level and extent of women's contributions to food production are central rather than complementary to the household economy (Edwards 1980; Ellis 1988; Forde 1988; Knudson and Yates, 1981; Rajack 1990, 1996). This is because women earn money from the sale of produce in the local markets; they save money by growing some of the food for their families, and provide free labour on the family farm. These are all major contributions to the household economy (Ellis 1988; Forde 1988), yet development agents, planners and policymakers often see their contribution as subsistence and/or marginal to the farm household's income. Additionally, women play crucial roles in food security in the domestic market of most Caribbean societies (FAO 2006; Rajack-Talley 2015).

## Gender Barriers

Despite the important roles that women play in agriculture, they are unable to move much above subsistence to commercial levels that can provide the incomes necessary for a comfortable lifestyle. This is primarily because women's roles as domestic food producers are mitigated by restricted access to agricultural resources and services such as land, credit, training, technological assistance and institutional support (Rajack-Talley and Talley, 2000). On the other hand, resources are allocated to the export-oriented agricultural sector in which men typically are more actively employed. In particular, *land distribution* patterns are very uneven with respect to farm size, and limit women's access to credit and other farming resources (Alleyne 1994; French 1988b; Kleysen 1996; Kudson and Yates 1981). For example, while a high percentage of all agricultural activities by women farmers take place on farms that are less than five acres, the production of export crops controlled mainly by men farmers, takes place on the larger pieces of farmlands (Beckford 1984; Gomes 1984, 1985). Generally, the domestic food sector in which women dominate occurs on small and fragmented pieces of land and is either rented, occupied without permission, or family-owned (French 1988b; Kleysen 1996; Kudson and Yates 1981).

For farming women who do not have access to, or the means to purchase farmlands, the use of family-owned land is particularly important. Sharing family-owned lands for farming is a common trend in the Caribbean although there are variations from country to country. Family-owned lands, however, cannot be individually owned and, as a result, their use as collateral in accessing loans and other services is limited. This situation is changing in some countries where specific land management policies are being introduced that offer some guarantee to women in the right to use family-owned farmlands under common law (Alleyne 1994; Cole 1994). For example, in Barbados, the Succession Act of 1975, the Property Act of 1979, the Family Law Act of 1981, the Tenancy Freehold Purchase Act of 1980, and the Agricultural Holdings Options to Purchase Act of 1982, all address the legal recognition of women in tenancy, in inheritance and in ownership of land (Alleyne 1994). However, throughout the Caribbean, Rajack-Talley (1998) found cases where when women purchase land, the land titles are often registered under the man's name or as joint ownership. Consequently, data collected on landownership show that more men are land titleholders (IICA 1996; French 1988b; Kleysen 1996; Rajack 1998).

Among the farming community, land ownership and tenure are important in accessing credit. Very often, the criteria for credit specified by lending agencies require collateral, which for small farmers is usually their land title (Alleyne 1994; Cole 1994).  The absence of land titles and tenancy by women, limit their ability to access *credit* and improve and expand their farming activities to levels that allow them to live well above the poverty line. In general, the economic terms of most credit schemes favours either middle- or large-scale farmers many of whom are men engaged in export production, and who own their lands. The literature shows that women respond to credit barriers from the conventional lending agencies (e.g., banks) in three ways. Some seek the assistance of a male partner in applying for a loan, others apply for loans from community-based credit unions and a fair number of women participate in indigenous saving schemes such as the 'sub' in Dominica, the 'box' in Guyana, and the 'sou sou' in Trinidad (CARDI 1997; D-REP 1998; Rajack 1998).

The three strategies are not mutually exclusive or are exhausted avenues. Monies accessed from the alternate sources are used both for farming and home use. Women who do receive loans have good credit ratings (D-REP 1998), and are more aggressive in accessing other loans and resources (CARDI 1997; Rajack 1998). With limited access to land ownership and credit, women's economic progress in the field of agriculture remains at the subsistence level. As such, women are kept out of the money-making agricultural systems and lack the requirements to ensure a decent standard of living for their families.

Another limitation facing women small farmers is that very few of them receive agricultural training, technology and technical assistance. There is also little data on agricultural training of women. What exists shows that between 1991 and 1993, less than ten per cent of all Caribbean women farmers, received training in crop production, chemical use, post-harvest technology and marketing, animal production and farm management (Kleysen 1996). When the data on the number of women engaged in farming activities are compared with the number of women who received agricultural training, technology and technical assistance, there is a wide imbalance. This gap sometimes influences the stereotypical belief that women do not adopt modern technologies and use machinery because they are by nature resistant to technology. Contrary to this belief, Caribbean studies show that women farmers are more embracing of new technology and are less resistant to moving away from traditional farming practices, compared to men farmers (CARDI 1997; IICA 1995; Rajack 1996, 1998). In general, men farmers tend to believe that they are quite knowledgeable about farming and, as such, do not see the need for training in the use of new practices and technologies, nor are they convinced that these are worthwhile additional investments for the farm (CARDI 1997; Rajack 1996, 1998). On the other hand, because women tend to believe that they lack adequate farming knowledge, they are willing to try new and recommended technologies.

More recently, the recognition that rural and farm women are left out of training and technological advances has led some regional agricultural research and development organizations to support training for farming women (e.g., CARDI, IICA). This includes training in organic farming, agro-processing and agribusiness. It has also spurred the formation of farming women's organizations such as the Network of Rural Women Producers who also advocate for women's access to credit, participation in government policies, micro-enterprise development, and the elimination of gender bias in land ownership and tenure practices. Enhancing women's access and control over technology, as well as to credit, land and other productive resources is integral to food security of the Caribbean region (Rajack-Talley 2015). It is also crucial in poverty alleviation and the well-being of families, particularly in rural areas.

Studies have shown that resources controlled by women are more likely to be used to improve family food consumption and welfare as well as to reduce child malnutrition (FAO 2008). As such, increasing women's income from farming and agriculture-related activities is important to sustaining many farm households across the region and preventing abject poverty. But, the age-old problem of gender inequity has not gone away. Caribbean women farmers, like female farmers worldwide, control and own less land, less livestock, use less improved seed varieties and fertilizers, access and use less credit, and are in need of extension services (FAO 2011). Compared to men, they are more likely to operate smaller farms, on average one half to two-thirds the size of men farmers; farm on small and fragmented pieces of land either family-owned, rented or occupied without permission; keep fewer livestock, typically of smaller breeds; and earn less from the livestock they do own (Rajack-Talley 2015).

Since historically, as well as in contemporary times, financial services and credit schemes favours middle to large farms which are owned predominantly by men for commercial production of crops and livestock, women are less likely to have access to credit and therefore less able to purchase inputs such as fertilizers, improved seeds and mechanical equipment so as to expand their farming business. They also have less education, and less than ten per cent have access to agricultural information, extension services and technology. Often, because of their low levels of education and their disproportionate workload in the domestic spheres of their lives (family and home), they are most likely to be employed in part-time, seasonal, and low-paying jobs that make it difficult to support their families on their own.

According to the FAO (2010):

> If women had the same access to productive resources as men, they could increase yields on their farms by 20–30 percent. This could raise total agricultural output in developing countries by 2.5–4 percent, which could in turn reduce the number of hungry people in the world by 12–17 percent.

## Women in Non-Agriculture Employment

The notion that men are the breadwinners is also challenged when one looks at women's participation in the non-agricultural sectors of the Caribbean. According to Massiah (1986), this idea was historically both unattainable and unrealistic, as the individual wages for most working Caribbean men were insufficient to maintain a household. As a result, women and men worked in specialized sectors that emerged since the post-emancipation and urbanization era. For women, this was in the domestic services sector and, later, the garment and manufacturing industries. Fuelled by W. Arthur Lewis's (1955) argument popularly referred to as *industrialization by invitation*, the region experienced economic restructuring moving from a more agrarian base to urban industrialization. Lewis's recommendation was based on the premise that there was a need to shift an overpopulation of labour from agriculture into a manufacturing sector, and develop a complementary industry.

Lewis's strategy was also rooted in the belief that there was a ready and cheap source of women's labour in the urban centre that can be employed in manufacturing (Reddock 1994). Interestingly, from the very onset of industrialization, the assumption that women should be housewives and men the principal economic provider for working and poor households was unreal. Instead, women's paid employment became more visible and necessary to the urban household and to the economy. A feminization of the labour force was realized because of: (i) the increase in demand for women's labour as a direct result of export led industrialization; (ii) the increase in the availability of women who were educated and choosing to have low fertility; (iii) the increase in the cost of living which made living off one wage extremely difficult; and (iv) a decline in men's employment during structural adjustments (Momsen 1993; Safa 1995).

Although women from very early in the Caribbean industrialization process played major economic roles in the non-agricultural sectors of both the informal and formal economies, their contributions were neglected and/or undervalued. This was due, in part, because studies from the 1950s to 1970s conducted on Caribbean women were preoccupied with the reproductive roles of women in lower-income black families (Braithwaite 1957; Clarke 1957; Smith 1956). As a result, it was not until later that scholarship emerged that highlighted women's participation in economic activities in the formal sector (Barriteau 1994; Barrow 1986; Gill and Massiah 1982; Reddock 1994), many of which were piloted through the Women in the Caribbean Project (WICP).[3]

These studies found a pattern of flow and ebb of women's participation in the labour force as women responded to changes in the socio-economic conditions over specific time periods. For example, in the post-emancipation era as ex-slaves migrated in large numbers to urban centres, Afro-Caribbean women moved out of the plantation economy and sought wage employment in nearby small towns. Momsen (1993) found that in some instances women workers outnumbered men workers because they were concentrated in occupations such as domestic servants and vendors. In the post-war period, 1947–60, the Caribbean region embarked on a process of industrialization and women again migrated at a faster rate than men out of the agricultural sector and into a growing manufacturing industry, the service sector, and other non-farming activities.

Inexplicably, while Caribbean women shifted in and out of the formal and informal labour markets, discrimination based on the Western gender roles followed women wherever they went. As a result, they were hired predominantly in occupations linked to stereotypical 'feminine' responsibilities in the home. They worked as domestic servants, nurses, teachers, and other sections of the public services (Ellis 1986). They were also found in large numbers in personal services such as hair stylists, dressmakers, washers, and in child care and nurseries. They were food vendors and caterers, produce and haberdashery traders, hucksters and higglers. Women currently dominate in these same stereotypical female jobs and form the backbone of the Caribbean tourist industry working as maids, cooks, launderettes, and general custodian employees. High rates of women's employment have also consistently been found in the garment and textile industry and other light manufacturing of food, apparel and accessories (Ellis 1986; Massiah 1986; Momsen 1993; Safa 1995). According to International Labour Organization (ILO) (2003) data, the share of women employed[4] in the non-agricultural sector in Caribbean small states is approximately 45 per cent in the previous decade.

## Industrialization and Women's Labour

Garment and textile production is the most consistently feminized of all non-agricultural industries. Hiring women over men, in textile production, is based on the understanding that the work involved suits women because: (i) it requires low skills that are acquired through home schooling; (ii) they have the natural dexterity for the job; and (iii) their labour is dispensable and cheaper. Nevertheless, women's employment in the textile industry has benefited many low-income households as well as the development of the textile industry and the labour movement of the Caribbean. Reddock (1994) advocated that any reconstruction of Caribbean labour history must feature women's roles in the garment and textile industries. For example, she pointed out that during the late nineteenth and early twentieth centuries, garment production in Trinidad was almost entirely controlled by petty commodity producers whose skilled labour force was predominantly female. At that time, garments were not produced in factories but by self-employed dressmakers who worked from home, with periodic visits to clients. The cost of garments were based partly on the means of the client, the clothes design, costs of materials, time spent in making the garment and location of the business (Harewood 1975; Reddock 1994). As a result, this arrangement was most cost effective because women's labour was cheap; working at home meant that the time to make a garment was not accurately counted and the overhead cost of rent for a business was reduced.

The rise of the garment and textile industry using local capital and entrepreneurship occurred in the post-war period (1947–60) in what is often referred to as Lewis's *industrialization by invitation* or *import-substitution*. Reddock (1994) points out that Lewis made his argument using the data that showed Caribbean women were becoming unemployed and returning to their homes because employment opportunities were not keeping up with population growth. Interestingly, Lewis encouraged establishing garment-related industries because he believed that women could be hired as cheap labour. Indeed, when the garment and textile industries expanded, 90 per cent of the workers employed were women. Women's work in garment making contributed to the household economy in two ways. First, the wages earned as factory workers or independent dressmakers were central to the household economy. Second, by making clothes for the family and not having to purchase these, a reduction in household expenses was observed, particularly when clothes were sometimes one of the most expensive item for working families with children at that time.

Over the years, women's self-semployment as dressmakers and seamstresses has persisted with periods of expansion and decline. Economic restructuring, under the structural adjustment policies of the IMF in the 1980s, saw another resurgence of garment and textile manufacturing. While the *industrialization by invitation* model was based on local capital, this new wave of industrialization was established as export manufacturing in Free Trade Zones (FTZs) throughout the Caribbean. The intended objectives of FTZs were to alleviate unemployment caused by the economic downturn and to produce desperately needed foreign exchange as avenues to assist in economic development. Whether or not these objectives were met successfully, the FTZs created jobs primarily for women. For example, Safa (1995) reports that by 1992, there were 27 FTZs in the Dominican Republic, which employed approximately 140,000 workers, of whom 60 per cent were women. These jobs re-incorporated women into the urban labour force.

On a global scale, women still constitute the bulk of workers in FTZ jobs, but wages and occupation are differentiated by gender. Women receive low wages, work in poor conditions, are forced to do overtime work with no child care services and have limited labour union access and support. The preference is usually for young, single, educated women, new to the industrial work force. The women who are married and employed in the FTZs are also the major economic provider for their family, and women who are single head of households carry a heavy financial responsibility. While the contributions to the household economy by these women are crucial to the survival of their families, their low wages compete with a constantly rising cost of living. As a result, the women engage in several other additional income earning projects, including entrepreneurial activities to supplement their low-paying FTZ and other low-wage jobs. According to Sybil Douglas-Rickett (2002, 127), 'the women earn enough to make ends meet but not to pay for the basic necessities of life', and so must seek additional ways to supplement their incomes. In many instances, this consists of small-scale and creative entrepreneurial projects.

## Women: Necessity Entrepreneurs

Many women from resource-poor households engage in activities in the informal sector as a survival strategy, and a large number are small business owners and operators. As a general rule, working women are three to four times more likely to be involved in entrepreneurial activity compared to women who are not working. Elaine Allen et al. (2007) explained that working provides women with access to resources, social capital and ideas. They also found that a high percentage of women in the Caribbean and Latin America were involved in entrepreneurship activities. Using the Gender Entrepreneurship Monitor (GEM) data, the researchers suggested that female entrepreneurship was increasingly becoming an integral part of the economic make up of the Caribbean, Latin America and all developing countries.

Allen (2008) described Caribbean women as 'necessity entrepreneurs' who embark on free enterprise because they are not able to find sufficient income in any one job. She and others see entrepreneurship as a way out of poverty. For women, it is easy to establish a small business in the informal economy because of the lack of 'red tape' to do so in the Caribbean compared to other parts of the world and/or in the formal sector. Caribbean women discovered from very early that through entrepreneurial efforts they can supplement and/or maintain a family budget, as their foremothers had done during slavery, trading extra food grown for the slave populations in weekend markets.

The type of entrepreneurship that women usually operate varies. Barriteau's (2001b) study on women entrepreneurs in Jamaica found that most women venture into social and personal services, manufacturing, and then some type of wholesale or retail trade. Women's small manufacturing and sale businesses are commonly referred to as 'cottage industry'. The women are popularly known as 'vendors', 'hucksters', 'hagglers', and 'island traders.' While the items or service that they offer widely differs, there are some common characteristics of their businesses such as scale of operations with a small number of employees, usually no more than 15, and who are primarily family members and female. To keep capital cost and expenses low the business operations usually depend on manual labour and are run from the individual's place of residence (ILO 2002). Revenue is also low and is based on returns from sales from personal orders delivered or picked up by a customer, and/or from sales in the neighbourhood, workplace, on a busy street, industrial site, or local market. Such enterprises operate on a small-scale and tend to dominate in specific sub-sectors such as retail distribution in fruits and vegetables or light manufactured items.[5]

Women entrepreneurs are also concentrated in small food processing businesses, garment construction, and in professional services such as in hairdressing and catering (Lashley 2010). Women's prevalence in these specific areas has been attributed to the idea that they are compatible and familiar 'traditional' or 'home-based' activities linked to their domestic and reproductive roles. Moreover, initial overhead costs are low because they already possess much of the start-up equipment for their businesses such as cooking utensils and sewing machines. This is not to say that there are no female entrepreneurs in the formal sector who own medium to large successful businesses. However, when looking at women or female-headed households and poverty, the attention is on women with low-income businesses operating mainly in the informal economy.

Although entrepreneurship activities managed by women provide supplementary incomes to the household economy, over the years, they have become more relevant in economic terms as potential employers and job creators. An ILO (2001b) study of three Caribbean countries (Trinidad and Tobago, Suriname, and Barbados) found that there were no comprehensive estimates on the number of small businesses since official statistics do not take into account the many unregistered establishments in the informal sector, a significant number of which are owned and managed by women. The report, however, acknowledged that women's entrepreneurship activities are important to the economic development and transformation of Caribbean households and societies. Another study conducted in the Caribbean and Latin America by Siri Terjesen and José Ernesto Amorós (2010) suggested that policymakers should encourage female entrepreneurship and provide incentives for women to start high-value-added ventures. They concluded that women's entrepreneurship, particularly when focused on high-value-added activities, was fundamental to social and economic progress and poverty reduction in developing countries.

High-value-added entrepreneurship activities have been more common among men but there has been some diversification by women into what was once considered the domain of males. These efforts are being supported by both non-government and government organizations. However, research shows that women entrepreneurs who operate on a small scale still lack technical and vocational training. As such, chances of moving from subsistence levels to profitable commercial levels are difficult. In this regard, women entrepreneurs supplement their wage employment and/or household budgets as a strategy to offset increases in the cost of living and fight off abject poverty. However, because of the lack of financial and other resources, they are unable to comfortably improve the standard of living of their families and/or move out of the reach of poverty.

Just as women's work in the home is given low status, so too are women's entrepreneurship ventures. Such ideologies which are pervasive across the Caribbean and Latin America limit the access of women entrepreneurs to productive resources (physical and human capital), and preclude them from exploiting opportunities for innovation and enhanced competitiveness. Accordingly, on a global scale, women's entrepreneurship is an untapped source of economic growth. Women have a lower participation rate in entrepreneurship than men, and choose different industries perceived as being less important to economic growth and development compared with those selected by men. Further, mainstream government policies and programmes do not take into account the specific needs of women entrepreneurs (ILO 2003).

Access to finance from the commercial banking system in the Caribbean presents yet another barrier for women entrepreneurs who rarely have the collateral required by the banking institutions. Sometimes the women lack the 'business skills' to communicate effectively with finance providers and deal with the bureaucratic conditionalities. As a result, women tend to rely more on informal sources for 'soft' loans, such as from family members or local credit schemes. In Barriteau's study on Jamaican women entrepreneurs, she also found that one of the main sources of investment capital was women's own savings. These sources were, however, unable to provide large sums of money to women to expand their business from subsistence levels to commercial enterprises. Consequently, women's businesses were often kept at a 'small scale', and were labelled as not being very entrepreneurial (Barriteau 2002). Their entrepreneurship was considered peripheral to the 'real economy' and their economic contributions marginal to the national economy (Barriteau 2001b; Lashley 2010).

The operating size of women's entrepreneurship has generated several theories and myths to explain why they have not expanded their businesses over the years. Many of these were noted by Nicholson and Garvey (2006, 48) in their study on women's entrepreneurship in Jamaica, and included the following negative stereotypes:

Women do not want to own high-growth businesses.

Women do not have the right educational backgrounds to build large ventures.

Women do not have the right type of experience to build large ventures.

Women are not in the network and lack social contacts to build credible ventures.

Women do not have the financial savvy or resources to start high-growth businesses.

Women do not submit business plans to equity providers.

Women-owned ventures are in industries unattractive to venture capitalists.

Women are not a force in the venture capital industry.

On the other hand, the Small Business Development Committee in Barbados (1989, 7) identified financial problems, low labour productivity, inadequately trained staff, not enough advertising, variable quality of material, and frequent unavailability of commodities and materials, as the main limitations that women entrepreneurs faced.

Jonathan Lashley (2010) rightly pointed out that women's entrepreneurial activities tend to be small scale, but there are several reasons for this. Women do exercise agency and some women entrepreneurs prefer to keep their businesses small and manageable. Their main goal includes survival and offering a good service or product. They believe that the capacity for hard work, determination, perseverance and self-confidence are the core to a successful business (Barriteau 2002). But at the same time, in many instances, women's businesses are small because they are not made aware of potential support for growth and development and Caribbean societies do not give adequate support to women's entrepreneurship (Lashley 2010). They lack government assistance, access to financial resources, an education that can prepare them for entrepreneurship, and access to information and professional networks.

Despite the many hurdles that women entrepreneurs face, they continue to engage in several income-earning activities as a survival strategy, because the income earned from any one source cannot support their household. Entrepreneurship offers women economic independence as well as a chance to improve the standard of living for themselves and their families. It is particularly important for single-female-headed households that need more than one source of income but have only one income earner.

The practice of informal entrepreneurial activities as a strategy to supplement low wages is also observed among Caribbean women who have migrated in search of work. They too experience similar problems in their attempts to operate small businesses as those back home.  These include a lack of financial support, education and technical training. In addition, studies on women entrepreneurs have found that Afro-Caribbean women in Canada lacked confidence and family support. Not having immediate and extended family members, particularly other women, to help with childcare and housework. Jacqueline Scott's (1994) research in Canada and Lashley's (2010) work in the United Kingdom have both identified the absence of family to support women as a serious barrier to successful entrepreneurship activities by Caribbean women. In situations where women were married or had partners, the small businesses were usually jointly owned, but women managed. This allowed the women to access resources as a couple, while managing the enterprise independently of their husbands and partners.

Overall, the many limitations that women entrepreneurs face are linked to the pervasive gender stereotyping that women's economic ventures are not as capitalistic-based as those of men, but more nurturing, domestic and supplemental. Similar to women's work in agriculture and its link to a domestic economy, women's entrepreneurship is compared to men's and deemed as economically inferior, lacking the potential for commercialized ventures. As such, they are criticized and labelled as 'cottage industries' that do not require high levels of support and financing. These misconceptions of women entrepreneurs and the important economic and social roles that they play are due, in part, to there being very little research or data gathering on these dynamic and talented women. Moreover, the approaches that do exist are not centred on the lived experiences of women entrepreneurs and, as such, are not agency-centred because they are not interested in what these women do. Consequently, women's abilities in planning and developing small businesses that require financial, marketing, creative and management skills, all of which can be further enhanced, is often unnoticed and undervalued.

Rather than minimizing the importance of women's entrepreneurship in the region, attempts for economic growth, women's advancement, and poverty reduction should validate and support their businesses. Truth be told, their entrepreneurship provides incomes for their households and contributes to economic development of their countries and the region as a whole. Moreover, Caribbean women entrepreneurs are experts on using local materials, resources, and markets to generate incomes while providing a service to the local needs of their communities and creating employment for those in most need. Without this very important segment of Caribbean societies, many more women, men and children would be unemployed, unable to feed and sustain themselves, fall below the poverty line, and/or become dependents on state welfare.

## Migrant Women and Labour

From the beginning of the twentieth century onwards, migration and the remittances that resulted supported many Caribbean families during times of high unemployment and economic difficulties. Caribbean men initially sought work in Panama, Costa Rica, Nicaragua, Cuba, the US, Great Britain and Canada. Male migration dominated for a while during the 1900s–1950s, but, in the post-war years, women started migrating in increasing numbers reaching a peak in the 1990s (Barriteau 2001b). Although female migration increased when economic opportunities for migrant men declined, in some cases, women migrated because their husbands ceased sending monetary support to the household, leaving the burden on the mothers of their children.

Caribbean women migrated from rural to urban centres, intra-regionally, as well as to foreign countries mainly England, Canada and the US. They sought a wide range of wage employment from casual labourers and domestics to nurses and other professional jobs. Support from migrant women and men included financial contributions as well as 'barrels' of food, clothing and other items which arrived periodically at the homes of families. The education of children and the maintenance or improvements of homes were also direct benefits of remittances. They pursued this option so that they could support their families, but indirectly the remittances that were sent home also supported the economies of their homelands (Aymer 2005).

Female migration for employment reasons is a survival strategy that many Caribbean women have adopted, but it is one that is emotionally difficult. Also, their economic experiences have always been challenging and exploitative, including when they moved from their rural communities to urban settings in the same country. Ester Boserup (1970), in her pioneering work on rural women, found that rural-urban migration does not better women's economic positions because job opportunities for women in towns are limited. A similar conclusion was drawn in a study conducted on women who migrated from rural villages to town centres in Jamaica. The study found that women in these situations did not really earn a lot of money (Foner 1975). As a result, women were forced to work longer hours and/or work multiple jobs. Consequently, women's other contributions to the household were reduced because they simply did not have the time to make clothing, linens, bakery products and other home-made items for the family, as they did back home. Instead, because many of these items now have to be purchased, they become a new expenditure to the household budget.

Before the trek to the North, Caribbean women moved intra-regionally, from one Caribbean country to another. They migrated either to support their husbands or in search of work themselves to sustain their families. For decades, women followed male migrant workers to the Panama Canal Zone (Brizan 1984; Conniff 1985; Richardson 1983), to the sugar-cane camps in Cuba, Dominican Republic and other large sugar producing plantations, to the oil fields of Trinidad (Brereton 1979; Brizan 1984), and later to the Dutch Islands of Curaçao and Aruba (Aymer 2005; Green 1974). At first, gender discrimination reared its ugly head and policies were enforced that debarred migrant women and their children from foreign residency, unless they were accompanied by a male husband (West Indian Royal Commission 1942).

Sometime later, women immigrants were allowed to work in male-dominated jobs as well as those stereotypically defined as women's work such as cooks, washers and in personal services. Similar to the experiences under slavery, indentureship, and post-colonialism, the gender paradox of trying to enforce gender norms and a family model that did not, and could not, reflect the socio-economic realities of Caribbean women, persisted. Moreover, immigrant women consistently faced gender discrimination and stigmatization while trying to maintain their economic worth. For example, when they were employed in stereotypical male jobs, such as construction, they were considered to be non-feminine women (Mack 1974).

Intra-regional work eventually declined in the post 1960s and so too did male migration. However, women continued to migrate intra-regionally, drawn to wherever there were economic investments particularly in tourism. There, they could find work in the service industry of both the informal and formal tourist and tourist-related sectors (de Albuquerque and McElroy 1982; Olwig 1993). During this period, women also began to migrate to Britain and North America as domestics, nannies, and caregivers of elderly persons. It was easier for women to find work in these job categories because the demand was for work closely associated with women's reproductive roles. While these jobs were low paying, the higher rates of economic activity and the regularity of having independent incomes did enhance women's economic position in the home. According to Nancy Foner (1975), wage-earning wives were more likely to be treated as partners rather than as dependents. She further concluded that when women work the whole family gains, as the total household income is greater and families are less likely to experience absolute poverty.

While much of the literature on Caribbean migration focuses on the Afro-Caribbean population, patterns of migration as a form of economic survival are also observed in the Indo-Caribbean population. Lomarsh Roopnarine (2003) identified three distinct periods: (i) Migration under indentureship (1838–1917), (ii) Inter-Caribbean migration (1917–62), and (iii) Migration to Europe and North America (1962–present). East Indian women's economic contributions under indentureship have been studied, documented and discussed, but their economic roles as immigrants are severely under researched. What is known is that historically Indo-Caribbean women worked as indentured servants and later as female labour on the sugar plantations and on small family farms, something which they continue to do today. What is less known is that after indentureship, women from working-class Indo-Caribbean families worked as domestics, factory workers in textiles and manufacturing, and as migrant workers in low-paying jobs in North America.

The concept of a male breadwinner in the Indo-Caribbean family has been challenged by Rajack (1990, 1999) and others who attempt to bury the myth of the docile East Indian wife. The economic contributions of Indo-Caribbean women to the household, the informal and formal economies are significant and important to poverty alleviation. Nevertheless, the gender and ethnic barriers they face are similar to Afro-Caribbean, poor and working-class women, and have kept them on the margins of society's wealth as their households struggle to stay out of poverty. Contrary to the stereotype, there are single-female-headed Indo-Caribbean households, many because of widowhood, that are masked by their residency in extended family homesteads. Although a different type of migration, the burden still lies on the single female to do whatever it takes to support her children and survive poor living conditions.

Overall, the migration of one or two parent abroad whose children remain behind with other family members is an old economic strategy practised by many Caribbean women and men for decades. There is an increasing amount of research on the positive and negative social and psychological impact of this practice on parents, children, and families in general. The analyses of this body of literature remains inconclusive (see discussions in Barrow, 2010 on Caribbean Childhoods). There are those who found that migratory separation is destructive to the family (Larmer and Moses 1996; Lowenthal 1972; S. Mohammed 1998), while others focus on the resilience of family members (Thomas and Bauer 2000; Wiltshire-Brodber 1986). They all, however, agree that for low-income families, migration is an economic choice that is accompanied with the pain of having to take the risk of emotional distancing from their children. They too are socially isolated in their adopted home and face the risk of exploitation, having to now support two households, and with little or no support from family, friends and community. On the other hand, members of a different social class who also migrate can do so with their entire families and are more quickly assimilated into their new country of residence.

## Summary and Conclusions

In this chapter, the economic experiences of women demonstrate a need to re-examine the extent to which a double standard is applied to working women in the Caribbean. First, the numerous examples of female breadwinners in both the agricultural and non-agricultural sectors show that very often women's realities are in contradiction with the prevailing perceptions about their gender roles. Despite years of proving their economic worthiness, Eurocentric notions still influence the idea of the male as the breadwinner in Caribbean families. Obsessed with women's reproductive roles it is believed that without a male breadwinner, households are more likely to experience poverty because women cannot economically support themselves and their households. Consequently, women are not often given the support as important income earners.

Secondly, when women's economic roles are encountered they are usually compared to those of men and are inherently devalued. Interestingly, the criterion used for diminishing what women do is seldom identified as sexism or gender discrimination. Instead, women's work is categorized and placed in more socialized roles rather than economic, or at least described as having a non-capitalistic modus operandi. For example, although Caribbean women have historically played and continue to play important roles as food producers, they experience severe constraints because of the 'type of agriculture' that they practise. This is a direct outcome of the plantation system and its patriarchal ideology in which male-dominated commercialized systems of production are viewed as more important compared to female-dominated food production systems geared to local and regional markets. Farming women, therefore, are vulnerable to double discrimination; first, because they work mainly in a neglected food sector that is in direct competition for resources with an export cash-crop sector, and second, the gender division of labour that developed under colonialism trivializes women's roles in both commercial and subsistence production.

In the non-agricultural sectors, women also face double standards and are twice disadvantaged because of their gender and job categorizations. Historical gender discrimination steered women into gender-specific employment in the labour market where because of low-educational attainment and little technical skills training, they were placed in job classifications that were the lowest paid. In many instances, women were also paid less in the same job category. This included the garment and manufacturing industries as well as occupations as domestic servants, petty traders, laundresses, and other professional services in both the formal and informal sectors. Today, although women can be found at all levels of employment, women from resource-poor households are still more likely to be employed in lower-level jobs while men are recruited into higher yielding income activities within the same field. Sandra Sookram and Patrick Watson (2008) attributed these gender labour patterns to wage discrimination rather than human capital differences between women and men. Specific to entrepreneurship, they found that men tend to dominate in what are labelled as the 'business informal sector' and women in the 'household informal sector'.

The labelling, classification, and the arbitrarily placing of hierarchical values on work is a clear indication of gender and social class discrimination where what is grouped as women's economic activities are considered to be 'not that economically important' to society. As such, little attention is placed on resource distribution, including financial assistance and credit, skills building, training and other support services for women's economic activities. Consequently, women rely on themselves, family, friends and community members, many of whom are in the same socio-economic bracket (chapter seven discusses further the impact of social networking, cooperation and social capital). While these women continue to support their families, without government and other sources of support, it is difficult to attain economic and social mobility.

The women also continue to rely on work in the less regulated informal economy where they have greater flexibility to manage their activities. The perpetuation of women's work in the informal economy shows that while women have made some advances in employment in the formal and private sectors, traditional and new forms of gender discrimination continue to undermine women's income and push them out of the formal labour market. According to John Humphrey (1985), 'objective economic laws of market competition work through and within gendered structures' (219). It is because of these gendered structures and discrimination in the formal sector that women seek refuge in the informal economy as a way to survive economically.

Overall, women shift between the formal and informal job markets, continuously working long hours, engaging multiple economic activities, building entrepreneurship, and/or migrating in search of work. This they do along with feeding, clothing, educating and providing shelter for their immediate and extended families. Simply put, women must work and produce for both use-value in the home and for exchange-value in the markets. Their fluidity and range of activities along a continuum imply that they are neither peasant, proletariat nor housewife but all three. While this is empowering for women it also means that (i) they have to negotiate the difficulties encountered in all three roles; (ii) bear the burden of having to carry all three at the same time; and (iii) deal with the relational tension embedded in these roles.

In these resource-poor households if women falter in any one of their many roles this could result in greater impoverishment of the family. There is no social capital to fall back on, no family member that can buffer, no health insurance, annuities, stocks or bonds. Worse yet, there is no savings account or government public assistance that can compensate. They have nothing to sell except their labour. As a result, not only are the women carrying an important financial responsibility, but this responsibility comes with great risks to their physical and mental well-being. They consistently have to assure their children that 'all is well' and try to hide the economic vulnerabilities of the home from other family members and even the public. Further examples and analyses of the socio-psychological dimension of poverty were discussed in chapter three.

This chapter focused on women in these specific areas of employment because it is where women in resource-poor households work. When gender analyses are conducted broadly for the region, the advancements made by women, educationally, professionally, politically and legislatorially, can place a shadow over the challenges and difficulties that women in low-income-earning activities experience. As a result, the plight of low-income, working women can easily be interpreted as not linked to gender discrimination. The information, discussions and analyses in this chapter show otherwise by exposing the difficulties that women, who belong to households in the poorest quintile of the population or in those close to the poverty line, experience daily as they try to earn a living wage. In some of these households, it is because of women's economic activities that families avoid falling near or below poverty estimates; others may have crept up to middle-class rankings. It is, therefore, important for us to look at what they do, and how they do what they do. In other words, research approaches need to place greater focus on these groups of women and their agency.

The various economic activities and strategies adopted by women within any one job category are illustrative of their human agency. This is further observed in women's resilience in supporting their families, with or without a male breadwinner, as changes occur in the broader economy and in their domestic situations. Their financial contributions to the home may be small, but they do not allow themselves to become marginalized in the home budgets as is often alleged, simply because their families (and their societies) cannot afford for them to not have an economic role. This is of greater significance in single-female-headed households where the likelihood of poverty is directly linked to women's economic capabilities.

As a whole, women do not only experience double discrimination based on their social class and their gender, but also the interactive effect of both. Yet, through their agency, they persist and continue to support themselves and others, as well as contribute largely or meagrely to the economies of both the formal and informal sectors. It easy to socially exclude them from macro-economic analyses when gender-disaggregated data is used by itself and where women's advancements are assumed to be broad-based. The specific experiences, conditions and challenges faced by the most vulnerable, yet hardworking and surviving groups of women need to be researched to better understand the female breadwinner in resource poor households, with or without a male breadwinner. The economic roles of these women, who are sometimes called 'matriarchs', need to be examined from both their strengths and their needs, and to always address the multidimensional aspects of their lives. In particular, more research is needed on women's work in the informal sector as studies have found a positive correlation between informal sector employment and poverty.

# 6. Women, Change and Power

*You have to hear for your own interest, nobody can listen for you.*
– Female Sugar Cane Worker (1991).

*You have to learn for yourself, nobody can learn for you.*
– Female Sheep Farmer, (1996).

Over the last few decades, feminist theorizing on gender has come to reject the understanding of gender as a social relation devoid of power (Barriteau 2009). Feminist theoretical approaches now question absolutist notions of male domination. The theoretical thrust of this literature has put forth the argument that gender power relations are negotiated, and that domination and resistance are part of the negotiation process (Deveaux 1996; Heckman 1990; Rajack-Talley 2004; Sawicki 1988). Much of the evidence for this research can be found in Caribbean women's history of resistance to slavery and colonization (Beckles 1989; Mair 1975; Rajack-Talley 2004).

Caribbean feminist and scholars further argue that power negotiations occur in both the public and private spheres of society and include both material and ideological factors (Barriteau 2001b, 2003, 2009; Collins 1991; Walby 1990). Over the years, a great deal of research on women and gender relations in the public domain has been published in the areas of history, politics, culture, education, labour and ideology (Barriteau 2001b, 2003; Leo-Rhynie, Bailey, Barrow 1997; Reddock 1994, 2012; P. Mohammed 1998; and others). Research focused on the private spheres of women's lives has concentrated on understanding the dynamics and nuances of family life, conjugal unions, childrearing, sexuality and health (Bailey 1998; Barrow 2010; Barrow, de Bruin and Carr 2009; Kempadoo 2004; Roberts, Reddock, Douglas and Reid 2009). These studies and others employ human agency, women's agency in particular, and, as a result, examine the rationale and processes involved in decision-making. Few studies, however, have closely examined social relations and gender power in economic decision-making in the private domain of the home.

On the other hand, research on household decision-making has been dominated by the economic literature where the focus is on intra-household bargaining models and the distribution of resources. Cheryl Doss (2012) identified four different models that can be measured, including the notion of the family as a unitary unit which has been slowly rejected since the 1980s. The alternative models focus on the bargaining of resources and decision making on all aspects of family life within several different types of complex household arrangements. The shift away from treating all households as unitary units has led to the need for more research on what are the factors that determine how resources are distributed, and for a greater understanding of decision-making processes.

I argue that within this framework, social relations of gender and power as well as gender ideologies, should be considered important contributing factors in household bargaining and decision-making. As a result, this chapter pulls together all three areas: social relations and gender power, negotiation of material and ideological factors and bargaining models. I use five case studies to show that bargaining in households involves both material and ideological dimensions. The bargaining of material resources is linked to the income earner, who in most resource-poor households, comprise both women and men as was explained in the previous chapter. Additionally, social relations and gender power and identity in the home – the ideological factor – are connected to women's persistence in wanting to maintain certain economic independence and autonomy. This is reflective of the prevailing gender ideologies in the wider society.

The discussions and analyses presented here fill the gaps in the research but also to show the interrelatedness of the three areas and why they are important in poverty studies. For example, if the social relations of gender and power are not carefully examined in households, then the bargaining of material resources, including the efforts of poverty reduction strategies will not be captured. Consequently, given that not all households are altruistic units, then it is possible that measures of poverty can in reality underestimate women's poverty in the home. On the other hand, if Caribbean gender ideologies and identities founded on women's history also play out in household bargaining, then we can expect interesting negotiations and outcomes in household decisions which can also affect poverty assessments of households.

Further, looking at intra-household dynamics is important because we do not adequately understand the extent to which the desired effect of projects and programmes aimed at poverty reduction are mediated by the gender-power dynamics in the home. In fact, these projects and programmes, including the introduction of technology and other resources from the outside, can act as bargaining chips for certain individuals in the household, and can have unintended effects for beneficiaries, or unintended beneficiaries. For example, the case studies show that intra-household negotiations affected the outcomes of an agricultural project designed to move women farmers from subsistence production to market sales and increased incomes.

While the previous chapters in the book looked at women breadwinners in households where male income earners may or may not be present, this chapter is centred specifically on two-parent households. This is important because one of the critiques of the *feminization of poverty* approach is that it failed to address intra-household dynamics and the gendered distribution of resources that occur in the private sphere of the home. The five case studies are used to get a close up view of what takes place between women and men in the same home. Typical of many Caribbean families, members were engaged in both wage employment and farming, and household budgets were sustained through incomes from wages and agricultural production on small family farms as well as through innovative expense saving strategies such as home production of haberdashery items and food for family consumption and sale (Deere, Safa and Antrobus 1997).

This chapter builds on the previous ones that captured the scale and prevalence of the economic contribution of women in resource-poor households and the barriers that they experience because of their gender and socio-economic status. The findings show women as social actors, who are not mere victims of male domination, but who sometimes resist, maintain, and/or alter systems of patriarchy while negotiating their living conditions and social relations. Note, however, the types of negotiation that occur in households vary greatly from what occurs in the workplace, as intimate social relationships are involved. Negotiations of economic roles and power relations in the home are intricate processes and are often directed towards keeping harmony, because if not successful they can lead to family conflict and unpleasant social relations as well as a worsening of material living conditions for the entire household.

## Gender Ideology and Women's Power

Discussions on gender ideologies and gender power have brought to the forefront, issues of male domination and female resistance, within the parameters of patriarchal societies. Feminists argue that the dominance of male privilege and values continues in the twenty-first century under the system of patriarchy. Patricia Mohammed (1998) squarely puts this responsibility on the feminist agenda to demonstrate more concretely how patriarchal privilege is a disadvantage to women, men and society. Alternatively, there are more fruitful ways of organizing the sexual division of labour in the public sphere and managing households and families in the private spheres. Undoubtedly, a direct relationship exists between patriarchy and gender, which is important to women's positions in both the public and private arenas (Barriteau 1998, 2001b, 2003, 2009; Seidman 2007; Walby 1990, 1997, 2001). However, the form and relationship of patriarchy in the public sphere is different from that in the private sphere because structures of public institutions such as the workplace are different from the household as a private institution.

According to Sylvia Walby (1997), in the public sphere, patriarchy operates at the structural level where the approach is one of separatism. Women are separated out of the public arena through structures that are used to subordinate them and deny them access to public spaces. In the private sphere of the household, patriarchy operates at the individual level and the strategy adopted is one of exclusion based on stereotypical gender roles and household incomes of individual members. Domination and subordination in the private sphere, therefore, takes place at the individual level and depend on a patriarch who may control the woman's experiences in the home. In this context, the patriarch is both the oppressor and the recipient of women's subordination. Walby (1990, 1997) contended that while patriarchy operates differently in the public and private spheres, the strategies used reinforce each other towards the same end, namely male domination and female subordination. In other words, the segregationist strategy in the public sphere maintains the exclusionary strategy in the private sphere, which, in turn, supports the segregationist strategy used in the public sphere.

## Domination and Resistance

The feminist literature on patriarchy and domination also generated discussions focused on Michel Foucault's thesis that posited; 'where there is power, there is resistance' (1978, 93). The work of Foucault on power provided a starting point for conceptualizing domination and resistance. Caroline Ramazanoglu (1993) and Rachel Alsop et al. (2002) explained that Foucault invited us to think differently about power, and indirectly the way in which feminists had understood it. Although, his model came from outside feminism, it does raise the question of how can women wield power if the power system is patriarchal? They suggested that leaving patriarchy 'to one side' allowed exploration of different aspects of social relationships, especially at the micro-level, and provided more opportunity to focus on the agency of women as a subordinated group.

This perspective opened the way for a better understanding of women's resistance to male domination in everyday life experiences (Deveaux 1996; Heckman 1990; Rajack-Talley 2004; Sawicki 1988, 1986). It allowed for a shift in focus from women as subjects of the exercise of power (McNay 1991), to women's interpretation and mediation in power relations, both in society and in the household (Deveaux 1996). The notion of women as 'victims' is rejected and, instead, the resistance of women to male domination is viewed as an act of human agency. Within this perspective, women are not treated as a uniform group of dominated and passive victims but as active individuals who negotiate their experiences. Some researchers suggest that there may be more than one process going on at the same time, and that domination and negotiation are interdependent and can exist concurrently (Gerson and Peiss 2000). For instance, women can respond to male domination by actively participating in, setting up, maintaining and altering systems of gender relations.

Feminist writings also link women's resistance to subordination in everyday life to women's resistance to domination in the public arena. They stress the interconnectedness of power and resistance in the two spheres. For example, Bell Hooks (1990) argued that women should be encouraged to feel personally empowered and exercise this daily power to resist domination and exploitation in the public arena. She also believed that the transformation for women in the public sphere can arise out of transformations for women in the private sphere. Similarly, Patricia Hill Collins (1991) wrote that the empowerment of African American women is an outcome of their rejection of theories on domination, and a re-conceptualization of power within both the public and private spheres. Taken as a whole, these perspectives on women's empowerment question the hegemonic nature of patriarchal domination in all societies. They give credence to the role women play in understanding and arbitrating their own experiences. Examples of this are best illustrated in the discourse on the development of a gender ideology indigenous to the Caribbean which has emerged as a result of women's resistance to domination and patriarchy.

## Caribbean Gender Ideologies

Caribbean scholars identify the region as diverse, but nonetheless speak of the existence of a common Caribbean gender ideology that cuts across geographical and social boundaries (Barriteau 2003; Barrow 1998; P. Mohammed 1998; Momsen 1993; St Hill 2003). These scholars explained that the Caribbean is one of the earliest areas of European colonization and the countries of the region have a similar ethos. The commonality stemmed from a shared history of colonialism, slavery, labour migration, economic and political structures oriented toward plantation production, and a peripheral status in the world economy. Included in this ethos or culture, is a shared gender identity that varies by class and ethnicity within different societies (P. Mohammed 1998; Momsen 1993; Reddock 1998; St Hill 2003). Gender identity and ideology can also be linked to the survival of traditional symbolism, beliefs and practices (Besson 1998; Massiah 1984; P. Mohammed 1998; Momsen 1993; Reddock 1998). Specific to the Afro-Caribbean women, is the cultural survival of the matrifocal and matrilineal[1] characteristics of the African societies from which the enslaved women were brought to the region. The effect of these cultural survivals is the continued dominance of female-headed households and female-centred family structures (Rajack-Talley and Talley 2000). On the other hand, some aspects of traditional East Indian cultural practices and gender roles are still practised in Indo-Caribbean households (Baksh-Soodeen 1998).

Despite these cultural and ethnic variations, a common Caribbean gender identity is still possible because irrespective of origins, the women inherited disrupted gender systems from their homelands, and had similar economic and social experiences in their new environment. Interestingly, the mutual work experience of the women included having high levels of economic autonomy (Momsen 1988; Patterson 1967; Rajack 1991, 1999; Rajack-Talley 2004; Reddock and Huggins 1988). This allowed Caribbean women to play central social and economic roles in households, regardless of ethnicity. While Caribbean feminist and scholars have made excellent progress in teasing out indigenous gender ideologies and possible variations based on ethnicity, much work is still needed to look at how social class forms part of this organic ideological growth. This is particularly important as the birth of Caribbean gender ideology stemmed from a working woman's standpoint (slavery and indentureship), but since that time, advancement in education and professional employment for both women and men have created fairly wide middle classes and smaller elite groupings throughout the region. Similarly, while research on social class has linked colour of skin to upward social mobility, they are yet to make this link to gender ideology and identity.

Nonetheless, Caribbean gender roles, identity, and ideology can best be described as paradoxical, with patriarchy coexisting with other gender ideologies (P. Mohammed 1998; Momsen 1993). It is within this social milieu that decisions are made and resources allocated in the formal economy and the informal economy as well as within the private sphere of the household.

The coexistence of patriarchy with this indigenous Caribbean gender ideology produces interesting but complicated outcomes in both the material and ideological progress of women in the public and private spheres of life.

## Material and Ideological Relations of Gender

Eudine Barriteau (2009) further elaborated on the interconnectedness of the public and private sphere and gender power relations. She asserted that there are two dimensions that combine to create and maintain gender relations of power in both spheres. First, there is the material dimension that determines how women and men gain access to material resources, and are allocated status and power in society and in the household. Then there is the ideological dimension. This constructs what is accepted or contested as the appropriate expression of masculinity and femininity. According to Barriteau (1998, 2003), the gender relations of any society are made up of the social, political, economic and cultural expressions of the material and ideological dimensions of a gender system.

The material and ideological dimensions that Barriteau (1998, 2001b, 2009) discussed reinforce each other and a change in one affects the other. Similarly, change in the material and ideological dimensions in the public sphere affects change in the material and ideological dimensions in the private sphere. Bina Agarwal (1997, 2001) referred to this as the quantitative and qualitative determinants of households bargaining powers. She argued that the material determinants interact with each other, and also with the ideological determinants. Together the effect gives rise to interesting and complex gender dynamics. These perspectives suggest that (i) bargaining takes place in households, (ii) that the processes are complex, and (iii) that they involve negotiations of gender power. It was further argued that determinants of gender power, weigh in bargaining processes found in both the public and private spheres of patriarchal societies. According to Barriteau (2001b, 48), 'when the material and ideological dimensions of gender systems advance opposing interests, major ruptures occur'.

Over the years, material relations of gender have improved significantly much to the credit of the governments of the region which have implemented policies and legislations that both provided more resources and removed structural barriers for women. However, Barriteau (2001b) pointed out that despite the material gains, particularly in education and professional employment, Caribbean gendered systems continue to be unstable and unjust. Moreover, Barriteau suggested that ideological relations are currently at their worst and that women now exist in a hostile climate because of women's advancements. In reality, expanded educational opportunities, increased employment possibilities and political and legislative progress for women have 'deepened the divisions and contradictions of ideological and material relations of gender' (67), and are sometimes manifested in the rise in domestic violence and the anger that some men feel towards women's gains.

Women, female-headed households, women's organizations, and feminist scholars are now being blamed for emasculating men and for boys falling behind girls in education and becoming involved with criminal activities. Statistical reports on women's progress and men's regress are associated with women's supposedly new gender identities in the home and in public. As a result, social relations are strained and gender power negotiations continue at all levels of society. These negotiations often go unnoticed until there are economic consequences that spot light the position of men viz a viz women either in public or in the home.

In this chapter, material relations of gender are centred on the roles of women and men on small sheep farms initially managed and controlled by women. The social relations, gender identity and gender power are treated as the ideological factors that are observed as changes takes place and roles, including farm decision-making are negotiated/bargained. Further, the research took place when the region was going through serious economic downturns that affected the way that working men and women survived.

## Gendered Responses to Change

The Caribbean region sits at the periphery of the world economy consistently responding to changes with fluctuating periods of economic growth and recession. In chapter one, theories on causation of underdevelopment and poverty were discussed, and in chapter five, the evolution of the female breadwinner was analysed. Each phase of the region's political economy was met with gender responses to roles and identities, including during the 1980s when many 'Third World' countries were faced with huge and mounting debt crises. As a result, a number of political and economic strategies, known collectively as Structural Adjustments Policies (SAP),[2] were mandated to debt-ridden countries, including those in the Caribbean. Women scholars such as Carmen Diana Deere (1997), Helen Safa (1995), Peggy Antrobus (1990) and others have argued that the implementation of Structural Adjustment Policies (SAPs) were particularly devastating to whatever gains Caribbean households and women had made by then.

According to Deere, Safa and Antrobus (1997), the economic crises and the implementation of the structural adjustment policies made it extremely difficult for households to survive. While the SAPs negatively affected all households, many working-class families were pushed closer to the poverty line. The combined effect of the SAPs resulted in growing hunger and poorer health in many developing and underdeveloped 'Third World' countries. The cutbacks particularly in health, education, transportation, and food subsidies have resulted in a shifting of economic and social responsibilities from states to households, increasing the burden on the poor, especially women. Despite this, households have survived and continue to do so.

Faced with economic downturn and structural adjustments, many households were forced to become innovative, continuously devising strategies to deal with economic hardships. At the heart of the survival strategies were the wives, mothers, daughters and sisters who lived in these households. These survival strategies included the gravitation of women from resource-poor households into the export-processing zones and service industries. Women also migrated in search of wage employment, particularly to the US. The greatest survival strategy, however, was to increasingly engage in a wide variety of economic activities in the informal sector where many women established small-scale entrepreneurial activities or return to small family farm agricultural systems. Women also saved money by modifying their households' living and consumption patterns.

The home became an important domain to develop and implement economic strategies. It was where women and men conceptualized strategies for generating income and coping with worsening living conditions and tenuous situations. The home became the main site where many of these survival projects were launched with minimum capital overheads. For example, in the home, food was grown and prepared for sale in local markets. Women also sewed, embroidered, and along with other family members, produced art, crafts, jewellery, food items and ornamental plants for sale. In some instances women, men and children were contracted by larger businesses and corporations to manufacture garments, toys and other items at their homes. Many of these activities were by no means new to many Caribbean households, but during hard fiscal times the intensity and urgency of these activities increased.

Other ways in which women, men, and households survived cutbacks in services and economically difficult times was by increasing their reliance on their social networks and their dependence on family, friends and neighbours. In the Caribbean, the concept of family extends beyond the household unit or the nuclear family, beyond the boundaries of neighbourhoods and villages, and even beyond the country in which they live. Similarly, the concept of community transcends any spatial boundary. People are linked together in many ways, by blood relations, by extended family relationships, through savings groups, sports, religion and other social, economic, and cultural associations. The persistence of these networks and the strengthening of these in trying times are crucial to the survival of resource-poor households. In many instances, food, clothing, services and cash flow through these networks. Financial investments and loans to start up small businesses are also filtered through these relations.

Alternatively, some households increase their household size because when the number of people living in a household increases, the household gains from the income of prospective new wage earners. In some instances, the new member may not be working but can assist in the household chores and responsibilities, particularly childcare, thus freeing other members to look for wage employment. It is quite common for households to incorporate additional kin, particularly small children or elders, in exchange for cash, kind, or services from relatives. Additionally, in most agrarian-based developing countries, including the Caribbean, households also return to, or intensify farming practices and grow some of their own food. Here, improved farming practices and the introduction of farm technologies are important in meeting the food needs of families as well as growing provisions for the domestic markets. The introduction of technological interventions, however, does add yet another dimension to gender reactions to economic shifts in farm homesteads.

Amartya Sen (1990) argued that technology is often defined in very narrow terms as either a mechanical, chemical, or biological process. Often, the social aspect of the use of technology is neglected and/or reduced to a cultural phenomenon, in which gender stereotypes about the fear, inability, or forbidden use of technology by women are assumed to be true. As a result, the social organization that surrounds the use and control of technology is ignored in research, agricultural extension, and by policymakers and planners. This is particularly important to the world's rural people, including those in the Caribbean, who are dependent on farming interventions as a way out of subsistence production and poverty. Moreover, peasant households are commonly organized around kinship lines and rules and, in some contexts, 'household' and 'family' can still be taken as synonymous terms.

Households and kinship ties significantly affect resource availability, particularly land, labour and technology. Because of the limited credit available from finance institutions, peasant producers rely heavily on household members and other relatives and friends for labour, financial assistance and security. Family members are also depended upon to pass on knowledge and technology, from one generation to another, and from one household member to another. Technology is considered an essential tool for change, and critical to the shifting of the farm enterprise from subsistence to commercial levels. In the application, it is assumed that technology is value-neutral and shared in a cooperative manner, among all the household members who are involved in farming (Rajack-Talley 2015).

On the other hand, research has found that technological interventions usually have a gender shift in labour and a negative effect on the status of women's work. Ester Boserup (1970) in her seminal publication, *Women's Role in Economic Development*, argued that activities that were once dominated by women are often readily transferred to men when new technology is introduced. She found that a single technological change in farming systems could entail a radical shift in sex roles in agriculture. These changes included increased mechanization, specialization and differentiation of non-agricultural tasks by gender. As a result of these changes, women were separated from production for market value and subsequently experienced a decline in socio-economic status.

Boseurp's findings along with others suggest that women are marginalized by technology because technology is not socially neutral and cannot serve the goals of gender equality, unless consciously designed to do so (Dauber and Cain 1981; Everts 1998; Goulet 1989; Rajack 1996; Rogers 1980; Sen 1999; Tinker 1990). In reality, the gendered control of technology can perpetuate social inequality and possible conflict, between men and women in the same household because it can change women's status. Women are often removed from the major income-generating farm activities to which technology is directed and relegated to subsistence production with low levels of technology use (Dauber and Cain 1981; Everts 1998; Tinker 1990). Nonetheless, farming technology is considered an important resource in moving farming families out of poverty, and women are aware of this potential.

Alternatively, there are those who argued that science and technology in general has had a two-fold positive impact on women. According to the United Nations University for the Advanced Study of Sustainability (UNU-IAS) (2005), technology can offer new employment opportunities for women and, secondly, it can reduce the market demand for unskilled female labour. These two different predictions placed gender issues in a new perspective and warrants further investigations on gender and technology. It is not only how women do science but also what science does to women and the interrelationship between women's power, or lack thereof, and the effect of science and technologies. Is the adoption of (farm) technology therefore gender neutral? In a case study of fish farming in Tanzania, Kitojo Wetengere (2011) found that although the probability that women would adopt the technology was higher than for men because it was linked to food security and accommodating to women's household responsibilities, women had less access to the resources needed to adopt the technology, including extension services.

These studies on women farmers provide important insights into peasant household dynamics and question the internal heterogeneity of households as well as the level of cooperation in the sharing of resources in all types of households. The socio-cultural foundation of peasant production in the Caribbean adds to the complex matrix of economic and social variables of household economies. The studies also found that personal relationships affect: the division of labour; rights to the use of land; mobilization of labour; the objectives of the decision-maker; the accumulation of capital; the size of technology and level of adoption; the disposal of output; resource allocation and product allocation. The women and gender studies that examined women's economic roles in agriculture and technology use, however, are not usually designed to examine the role of gender identities and ideologies in negotiating these situations and their outcomes. Consequently, women's agency in negotiating the distribution of power and resisting domination and marginalization when technology and other changes are introduced in farm households are rarely documented and understood.

## Intra-Household Dynamics: Bargaining Models

The nature of gender relations of power is highly complex and is even more difficult to grasp within households where personal ties also have to be considered. The exercise of gender relations of power are often noticeable when economic outcomes are at stake; however, it embodies both material and ideological factors (Agarwal 1997; Barriteau 2001b, 2009). Studies embedded in various disciplines have examined household social relations to determine whether they operate as unified or non-unified entities and reached different conclusions (Agarwal 1997; Barlette 1989; Collins 1988; Doss 1996, 2012; Guyer 1981). Many of the initial works were empirically focused and centred on the economic functioning of households, and assumed that households have certain rules that are applied, so that the most efficient household decisions are reached (Chiappori 1992).

One perspective suggested that households are unified with a 'benevolent dictator' altruistically pursuing everyone's best interest, or one in which all household members have identical preferences. Another perspective presumed that households are non-unified units consisting of individuals who may have diverging preferences (Kabeer 1998; Chiappori 1992; McElroy and Horney 1981, 1990). Within this research, there were disagreements about how decisions were made to resolve diverging preferences. One suggestion was that household members make what they believe to be the most efficient decisions for that household, while another proposed that householders engage in a bargaining process when making household decisions.

In households where members bargain, gains from co-operation are weighed against gains from non-cooperation. Gains from the co-operation are then allocated among household members; a corollary to this perspective is that the household member with the greatest bargaining power will benefit the most. A third argument is that in non-unified households, members have individual preferences and operate separate and autonomous sub-economies. As such, each member controls and disposes of the individual incomes gained from the sub-economies (McElroy and Horney 1981, 1990). Here, the assumption is made that there is no need for co-operation, but that there is still some level of equilibrium in these 'non-cooperative' households. Marjorie McElroy (1992) suggested that the three scenarios are not mutually exclusive, and they all reflect some level of co-operation within households.

These economic models are useful in that they highlight household decision-making as a bargaining process; that household members can have different preferences; and that the bargaining power in decision-making can be affected and effect differential access to resources. However, Doss (2012) found that to better understand intra-household bargaining, it would be very useful to have research that includes outcome measures as well as measures of women's bargaining power. This would allow for analyses of how changes that may affect women's bargaining power affect outcomes.

Alternatively, sociologically oriented research broadens the focus on the distribution of resources within households, and suggests that where patriarchy exists, males will have greater bargaining power because of their greater access to, and control of resources (Agarwal 1997; Boserup 1970; Donham 1990; Halperin 1994). Bargaining powers, therefore, can be derived from gendered disparity in access to resources (Folbre 1984). Nevertheless, this perspective argues that bargaining power is not determined solely by individual possession of resources, as individual contribution to the household economy is also important (Boserup 1970; Folbre 1984; Lipman-

Blumen 1984; Safa 1995). In most developing societies, women's financial contributions to the household economy are central to their household's survival, and this may provide another bargaining factor in decision-making processes. Along with the bargaining of access and distribution of resources, household members also negotiate the gender division of labour, gender identity and power.

Feminist theses argue that, in all households, both non-capitalist and capitalist, there are structures of hierarchy, and that mutual obligation often has to be negotiated or enforced based on power and authority (Boserup 1970; Folbre 1984; Lipman-Blumen 1984). The social stratification within families is therefore important because at a more micro level where the focus is on the individual, the assumption of a unified unit could be false and misleading. Women and men do not just respond to change but actively engage in a process of negotiating change. Household members bargain over gender division of labour, roles, responsibilities and access to and control over resources. It is not simply the case that women are subordinated and men dominate, although this trend is present. There is also no single outcome as the bargaining process involves interplay of gender identity and power. The nature of the social relations is personal and, as a result, the negotiation process occurs in various verbal and non-verbal ways (Rajack 1996). This is different from what takes place in the public sphere and is more complex and indeterminate. The discourse raises more questions than answers about the distribution of gender power in households. Are decisions in households altruistic, male-dominated and patriarchal? Or are households in the Caribbean and in other developing societies, women-dominated and matriarchal, or gender balanced?

In the following sections of this chapter, case studies are used to illustrate various models of gender roles and identity within resource-poor Caribbean families, before and after economic shifts and technological interventions. They are useful in understanding the personal settings, the social relationships and the role of agency that are all part of complex household bargaining of both material and ideological factors.

## Case Study of Women Sheep Farmers in Caribbean Households

The case studies cited are all peasant households located in one Caribbean country, but they tell the story of others throughout the region. The data were collected from five households over a four-year period and traced the impact of economic changes in society on the home-based farms. In-depth interviews and group meetings were used to capture the perceptions, views and feelings of the women and men from the farming households. The sustained nature of contact allowed for ethnographic type data collection and first-hand observations of the process and outcomes of gender negotiations. In all cases, women were the primary subjects, but reports from male partners were used where appropriate, in the citations and analyses. All of the households were part of an agricultural research project where technology transfer and improved sheep farming practices were introduced.[3]

The households selected shared the same demographic characteristics of race/ethnicity, class, age and religion and thus allowed for gender analyses in everyday life experiences. The subjects were Afro-Caribbean, practised the Christian faith, possessed primary and secondary school education, were between the ages of 45 and 60, and had children who were either teenagers or adults living outside of the home. The couples reported stable relationships although they were not all legally married. They lived in low-income housing and communities, and supplemented their wage incomes through subsistence agricultural production, typical of most rural Caribbean families. They grew a mixture of food crops mainly root tubers and vegetables and reared a small number of livestock (poultry, dairy cows, sheep and other small ruminants). Some of the food items grown were used for home consumption and the extras sold in the local farmers' markets. The examples of change in gender roles, activity-specific division of labour, use and control of technology, decision-making, and management control of an income-earning project were primarily from a sheep farming project, common to all five households.

## Gender Identity and Gender Roles

At the start of the research period, the household economies were supported through a combination of wage employment in the formal sector and subsistence farming located in the informal economy. All the men were employed on a full-time basis as unskilled labourers or machine operators on government-owned farms, public servants, or as taxi operators and service workers in Tobago's tourist industry. On evenings and on weekends, the men assisted the women with the farm work and in small cottage industry activities located in the home, thereby moving between the formal and informal economy on an everyday basis. It is unclear why only the men and not the women in these households were employed in the formal sector. This may be due to traditional practices in peasant households, or to peculiarities of these women's familial situations where, for example, the women were also taking care of young children or grandchildren. On the other hand, women's involvement in home-based cottage industry located in the informal economy has been described as typical of Caribbean low-resource households (Beneria and Sen 1981; Deere, Safa and Antrobus 1997). It is, therefore, not surprising that the women of this study contributed to the household budget by growing vegetables, raising small livestock, including sheep, and from monies gained from cottage industry production. The cottage industry activities included sewing, making of candies, arts and crafts and other gift items for sale as well as providing childcare services.

At the beginning, the women were the primary sheep farmers who managed the farms and made all the major decisions for the enterprise. They often consulted with the men who assisted them on a part-time basis, but who understood that the sheep farming enterprise was the 'woman's project'. The common rearing practice was free range and the sheep grazed in open fields. Little maintenance was required other than providing water for the animals. Feeding, breeding, animal health and all other aspects of sheep management were ad hoc, and based on knowledge accumulated through family and personal experiences. Sheep farming was not an organized activity and record keeping was absent or inefficiently managed. Sheep farming was seen more as an investment or savings that the household could 'cash out' in times of need. Income from sheep farming was not part of the routine budget but instead, animals were sold when extra money was needed, for example, for weddings, christenings, school fees and other expenses.

In the home, women did most of the housework and spent over six hours per day doing various domestic chores. On average, the men in the study spent less than three hours per week helping around the house. There were reports that when housework increased because of the addition of grandchildren, men did increase their contributions to housework.

> The men sometimes help in the housework mainly in the area of keeping an eye on the grandchildren. You would find that they would help you more in this area when the children mother or father sent money, clothes and other items for helping out. Sometimes my daughter who lives in America will send us tickets to come for a holiday.
> —Tobago Case Study 1.

Interestingly, while the women worked for their own incomes and experienced high degrees of economic independence, they did not demand gender equity when it came to housework, but were aware of the disproportionality.

## Shifts and Uncertainty

Over time, employment in the formal economy declined and the households became increasingly dependent on activities in the informal economy. The number of men employed in the formal sector decreased and, within a five-year period, many of the men either lost their jobs or were forced to retire. A few were unable to maintain their small private taxi businesses and other operations. The men immediately sought work elsewhere, mainly as casual labourers and/or returned to farming with their wives on the family farm. They felt pressured as the male breadwinners for their families.  For example:

> When I lose my work...what was I to do? I cannot sit at home and do nothing. I have to find work somewhere else or I have to make the farm work for me. A man has to provide for his family.
> —Tobago Case Study 5.

The loss of wage employment by men and the improvising on the family farm, previously managed by women, necessitated certain shifts in gender roles and a change in the gender dynamics at the farm and household level. This was further compounded by the fact that the substituted jobs were usually intermittent and poorly paid. As a result, contributions by men to the household budgets were considerably reduced, and men were no longer the major bread-earners in the home. As might be expected, the men responded by trying to find equally productive ways to occupy their time, even if this meant encroaching on the women's projects. Under these circumstances, the women expressed a certain amount of fear and ambiguity because:

> When my husband lost his job I did not know what we were going to do. I was afraid. I knew we always had the farm to rely on and that he could do more farm work...but I was not sure how this was going to work out for me.
> —Tobago Case Study 5.

As the men sought work in home-based enterprises and on the family farm, women were concerned that their own income-generating activities would have to be shared, or even be taken over by the men. They viewed their source of individual income as extremely important not only to their family budgets, but also to their economic independence.  According to the women:

> Women like to have control of their own money...they do not like to always have to ask how to spend the money. For example, if you want to give your mother or sister some money, you do not have to have a

discussion with anybody – you can just go ahead and give the money...
You too (the researcher) must also do this as a woman.
–Tobago Case Study 4.

The women adamantly stressed the importance for all women to have some kind of financial independence and control over income-generating activities that were not shared with partners. In this regard, cottage-industry-type activities are often used by women (farming or non-farming) as a means for them to have sole ownership of an economic entity, where men could assist but not control. One of the women explained:

> Sometimes the husband helps (making candies for sale)...he helps me by cutting and peeling the fruits and so on...but he knows that this is my thing and that he is only assisting. He cannot tell me what to do.
> –Tobago Case Study 5.

The desire for economic independence and to maintain autonomy in at least one income-earning activity were found in all the households. This belief is reflective of Caribbean women's historical experiences and gender identity, but contradictory to the region's patriarchal values. It also challenges the stereotypical beliefs that in poor households women are economically dependent on men. On the other hand, typical for most patriarchal societies, the women in the case studies continued to perform a disproportionate amount of the housework. Interestingly, there were little gender negotiations of domestic work even when the woman's economic contribution to the household budget increased in importance. The women never complained or expressed dissatisfaction with this domestic arrangement, although they did acknowledge in interviews that housework took up a disproportionate amount of their time. For example, one woman expressed that:

> I would be very happy when my husband retires and takes over most of the work on the sheep farm because it is really too much work for me to do both the housework and the farm-work...especially since the grandchildren came to live with us. I really have too much to do...but I will keep my little business of selling snacks to the school children on evenings.
> –Tobago Case Study 1.

The women recognized that the time spent in housework limited their involvement in other social and economic activities, but did not suggest a more equitable sharing of the housework by men as an alternative. Instead, many accepted housework as women's work. At the same time, the women did not perceive themselves to be mere housewives. In a focus group meeting, one woman (Tobago Case Study 1) explained:

> I do not call myself a housewife because what I do is more than
> housework and caring for my husband and family. I prefer to call myself
> a homemaker because that gives a better picture of all the things I do.
> I farm, I make candies and craft items for sale, I sew, I see about the
> grandchildren and do plenty other things.

The change in the economic attachment of the households to the formal
economy through men's wage jobs did not have an effect on gender roles
specific to housework and cottage industry production, but it did affect
gender roles on the family farm. As men turned to farming they began to
take more responsibilities with respect to decision-making and other aspects
of farm management. In particular, the men were attracted to the sheep
farming enterprise because:

> I believed that we could get more materials and technical assistance
> from the Caribbean Research and Development Institute Sheep Project.
> If this is true then I believe that this kind of assistance could turn the
> sheep farming around and eventually we could sell plenty more sheep.
> I think this could happen much faster in the sheep business than on any
> of the other farm business.
> —Male from Tobago Case Study 5.

Technological interventions were introduced with the intention of
moving sheep farming from a subsistence level to a successful income-
earning enterprise. The project was funded by the Canadian International
Development Agency (CIDA) and implemented by the Caribbean Research
and Development Institute (CARDI). Sheep farming was being transformed
from an open grazing system to intensive housing and feeding systems,
with accompanying improved breeding, animal health, record-keeping and
marketing strategies. The fundamental change in the farming practices meant
that the sheep enterprise now required more attention, time and resources
compared to the traditional open grazing system. The new farming methods
and technology were made available to both women and men. Training was
directed at the household rather than at the individual to ensure that women
also had access. The women generally agreed with the men that the new
methods required increased labour and resources but were more willing to
adopt the new methods. One of the women explained her own willingness
to adopt the recommended new methods over the ambivalent attitudes of
her husband:

> When I first started this business (sheep farming) I did not know very
> much. Keeping sheep was just something I did to earn a little extra
> money for when I needed it. So when the scientists from the CPS/M

> project show me and explain to me how to do things differently I am willing to give it a try. We are not like our husbands who feel they know everything – even more than the scientists.
> –Tobago Case Study 5.

Interestingly, the men all complained that the new practices of sheep production required a lot more record-keeping and saw no need for this. On the other hand, women who typically kept the farm records indicated that they preferred this aspect of the work, rather than the more physical elements of sheep production. However, because of the potential of the sheep enterprise to become a major income-earning source it was now a contested terrain. The men were attracted to the technology as well as control of the enterprise, and made it more difficult for the women to keep the sheep project as a separate income-generating activity under their control. Both women's economic independence and autonomy over the sheep farm enterprise were now on the bargaining table.

## Cooperation, Conflict and the Contestation of Gender Power

The examples highlight the gendered and social nuances observed in bargaining that take place in the home. They also illustrate how negotiations become heightened when there is economic change in the wider society, and/or when there are economic implications with the introduction of technology in home-based enterprises. Sen (1987, 1990) researched the nature of co-operation and bargaining that takes place in household decision-making processes, and identified different *co-operate conflict models,* to illustrate how household members bargain over material and ideological factors. In the study on the Tobago sheep farmers, material factors were taken as forms of income generation in the formal and informal economies, while ideological factors included gender roles and gender identity. Further, it is argued that gender roles and identities are influenced by the gender ideologies of the society, in which households are embedded.

Interestingly, linked to women's gender identity and power was the extent to which the women wanted to maintain their economic independence with or without the sheep enterprise as well as their autonomy in managing and controlling this potential income-earning business. Independent, a term often used to describe Caribbean women was explored by Christine Barrow (1986) on its merits, limitations, and in the way it reflects yet obfuscates reality. According to the women who were interviewed by Barrow in Barbados, independence is based on having one's own source of income, generally from employment and /or other income-generating activities. Autonomy, on the other hand, is linked to decision-making for oneself and having control over one's destiny with no strings attached (8–9). Economic self-sufficiency is, therefore, not the same as female autonomy as autonomy implies inter-dependency with other family member.

The case studies of the sheep farming households revealed three dominant social arrangements of co-operation, conflict and the contestation of gender power, when women-managed income-earning projects (sheep farming) were challenged. These patterns were neither mutually exclusive nor exhaustive, and could change from one situation to the next and across time, in the same household. The levels of co-operation and conflict were found to be linked to the extent to which women and men wanted to share control over the same income-generation activities, or to manage separate enterprises. The three patterns were: (i) Limited Collaboration and Conflict; (ii) Collaboration and Conflict; and (iii) Cooperation without Conflict.

## Limited Collaboration and Conflict (Households 1 and 2)

Limited collaboration and conflict were observed in households where women and men made joint decisions about family affairs, but agreed to operate and manage separate income-generating activities with limited input by the other partner. In these households, it would appear that there was not much conflict over the different income-earning projects, especially with the management and control aspects of these activities. Here, the division of labour was not based on stereotypical gender roles (except for housework), but on which household member could get wage employment outside of the home. Consequently, the other individual would work on the family farm. In other words, women from these households desired their economic independence and autonomy in their separate income-generating activities but not from general household decisions.

As a result, couples engaged in separate income-generating activities and were satisfied with this arrangement. For example, in one of the homes, the woman was identified as the sheep farmer and new farming methods and technologies were directed to her as the manager and owner of the sheep enterprise. Her partner continued to assist and participate in the training as well as in the use of the new technological interventions. Sometimes, this influenced him to become more interested and co-operate more in the farm enterprise. At the same time, the woman's role was not minimized nor was she displaced as the manager. There appeared to be little challenge for control of the technology and the enterprise and, as a result, there was limited contestation of gender power. In this arrangement, it is clear that the women were the primary decision-makers for the enterprise. The husbands contributed much appreciated time and labour.

> My husband helps me in the evenings and on the weekends but I do most of the work. On the government farm he works with machines so he was able to help me put together the feed chopper. Sometimes I ask him what he thinks but I make the final decision.
> —Tobago Case Study 2.

When the woman was not displaced from control over the income-earning project, an amicable social relationship resulted. Her status in the household was enhanced, something that appeared to be in the best interest of the home and family unit. The individual motivations behind the co-operative agreement in this household were not always clear, but in all cases the couple agreed to have separate income-generating enterprises. The woman consistently expressed strong feelings about retaining control of the income-generating project and her partner rarely challenged her but supported her endeavours.

> I want to help her build the new pens but I have not had the time. I hope to do this soon because I know she needs the pens to house the animals.
> —Tobago Case Study 2.

Interestingly enough, not in all cases of limited collaboration and conflict did the woman maintain her primary sheep farmer status. In one household, the couple agreed that the man of the household should take over the sheep farm from the wife. This occurred when the man lost his wage jobs and so the couple decided that it was time for him to take over the enterprise. In this case, the wife reported that she wanted the change but not the loss of her individual source of income and financial independence. As a result, she shifted her time, labour and other resources to a series of other income-earning activities that she preferred, and that she could completely own and manage. The arrangement of having separate income-earning projects with limited collaboration and input by the other partner allowed for continued amicable relationship. For example:

> In our house, I do my thing and he does his. I am in charge of the house and use to be in charge of the sheep when he was working. Before we started the sheep business, I use to do a lot of other things. The sheep kept me busy and some of the money-making things I use to do suffered. I was ready for him to take over...Now he has the sheep and I do my own

thing making and selling sweets to school children on their way to and
from school. We discuss most things but I make decisions on the things
I am involved with and he makes decisions about his business. We do
discuss a lot of things and on serious matters relating to the children and
grandchildren we sometimes make joint decisions.
—Tobago Case Study 1.

The couple in this case study had low levels of conflict in their relationship
and little contention for leadership for the same income-earning activity. In
this model, the strong personalities of one or both partners are resolved
by agreeing/co-operating to have separate income-generating activities as
well as identifying what these activities were. In these two households, the
women maintained their economic independence and autonomy in different
ways. One selected to do this by allowing her husband to take over the sheep
enterprise while she shifted her time and resources to another income-earning
activity. The other decided to maintain the sheep enterprise and continue in
the role of manager.

Models of limited co-operation and conflict are, therefore, observed in
households where gender roles are defined by choice or de facto. The role of
women's agency trumps the stereotypical arguments that women are simply
displaced by men in certain circumstances and her role in the household
economy minimized. Instead, we see that gender power is negotiated but
that there is little conflict when income generation is kept separate with little
need for co-operation in these projects. Households that fall into this category
can appear to operate on an egalitarian basis, which may or may not be true.

## Collaboration with Conflict (Households 4 and 5)

Co-operation with conflict was found in households where individual
members have diverging perceptions about gender roles. Here, the women
wanted to maintain both their economic independence and their autonomy
with the sheep enterprise. As a result, as men lost their wage jobs and returned
to the family farm, there were disagreements about who should control the
main farm income-generating activity, previously under the control of the
woman. In these homes, men were observed as wanting to take control of
sheep farming and shift from being part-time helpers to assuming the role as
manager and owner. In one case, household 5, the woman unwillingly agreed
to give the sheep farm to her husband because he was very domineering and
opinionated. She felt that this action was the path of least resistance and
conflict. In household 4, the woman was adamant that she wanted to keep
the enterprise and the man did challenge her but tempered his efforts for

the same reason, to minimize conflict in their social relationship. The women resisted and were unwilling to relinquish control but in the end there were different outcomes. They wanted to maintain their positions as the primary sheep farmer and not simply give it to their husbands because:

> It is us women who have spent the most time, labour and money in the sheep...it is therefore ours. We should not have to give it up. If the men want to help that is fine but I do not see why they should take it over from us...they could find something else to do.
> —Tobago Case Study 4.

These cases studies and examples reflected the gender thinking that tends to drive the contestation of power. Acts of domination and resistance were manifested in very interesting ways. Sometimes the negotiations were open and verbal and, at other times, they were subtle, silent and creative. In order to avoid open conflict and undesirable social relationships, men tended to use less confrontational measures such as quietly being unco-operative in sharing farm information with their wives. Since knowledge is power, wives not having knowledge meant that they had less control over the farming enterprise. For example, it was common for women to keep records as part of farm management (e.g., weight of animal, diet and nutrition, medical treatment and vaccination, etc.). This task allowed women to exercise some degree of control over the sheep enterprise. Consequently, data for record-keeping became another bargaining chip in the gender negotiations of power over the enterprise. When the sheep farming business was not contested, sharing information on farm activities was not a problem. Once the sheep farming became a contested terrain, men began to withhold information and keeping proper records became difficult for the women.

Thus, part of the negotiation for control involved a complex series of unspoken actions and interactions. In these instances, open discussions were never part of the negotiation process. The women and men did not verbally agree or disagree on record-keeping, or any other matters pertaining to the sheep enterprise, they simply consciously or unconsciously reacted. The absence of discussions, therefore, did not mean that the couples did not have opinions because they did report these to the researcher. However, they did not want to have unpleasant discussions with each other because they felt that this would hamper the social relationships between them. The situation, however, did cause conflict as one woman explained:

> I am totally frustrated at not being able to keep proper records. I have to be constantly asking him to give me the information and he is not willing to do this. I do not know how much more of this I am willing

> to take...he knows that it is important to record the information, yet he
> refuses to give me it. I do not know how he expect us to see the progress.
> —Tobago Case Study 5.

The men, on the other hand, rationalized their actions by claiming that:

> I forgot to tell my wife...or I don't see why it is important to keep records.
> —Tobago Case Study 5.

In the other household, the man bluntly refused to pass on important data on a sheep activity to his spouse to record.

> I did not have the time to keep records because the sheep keeps me
> busy...and anyway it is her role to keep the records.
> —Tobago case Study 4.

Interestingly, prior to losing their wage employment the men were not opposed to their wives being sheep farmers. However, it became noticeable that once conflict over control of the sheep enterprise sparked, the men attempted to rationalize why women should not be primary farmers using stereotypical gender arguments. These stereotypes often centred on the use of technology. One woman made the observation that:

> Men are particularly attracted to the new machinery like the feed
> chopper. They feel that the chopper is too dangerous for us women. The
> men also think that the feed chopper requires special skills that men
> tend to have. They think because it is a machine, it is men's work. But
> when he is not here I use the chopper with no problems.
> —Tobago Study 5.

The husband from household 4 suggested to his wife that the work was too strenuous for her. He believed certain activities such as providing medicines, hoof trimming, weighing of feed and so on, were more suitable for men. In this example, both the technical and physical aspects of the farm work were assumed to more suitable to men's capabilities.

The men sometimes blocked the women's access to technology and training. For example, one woman expressed her disappointment and hurt when she learnt that her husband knew about a scheduled training session but did not pass the information to her, and as a result she missed the workshop.

> Before, when the scientist came on the farm he would talk with me...
> now when he comes it is difficult because my husband who is now
> always home dominates the conversations. Sometimes I do not even
> know when the scientist is here because I am inside doing other things
> and my husband does not bother to let me know that he is here.
> —Tobago Study 4.

Despite the many deliberate setbacks as previously stated, the women from these households did not openly express their anger and frustration with their husbands, in the interest of maintaining a fairly peaceful coexistence. At the same time, the women resisted exclusion from technological interventions and opportunities to improve their income-earning abilities. Women's resistance to exclusion and their tenacity to remain in contact with the scientists, attend training workshops and participate in field demonstrations, resulted in underlying conflicting relationships with husbands and partners. Their determination was to a large extent based on their desire to maintain control over *their* sheep enterprise, despite the efforts of their husbands to dominate. Interestingly, women who negotiated to share the sheep project, and/or diverted their efforts to other income-earning activities were also determined not to be left out of the opportunity to gain knowledge and technological skills because:

> I still like to be involved. I especially like to go to the training sessions and farmers meetings. You have to learn for yourself, nobody can learn for you, besides I find the information useful and I can use it elsewhere outside of sheep farming.
> –Tobago Study 5.

These examples challenge the many gender stereotypes about women's fear and/or lack of interest in technology. They also contradict the argument that when technologies are introduced, men dominate and women are marginalized. In fact, they reflect women's agency in negotiating these issues. The case studies also revealed new and exciting knowledge about women's responses to technology, and demonstrated that women's interests in technology and new ideas were not necessarily linked to domination and control as is the case with most of the men. The women were interested in the broad application and usefulness of the technology, which may or may not result in direct material gains from the original project to which it was directed, but could be applied to other income-generating projects.

In this model of collaboration and conflict, women chose to remain involved at different levels and when contested by their husbands preferred to share/ co-operate rather than give it up altogether. As a rule, women in these case studies decided to work through any conflict, while most of the men tried to ignore the women's continued interests. They did not understand why the women wanted to still be involved in managing the enterprise or why they were interested in the new technologies. The situation was quite frustrating for the women who became dissatisfied with their men for deliberately excluding them from access to information and training. Within this model, co-operation in the same income-earning enterprise is more likely to exhibit conflict over control of the enterprise and in their social relationship.

The examples in the case studies are congruent with the literature that suggests when there are diverging interests in the household, bargaining power and decision-making are linked to what individuals contribute to the household economy (Agarwal 1997; Boserup 1970; Donham 1990; Halperin 1994). In patriarchal societies, males are cast in the role of major income earners and are, therefore, expected to have greater bargaining powers. In the case studies of the sheep farming households, it was unclear as to which members had the greater bargaining power in the negotiation processes. For example, in some of the households, women's income was central to the household's budget but men still exercised domination when bargaining for control of the sheep enterprise. The case studies also served to highlight how negotiation of gender power in the private sphere of the home is complex. Often, the viewpoints and feelings of individuals are not shared between partners because of fear of causing discord in an intimate and personal relationship. According to one of the women:

> I really do not know what to say, do, or think. I have mixed feelings. On one hand I resent that my husband is trying to dominate the sheep business because of all I invested in it...I do not hate him or anything. When he had his job it was okay that he helped on the evenings and weekends but I was in charge. Now more and more I feel as if I am losing the sheep business to my husband. I do not want to say anything because that might cause some conflict between us. Sometimes I think that it is best just to let him have it and devote my time to something else.
> —Tobago Study 4.

The sentiment expressed suggests that integral to the negotiation process is the weighing of individual material and ideological interests against those of the family. According to Naila Kabeer (1998), Pierre-André Chiappori (1992), Marjorie McElroy and Mary Jean Horney (1990), co-operation can be viewed as a condition of the bargaining process if the gains from co-operation outweigh the gains from non-co-operation. In the household case studies, some women selected to either compromise or share in the management of the enterprise, or shift to other income-generating activities. They chose these alternatives because unpleasant and undesired conflicts were emerging with their partners. Interestingly, whenever concessions were made, women were more likely than men to compromise their individual interests for the interests of the social relationship and the economic situation in the home. The women did not perceive their decisions as forms of subordination, but as conscious choices made in the interest of their familial and households' stability. The women loved their husbands and sometimes the negotiations and the outcomes were difficult and painful.

> I feel deeply hurt inside...I do not like how he is behaving. He has said hurtful things to me... but I don't want to tell him anything. I am just going to do my own thing. I really like the sheep business but since he has taken over I am not comfortable with it...so I just find something else to do.
> —Tobago Case Study 4.

On the other hand, the men of the households tended to be unaware of their partner's feelings and did not report any negative emotions from the negotiation process. Some even believed that their increased involvement on the farm was helpful to their wives and in the interest of the household.

> I doing most of the work...I don't expect her to do this kind of work while I am able.
> —Tobago Case Study 4.

> My wife is always working, looking after the grandchildren... seeing about her vegetables...making things to sell...and running the house. So this is how I can help.
> —Tobago Case Study 5.

The men of these households did not seem to be aware of the privileges they assumed in the negotiation process nor the compromises that their wives were making.

## Co-operation without Conflict (Household 3)

Not in all of the households where couples co-operated in the same income-earning activity did conflict arise. In this one case, the woman did not desire economic independence or autonomy with the sheep enterprise as this was not the *modus operandi* that was adopted for all other activities that she shared with her partner. In this household, the couple shared the sheep-farming enterprise and had a very amicable working relationship. The woman and her husband co-operated in the decision-making processes and in the use of technology in the sheep enterprise. However, while tasks were shared, there was no ambiguity in identifying who the primary farmer was. There was no competition for the use of technology and control of the sheep enterprise.

The woman maintained her role as the primary sheep farmer and was recognized by her husband and children as the manager of the enterprise. While the woman worked at home and on the farm, overseeing all the farm activities, her husband was still employed in a job off the farm. The man assisted his wife on the farm in the afternoons and on the weekends. The female sheep farmer reported that she discussed both farm and household matters with her spouse, and all decisions were jointly made. However, further investigations showed that it was usually the woman who made the decisions about the sheep enterprise and these were usually supported by her husband.

Interestingly, although there was no gender shift in position from female-managed to male-managed sheep enterprise, the introduction of farm technology did cause an increase in the husband's interest in the sheep enterprise, particularly in the use of technology. Although his interests and participation grew, he did not displace his wife as the primary farmer and user of the technology. Instead, both the husband and wife operated the machinery, and often the wife would do so by herself. As the identifiable primary farmer, she would also interact with the scientists, participate in training workshops, and take the lead in making technological recommendations and other decisions pertaining to the sheep enterprise. Over time, the sheep farming practices improved and so too did the income generated from the enterprise. In this household, it was difficult to identify conflict in the co-operative working arrangements on the farm, or in the social relationship in the home. It is also important to note that the male in this household still had his wage employment in the public services and, thus, his own economic independence.

## Summary and Conclusions

The sheep project was an attempt to improve the incomes earned by women in resource-poor households. It was attractive for the women because it meant that they could operate the enterprise close to home which made it convenient to balance their housework, childcare and other income-generating home-based projects. They did not resist improved farming practices and the technologies transferred because they understood that this would increase productivity and earned incomes, as well as decrease their labour input, saving time and physical work. In some of the homes, women were slightly more educated than the men and so improved record keeping, budgeting and other improved practices were not intimidating but welcomed.

However, the desired objective of improving the livelihoods of the farm women through improved sheep farming was not met in all cases. Moreover, there were varied outcomes from negotiations of both material and ideological factors. Material factors included a change in men's primary sources of income and the introduction of resources to the sheep enterprise. Ideological factors included women's identity linked to having their economic independence and autonomy in the sheep enterprise. Interestingly, while the extent to which women desired autonomy in the management and control of the sheep business varied, they all opted to maintain economic independence with or external to the sheep enterprise. The women's desire to have some level of power through economic independence and autonomy in what they did and how they did things can be linked to the encapsulating gender ideologies of the region. Nevertheless, both the material and ideological factors led to interesting household dynamics in which strained social relations were negotiated alongside economic ways to survive in stressed financial situations.

From the literature, it was anticipated that, since the Caribbean is identified as highly patriarchal, males in the case studies would have stronger bargaining power because of their greater access to and control of resources in the public sphere (Boserup 1970; Donham 1990; Folbre 1984; Halperin 1994). Men were also assumed to be the major income earners in the household (Boserup 1970; Folbre 1984; Lipman-Blumen 1984; Safa 1995), and may have been so initially before they lost their jobs. The examples did show that the men attempted in many instances to exercise control and dominance over the sheep enterprise when they were no longer able to be 'the primary wage earner' in the house. However, since in these households both women and men were making financial contributions and had access to the resources in the sheep enterprise, negotiations over management and bargaining over specific activities ensued and were mediated accordingly.

The bargaining process and the outcomes of the negotiations suggest that even within situations of male domination, women exercise choices. The findings support the feminist literature on patriarchy and domination that rejects the notion that women are mere victims of domination. In this study, women were active agents mediating gender power through a negotiation process in which both domination and resistance were present. As a result, different models of co-operation, collaboration and conflict emerged. In all cases, co-operation was present in decision-making when gains from co-operation were perceived to outweigh the gains from non-co-operation, which in most instances was simply the maintenance of an amicable social relationship. At the same time, while co-operation prevailed in all cases, conflict was also present when control of the women's economic enterprise was being challenged by their male partners. In other words, having autonomy in the same income-earning activity was negotiable but overall economic independence was not. They co-operated with the men, but resisted complete domination.

The findings and analyses highlight how important it is to understand the extent to which desired effect of projects and programmes, aimed at reducing poverty, are mediated by the gender–power dynamics in the home. The mediation process can result in unintended consequences, including the benefits of the poverty reduction programmes not reaching its intended beneficiaries, at least not in the way it was planned. As a result, it is equally important to monitor and assess how interventions are used in the bargaining process within varied household arrangements, and not simply assume that households are altruistic units. Similarly, women should not be seen as mere victims to male domination in the home but as social agents who consistently battle material and ideological gender barriers, while trying to stay central to their household needs and simultaneously keep cordial relations with their partners. More research is definitely needed to further understand the gender dynamics within poor households, and understand how interventions affect and are affected by human agency.

# 7. Social Capital, Agency and Poor Communities

*Sometimes it is not so much what you know but who you know.*

In this chapter, I move the level of analysis away from individuals and households as was discussed in the previous chapters, to examine the role of agency in poverty reduction at the community level. Here, the ability of a group of individuals to access what is required to improve the living conditions in resource-poor communities is explored. Prior research has found that although there are limited assets in poor communities, there is a range of diverse physical and social assets that individuals, households and communities draw upon in times of need (Narayan et al. 2000). In general, assets in the poverty literature are referred to as capital and grouped into several different but related categories that include physical, human and social capital, among others (Deosaran 2000; Narayan et al. 2000; Narayan 2002).

In poor households and communities that lack material and productive resources, and where literacy rates, educational attainment, employment and material wealth are low, having a healthy body is relied upon to make a living (Narayan et al. 2000), and co-operating with each other (social capital) is essential to survival. These understandings are important to both research efforts and strategizing for poverty reduction, and can only be achieved if the social networking and social capital available at the local level of communities are included in poverty studies.

For a long time, research on social capital focused on how it relates to economic development. However, over time, interest in social capital has moved on the radar of both social scientists and policy analysts concerned with issues of poverty and social inequality. The rejuvenation of social capital became glaringly evident when the World Bank endorsed it as an important asset to both social and economic development. The Bank reported that there was adequate empirical data to show that social capital is a significant variable in sustainable development. This led Ismail Serageldin, Vice President of Special Programs of the World Bank, in 2001, to declare that traditional forms of capital, such as physical and material assets, must now be broadened to include human elements in social capital. As a result, the Bank established a social capital initiative (SCI) unit within its structure where social capital is now being treated as an asset to be harnessed for the good of all stakeholders (World Bank 2001).

The endorsement of social capital by the World Bank, in the 1990s, stimulated further interests in the concept by policymakers in Latin America and the Caribbean. Subsequently, later in 2001, the Economic Commission for Latin America and the Caribbean (ECLAC) and the University of Michigan held a conference entitled, 'In Search of a New Paradigm: Social Capital and Poverty Reduction in the Region'. The contextual framework for the conference was that persistent poverty was endemic to the region and a major obstacle in achieving equality. Moreover, it was important to mobilize social capital in the poorest sectors, alongside economic and socio-political resources, as a strategy that was truly inclusive and could foster greater social equality.

These observations are congruent with the realization that global economic development is not being accompanied by satisfactory levels of social development. Joseph Stiglitz (1998), for example, argued that addressing structural inequalities requires both economic development as well as societal transformation. On the other hand, social transformation requires an understanding of the nature of social relations in economic development. It is within this background, that social capital has gained wide currency in research that looks at the relationship between economic growth, social equality and poverty.

Hence, while the concept itself is being revisited with new interest and enthusiastic hope, the focus on social capital, however, is not without interesting questions and controversial dialogues. This chapter discusses and analyses some of the complexities and elusiveness of the concept, including the difficulty in its operationalization, how it is used in resource-poor households and communities, and problems in trying to position social capital in any policy setting. Many of these issues depend on whether social capital is used as a political or an analytical tool. Interestingly in both circumstances, gender issues are subordinated and the structural and social difficulties that women experience in accessing resources are not well examined. Similarly, little is known about women's networks and forms of networking that are important for them to 'get by' and 'get ahead'.

The various intricacies, ambiguities and core issues that surround social capital are examined and analysed in the chapter using a case study of a small, undeveloped, agrarian-based community in Trinidad. Graphic examples are used to illustrate how the different types of social capital work in the everyday survival of individuals and households as well for the improvement of the community. The differences in women's access and use of social capital are also highlighted in the case study. In the last sections of the chapter, the limitations of social capital in achieving social equality and poverty reduction are examined, including the neglect of gender-analysis and gender equity as well as the link between social capital, social exclusion and poverty.

## Defining and Conceptualizing Social Capital

Although there is renewed interest in social capital, the concept itself is not new. There is a long intellectual history of social capital in the social sciences by those interested in social networks and life chances. Social capital can be traced as far back as the classical sociological and philosophical theories preoccupied with understanding quality of relationships and shared values. Hints of social capital can be found in the works of Alexis Tocqueville (1832), that focused on associational life, Emile Durkheim (1933), who espoused the theory on mechanical and organic solidarity; Ferdinand Tonnies (1887) in his work on purposive association or the Gemeinschaft community and instrumental association or Gesellschaft community; Max Weber (1989–56), who explored the concept of a shared lifestyle; and Karl Marx (1843–67), who discussed solidarity among the oppressed. Interest in social capital continued over the years and peaked once again in the social sciences research of the 1980s with the seminal works of Pierre Bourdieu (1980, 1986); Nan Lin (1999, 2001, 2008); James Coleman (1988, 1990); Robert Putnam (1993, 1995, 2000); and Alejandro Portes (1998).

While the conceptual focus of each of these scholars varies, they do provide a theoretical framework for understanding the effect of networking on the life chances of individuals, groups, communities and society. For example, Bourdieu's interest in understanding class conflicts sees social capital as a resource similar to economic and cultural capital used in class struggles. He argued that social capital as a resource is based on group membership and social networks, and is determined by the totality of the relationships (Bourdieu 1980). Later, Coleman (1988) defined social capital more as a function that facilitates certain actions by individuals who belong to the same social structure. Following these conceptual explanations of social capital, Putnam (1993, 1995) described it as a feature of social life where networks, norms and trust foster individuals to act together and effectively pursue shared goals and objectives. The way that each scholar conceptualized social capital is linked to their research interests, disciplines and orientations.

In the same vein, Else Oyen (2002) found that social capital can also be conceptualized based on whether the intention is to use it as a political tool or an analytical concept. For example, policy specialists and politicians who are interested in the economic effects of social capital define social capital as 'the glue that holds society together' (World Bank 2001). They incorporate the economists' rationale that social capital is social because it involves people being social and arises from non-market interactions, and it is capital because economic benefits accrue as people have greater access to information that helps them to perform certain transactions in a co-ordinated way. In the process, trust is generated, opportunistic behaviour reduced, and all players benefit from economic gains (Collier 1998; Dasgupta 2000).

On the other hand, social capital as an analytical construct in the social sciences shifts the level of analysis from the economic gains of the individual to the improvement of life overall in the community. Social capital is perceived as the collective asset of a community rather than the property of individuals. Individuals can contribute to and use social capital for their personal welfare but cannot own social capital (Warren, Thompson and Saegert 2001). As an analytical concept, the social stratification of society and the power differentials of groups are believed to impact the type of social capital accumulated and its use.

Notwithstanding the differences in the use of social capital, there is a general agreement that social capital is relational, that is, for a person to possess social capital they must have social relations with others. David Halpern (2005) pointed to three basic components that identify social capital, regardless of orientation and use. First, social capital is comprised of social networks; second, within these networks there are shared clusters of norms, values and expectations; and third, the norms, values and expectations are maintained through sanctions. Further, Claudio Cecchi, Luca Molinas and Fabio Sabatini (2009) suggested that the social environment in which people interact frequently encourages the building of shared values, norms, trust and reciprocity within the network, and that all aspects of people's lives are embedded in social networks. In other words, social capital is formed when networks facilitate collective action and allow groups of individuals to gain competitive advantages in pursuit of their aims.

Social networks can, therefore, be considered a resource that people can draw on to improve their living conditions (Flap and Volker 2004). However, the extent to which resources can be mobilized is dependent upon: (i) the number of people within the network who are prepared or committed to share their resources; (ii) the resources that individuals possess; (iii) the strength of the social relationships; (iv) the norms and values that govern interactions among people; and (v) the type of institution or networks in which interactions are embedded (Flap 1991; 1994; Serageldin 1998). The various combinations of these factors give rise to three distinct forms or subtypes of social capital – *bonding, bridging* and *linking social capital.*

## Forms or Sub-types of Social Capital

The three sub-types of social capital – *bonding, bridging* and *linking* – vary based on the strength of the ties and the level at which social relations are formed (Putnam 1993, 1995; Warren, Thompson and Saegert 2001; Woolcock 1998, 2001) as well as the nature of the social milieu in which individuals form social bonds (Temkin and Rohe 1998). Strong social bonds or *bonding social capital* are usually formed through the interaction of people who already know each other within a group, organization or community. Typically, individuals from a family or who are close friends and neighbours form social relations because they share similar lifestyles. Putnam (1993, 1995) argued that the main element in this form of social capital is trust and co-operation. The more people connect or bond with each other, the more they will trust each other and act collectively. For example, residents believe that their community is a spatially distinct place which forces them to interact with each other in various ways. They help with small tasks and exchange goods and services. The strength of the social bond among the residents is linked to the extent to which they have an attachment and loyalty to their community. So, for example, when residents in poor communities bond to help each other, they feel less vulnerable to their living conditions (Cleaver 2005).

Social relations, however, are not limited to internal and close relationships. While poor communities are often socially isolated from the rest of society (Wilson 1987), people from poor communities do join groups and organizations as well as interact with others in communities external to their place of residence (Warren, Thompson and Saegert 2001). This type of social relations among people who previously did not know each other produces what is called *bridging social capital* (Putnam 1993, 1995; Warren, Thompson and Saegert 2001; Woolcock 2001). *Bridging social capital* emerges from weak ties among people of different ethnic, geographic and occupational backgrounds, but creates greater resources than what can be garnered from *bonding social capital.* As such, *bridging social capital* is important in 'getting ahead' and creating public benefits (Briggs 1998; Cleaver 2005).

*Bridging social capital* can occur across local institutions within a community, between different low-income communities, between poor and more affluent communities, or between people and society in general

(Warren, Thompson and Saegert 2001). Interestingly, the capacity of any group of individuals or a community to collectively build bridges and leverage external resources is strongly dependent on the strength of the internal bond among the members of the group, or residents of a community (Temkin and Rhoe 1998). While *bonding social capital* is used as a survival strategy of the poor to meet the daily challenges of life, *bridging social capital* draws on the assistance of other people and their resources to help solve more long-term problems (Briggs 1998).

A third type of social capital, *linking social capital*, is a form of *bridging social capital* as it is accrued through transactions between individuals within a group or community and others outside who live in dissimilar situations (Warren, Thompson and Saegert 2001; Woolcock 1998, 2001). *Linking social capital* unlike *bonding* and some forms of *bridging social capital* is formed between groups or networks where there is unequal power and resources (Halpern 2005). This form of social capital is the type most favoured in research and policy orientations because social interactions can be useful for economic purposes. Further, any individual of the general public can benefit from linking social capital whether or not he/she was part of the social network and interactions (Halpern 2005). From an economic perspective, Frances Cleaver (2005) suggested that social capital can arise from interactions that can be categorized into four different models within a matrix. These are: (i) one-way relationships organized in a hierarchical order; (ii) reciprocal type organizations such as those found in a club; (iii) one-way-spontaneous types of social relations such as agent to agent; and (iv) reciprocal-spontaneous relationships found in networks.

Interestingly, the classification matrix is not concerned with whether social interactions are vertical or horizontal, which is important in the sociological and/or poverty perspectives on social capital. This is primarily because in economic understandings all the forms of the social interactions in the matrix have the potential to yield social capital, regardless of hierarchical power relationships. For example, individuals, groups and organizations within a community network can conduct transactional activities with government and private-sector agencies. Consequently, partnerships are developed with the various stakeholders and a synergy is created (Warren, Thompson and Saegert 2001). Regardless of whether economic benefits are derived equally among the different players, *linking social capital* allegedly provides poor people with the opportunity to promote their interests and needs with influential people in financial institutions, development agencies and government offices (Cleaver 2005). They can also potentially access information and other resources that are useful but are normally out of their reach without the 'linkage' (Cleaver 2005; Dasgupta 2000).

The three forms or sub-types of social capital are not mutually exclusive and all, or a combination of the three, can be found in any one situation. In the case study below, the interplay of the three forms is observed, analysed, and the dynamics involved in building and using social capital examined. Examples are used to show how *bonding social capital* is applied on an everyday basis by friends, neighbours and the community to 'get by', while *bridging* and *linking social capital* examples illustrate how individuals come together to make collective decisions and lobby for improved services for their community to 'get ahead'. The extent to which social interaction among residents is based on trust or simply to 'get by' is interrogated. In general, the case study adds to the discourse on whether the rejuvenation and high level of enthusiasm shown for social capital as an efficient poverty-reducing strategy is realistic.

## Case Study of Tumbasson Village

The community of Tumbasson Village was selected, in part, because of the advantage of observing and collecting data from a small and manageable community with limited resources. It was also chosen as it is geographically separated from the rest of society due to lack of proper roads and telecommunication, but possessed similar characteristics typical of poor and/ or rural communities throughout the Caribbean. The village is nestled in the foothills of the Northern Range within the Caura Valley of County St George, Trinidad and Tobago. It is approximately 20 miles east of the capital city of Port of Spain, with winding roads through the mountains – a 90-minute drive from the city. The highest concentration of poor people in Trinidad and Tobago is located in County St George, which also has the highest concentration of the country's population. The data for the case study is taken from a larger study commissioned by the United Nations Thematic Group on *Sustainable Livelihoods, Poverty Alleviation and Food Security* in 2000. The underlying aim of the project was to provide data and recommendations that can be used for the development of a broader national initiative that sought to adopt a holistic approach to poverty reduction.

The poverty participatory approach (PPA) framework was used to collect and analyse data on all aspects of the living conditions of the families in the community, as well as environmental management practices, gender equity issues, youth involvement, and food production and security, as part of an integrated community development plan.[1] A multi-method or triangulation was used to gather both quantitative and qualitative data from 19 male and four female respondents in 23 households. In addition, structured interviews with key community members and focus group interviews were conducted with the youth, women, and the men from the community and the environs.

## Community Profile

The residents of Tumbasson lived in small wooden houses of which 67 per cent were one-bedroom and 33 per cent two-bedroom abodes. Kitchens were located on the inside of the homes, but bathrooms and toilet facilities were located outside. There was no electricity in Tumbasson and no running water piped to the homes. Most of the households (85 per cent) used kerosene for lighting at nights and a small percentage (15 per cent) used battery-operated systems. Cooking was done mainly using propane gas, but 25 per cent of the homes used wood as cooking fuel.

There were no telephones in the community. Residents travelled to the nearby towns and used pay phones or the phones of family and friends. Public information was accessed through one or more use of radios (40 per cent), conversation with friends and neighbours (25 per cent), from newspapers (24 per cent) and from battery-operated televisions (15 per cent).

*Figure 6.1: Map of Trinidad and Tobago Showing the Location of the Tumbasson Community*

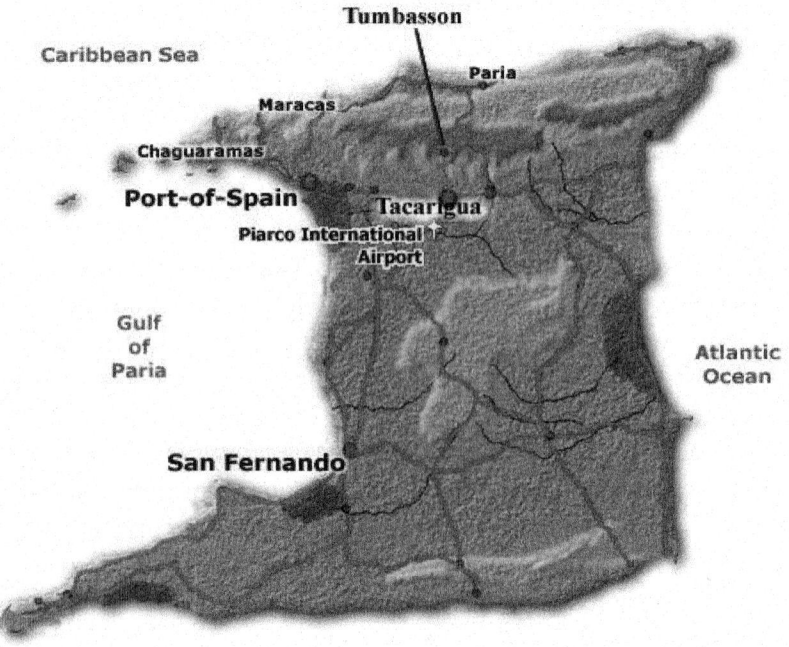

The main form of transportation was a rural bus operated by the government of Trinidad and Tobago and only 13 per cent of the residents owned vehicles. It was also a common practice to use private taxis or hitch-hike. The children who were attending either primary or secondary schools were transported by a school bus paid for by the government. Agricultural production was the main income-generation activity in the community with 60 per cent of the residents operating as full-time farmers. The main crops cultivated included a range of short-term vegetables, some root crops and an array of fruit trees. There are two main agricultural production seasons in Tumbasson, the wet season in which the vast majority of crop cultivation takes place and the dry season in which limited farming occurs. As a result, during the dry period, most of the residents (67 per cent) seek off-farm employment.

In general, the farming practices of the majority of farmers were believed to be environmentally friendly and almost half of the respondents derived all of their income from farming. Income earned from farming, however, was low and the reported average annual income per household was slightly below the average for the country at the time of the survey.[2] It was reported that an average of 35 per cent of household incomes was spent on food, 15 per cent on education, 16 per cent on transportation, and 19 per cent on agricultural inputs and 15 per cent on other expenditures.

## Households, Women and Children

The average size of the 23 households surveyed was 2.7 persons per household. Twenty-two per cent of the residents were legally married and 39 per cent lived in common law relationships. The total number of dependents of the household surveyed was recorded as 79, all of whom did not reside in the village. Interestingly, the female spouses and/or partners of the men, and many of their children, did not live in Tumbasson at the time of the study (1999–2000), but still considered themselves to be residents. Without basic amenities, it was difficult for the women to take care of their children in the village, so they lived with relatives in nearby towns. Also, none of the women were given land to farm; one eventually appropriated farmlands from a male resident. Since they were not farmers, although they assisted in various agricultural activities, the women sought casual wage employment and informal entrepreneurial income-earning activities outside the village.

Sixty per cent of the women had elementary school certificates and 40 per cent had attended various levels of secondary school. The educational attainment of the men respondents varied with 64 per cent having at least a primary-level certificate, 41 per cent with secondary-level certificates and one person had a university degree. Over 80 per cent of the adult population was between the ages of 36 and 55 years. The population consisted mainly of individuals of Afro-Trinidadian ethnicity (70 per cent), with a small group of residents (17 per cent) of Indo-Trinidadian ethnicity, and (13 per cent) of mixed ethnicity. The main religions practised included the Orisha/Spiritual Baptist/Bobo-Shanti faith (39 per cent), Christians (22 per cent), Muslims (13 per cent), Hindus (nine per cent), and Rastafari (four per cent). Three of the respondents did not admit to any particular religion and others who were Rastafarian also practised other faiths.

Typical of low-income households, the residents talked more about their assets rather than household incomes. In fact, they explained that one of the ways to cope with poverty was not to spend money that you did not possess. They also grew and shared much of the food that they consumed and adopted a lifestyle in which they did not have to pay many bills. For example, the residents did not have mortgages, rent payments, water or electrical bills, nor did they have health insurances, life insurances or annuity payments. Further, they did not spend much money on recreation or entertainment. The majority of the households did not receive remittances in the form of cash from family members or governmental agencies. Children benefited from a government-subsidized school transportation service, and the community benefited from a rural bus system that operated only during the week and on a limited time schedule.

## Social Networking

From the very beginning social capital was used to establish the village of Tumbasson. According to community informants, the village was founded by a group of Afro-Trinidadian men in the midst of the 1970s 'black power' movement. The young men were influenced by the rhetoric of 'black consciousnesses' and encouraged to adopt the political ideology of self-determination and become totally independent. Farming and land ownership were seen as avenues in which this was possible, at that time. Consequently, they approached a government official that supported their stance and was granted permission to live in a certain area of the watershed protected Caura Valley. The young men came from Laventille and the East Dry River, which lie on the periphery of the capital city, Port of Spain, and were considered impoverished communities. While the early residents were not farmers, permission was granted to live and farm the land, and to establish a village which they named Tumbasson.

Many of the earlier settlers were members of grassroots-oriented political groups but were not experienced nor trained in agriculture. Over time, they became frustrated and left the village. As a result, when the study was being conducted only a few of the original villagers were living and farming in Tumbasson. However, social networking continued and was integral to the survival of the community. All aspects of the lives of the individuals were found embedded in social networks. Moreover, social networks were an important resource used by individuals to cope with poor living conditions as well as to improve the community.

The outcomes of social capital were observed to be dependent on: (i) the number of people willing to co-operate and pool their resources; (ii) the material and physical assets that the residents possessed; and (iii) the strength of the social relations. The three forms of social capital, *bonding, bridging* and *linking* were apparent as residents formed networks among themselves, with residents from nearby communities who shared similar living conditions, and with individuals and organizations external to the community with whom there was little socio-economic similarity.

As most of the women were absent in the village, *bonding, bridging* and *linking social capital* activities were male dominated in the early phases of the study. The one female farmer did engage in networking with her counterparts and participated in *linking* and *bridging* activities. As the study progressed, external resources were mobilized through *bonding, bridging and linking* activities and the participation of women in social networking and use of social capital increased.

## Bonding Social Capital

The social capital observed to be the most dominant form used every day by community members was *bonding social capital*. Individuals developed social relations with each other and shared material and non-material resources. For example, the Tumbasson residents adopted a 'lend hand' system whereby they came together to build, repair or extend each other's homes, particularly those in a state of disrepair. The skills of men, particularly in carpentry and masonry were mobilized, but the main input was always their physical labour. This was not surprising as Deepa Narayan et al. (2000) explained that among poor households the main asset is often physical labour.

The terrain of Tumbasson was quite rugged and land preparation for crop production was physically demanding. The one female farmer did get assistance from her male neighbours and fellow-farmers in a range of physically challenging activities on her farm lands. In return, she sometimes assisted in selling the produce of other farmers in the weekend open-air markets. Transportation and communication support on a daily basis was also heavily relied upon from community members, family, friends and neighbours. Assistance in transportation was needed for farm produce as well as for individuals to commute to and from shops and businesses in the nearby towns. Community members who owned a vehicle would often offer passenger rides or assistance in the transportation of goods. Alternatively, community members would sometime hire a vehicle at a subsidized rate from another resident, a friend, a family member or an acquaintance living nearby. Children who lived in Tumbasson sometimes would get rides to school from neighbours or visitors to the village. Similarly, the women who visited often received transport assistance from whoever at the time was driving to and from the villages.

When the study was conducted, cell phones were not commonly used or available. There were also no telephone lines to the village. As a result, if a villager wanted to get a message out of Tumbasson they would ask anyone who was travelling to the nearby towns to make a telephone call for them, or they would hitch a ride to the nearest public telephone, or to a relative's home that had a telephone. Overall, these types of support were important to help people 'get by' or survive on an everyday basis (Briggs 1998).

However, while co-operation by community members was sometimes based on trust as suggested by Putnam (2000) and others (Flap and Volker 2004), this was not always the case. Some residents explained that while they had amicable social relations and helped each other willingly, they were not 'comfortable' joining the Tumbasson Improvement Committee (TIC), the only community-based organization with the aim of improving the living conditions of the Tumbasson people. Only 27 per cent of the residents were members of the TIC, others (35per cent) said that the TIC was not a 'real' community organization but a 'ghost organization', existing only on paper. Another 18 per cent reported that they were not invited to join the TIC and 20 per cent cited hostility towards the TIC leaders as a reason for not joining the organization. Twelve per cent said that they did not understand the role of the TIC and another six per cent suggested that the TIC was not well organized and had no desire to become members of the group. Only a few of the villagers said that they did not join the organization because of time limitations.

Conversely, the residents would periodically get together with members of the TIC for large community projects because they understood that it was important to help each other through harsh living situations (see also Temkin and Rohe 1998). The residents further explained that most of the people from Tumbasson and the Caura Valley in general depended on land and each other. Land was important to produce food and the people made sure that everyone had food on their tables. In agrarian-based poor communities like Tumbasson, food is often grown for home consumption with extras sold for cash.

Food produced was an important asset that was also shared among the families in the community. The villagers would exchange food items and in situations where a household had little or nothing to eat, food items were simply given as gifts, in anticipation that if they faced a similar situation their neighbours would reciprocate. Interestingly, the residents never identified trust as the reason why they co-operated and shared goods and services. Instead, they would speak about the necessity to do so, and admitted that they depended on each other on a daily basis. Some described it as the 'neighbourly thing to do'.

This form of *bonded social capital* was also observed to be important to the social life of the residents. With little or no income to spend on recreation, residents usually entertained themselves through animated discussions and various libations. Many of the youth came together on evenings and weekends to play sports on the unpaved roadway. For most of the adults, their social life was centred on religious ceremonies and activities where neighbours, family and friends would contribute food items and/or act as spiritual leaders, musicians and chanters. Frequently, residents would turn to those identified in the community as religious leaders, mainly of the Orisha faith, for consultation and counselling.

The villagers also turned to individuals within the community identified as spiritual healers for advice on local herbal remedies for common illnesses as approximately 90 per cent of the Tumbasson residents utilized what they called 'bush medicine'. Medical persons and services external to the community were only sought if the health issue required surgery or hospitalization. They did not visit doctors or dentists on a regular basis, and relied on their own knowledge, that of elders, spiritual healers and each other for advice, remedies and assistance. In this regard, there were elements of trust, respect and friendly relationships.

The strength and nature of the bonds varied but was sound enough for community members to help each and come together for important events, including those led by the TIC through *bridging* and *linking social capital.* While women participated in these events and played major roles in the organization and implementation of the activities, there were no female leaders, spiritual or otherwise. There were women who commanded high respect by all and were identified as potential leaders among the women. One of these, the lone female farmer, was also a member of the TIC. The others later played major roles in forming a women's organization.

## Bridging and Linking Social Capital

Congruent with the literature, the study found that the presence of strong *bonding social capital* could lead to accessing *bridging* and *linking social capital* (Putnam 1993, 1995; Warren, Thompson and Saegert 2001; Woolcock 2001). Social capital that reflected *bridging* and *linking* characteristics was observed in the way community members mobilized resources for more long-term and sustainable developments in their community. These included income-generating agricultural projects, improved farming conditions (farm roads, extension services, regularization of tenancy), improved infrastructure (main roads, water, and electricity) and improved domestic services (transportation and communication). There were also specific activities and resources for women that were accessed through *bridging* and *linking social capital.*

Residents networked with other nearby local community-based groups, nationally-based organizations, and international agencies. In addition, as farmers, they were also in contact with members of the Ministry of Agriculture, in particular with the Agricultural Extension Department. Linkages to organizations outside the village were possible because although there were communication challenges residents were not socially isolated. The household survey data showed that 50 per cent of the residents belonged to the Caura Valley Farmers' Association, and 61 per cent were members of the Caura Valley Village Council. Additionally, community members (approximately 40 per cent) either belonged to, or had contact with, national and/or international organizations. Within these groupings, only the one female farmer was a member of the Farmers' Organization, none of the women indicated that they had links to political networks of any kind, but a number of the women were active members of the Caura Valley Village Council.

Characteristics of *bridging social capital* were found to be prevalent among residents who had strong social relations with family members and/or peers who were living in the nearby communities of the Caura Valley. The residents of these other communities shared similar living conditions, worked in the same job types, were predominantly farmers and possessed limited resources. As a result, the main social capital that resulted from these associations was accrued because of the advantage of collective bargaining. For example, governmental agencies, as well as national and international developmental organizations, responded more positively to requests from organized groups or associations.

Collective transactions were used to leverage external resources that residents of Tumbasson could not otherwise access because of its small population size and its limited material and social assets. For instance, the Tumbasson farmers joined the Caura Valley Farmers' Association and with the other local farmers advocated for, and received government assistance for land preparation, farm subsidies, agricultural information, training and other services. The regularization of land tenure for the Tumbasson farming community was also being pursued through their membership in the Caura Valley Farmers' Associations. Further, the process of legalizing residency and land tenure arrangements of all Tumbasson's community members was being sought through national political networks. Community members who were affiliates of both the ruling party and the leading opposition party used their social relations with political leaders to treat their issues as a matter of urgency.

The residents spoke of several projects where the level of co-operation illustrates the close interaction between *bridging* and *linking social capital,* and how these are used to increase the incomes of individuals and households as well as leverage resources to improve the working and living conditions of residents in the village and environs. The data showed that it was the men from the village in leadership positions who made contact and networked with other men in government and non-governmental agencies to collectively bring social capital through *bridging* and *linking* bonds. This was not surprising as women's political status in most Caribbean societies are lower than that of men and removes them from having access to the same political capital as their male counterparts. However, the women who were either the spouses or partners of the villagers, and women in general from the wider Caura Valley participated and benefited from emergent activities.

Overall, interesting gender patterns of social inclusion surfaced when social capital was used to abridge some of the negative impact of historic gender exclusion. Developmental projects that were a direct result of *bridging* and *linking social capital* were centred on stereotypical gender roles and income generating activities. For example, the women used their membership in the Caura Valley Village Council as well as initiated a women's group to access support from the State for skills-building workshops and technical training in floral arrangement, cake decorating, food processing and handicraft-making programmes among others. Through their women's group they also accessed funds, equipment, and training in small business management in agro-processing from international non-governmental organizations. The idea was to use the extra fruits produced on the farmlands by the men and turn these into value-added products.

The women also made contact with a national women's organization that gave them additional training to strengthen their entrepreneurial abilities. Overall, the women found that membership in the Caura Valley Village Council was useful in accessing information to keep abreast of available governmental programmes and resources that can help improve their lives and that of their families; and that by having a women's group they qualified for a lot more assistance compared to any one individual.

Men on the other hand, benefited from projects that were directly linked to farming as an income-generating business. One important example was the TELEFOOD Project,[3] a viable agricultural project that involved the production and marketing of the papaya fruit of community members from six male and only one female-headed household. The social bond among the members was strong enough that each member agreed to have an equal but separate allotment of land, and to pool their labour efforts so that they collectively worked on each agricultural plot. At the same time, individuals were free to work on their own allotment outside the pooled labour efforts. The papayas were harvested and transported as a group effort but the income from the sales was distributed based on the quantities harvested per individual plot. The social capital in the form of labour and other resources that were invested in the TELEFOOD Project were coordinated and shared by all participating members.

Part of the finances and technological resources invested in the TELEFOOD Project were accessed through *bridging* and *linking* forms of social capital. The lead person of the TIC had a prior professional relationship with the organization and made the link between the TIC and the Food and Agriculture Organization (FAO) of the United Nations. Interestingly, while this income-generating project was successful and was built on the strong social relations of those involved, it did not involve all the members of the community. Reasons cited for not participating in the TELEFOOD project were linked to the nature of the social relations that individuals had with the TIC leaders. The lack of trust and a sense of alienation to the TIC and the TELEFOOD Project were reported as the main reasons for non-participation. All the members of the TELEFOOD Project were key personnel in the locally based TIC.

Despite, the unwillingness to directly participate in the TELEFOOD Project, all members of the community did benefit from the spin-off of the project. For example, the TELEFOOD Project promoted the Tumbasson farmers and other farmers in the nearby environs as suppliers of good quality papayas to potential buyers. In addition, non-participants were privy to any new technology adopted in the fruit-growing practices through direct observations, information sharing by participating farmers, and by attending training sessions. The TIC members also reinvested some of the income earned from the TELEFFOD project into the infrastructural development of the village.

Regardless of how villagers felt about the TIC or the TELEFOOD project, they came together to improve the living conditions of their village. From the inception, the community did not have access to pipe-borne water and residents were forced to fetch water by hand from a nearby river. Subsequently, a water system was built through the efforts of the community members, a non-governmental organization and the government agency for water and sewage services. The project was a result of the social relations between one of the women from Tumbasson and a non-governmental organization, the Caribbean Network for Integrated Rural Development (CNIRD). The female resident had previously worked for the NGO as a community development officer.

Through this network, a viable proposal for a water system for the community of Tumbasson was designed and implemented. CNIRD agreed to provide the basic funds and act as a mediator, and the water and sewage company provided technical assistance. Physical labour was the major resource provided by community members to the water system project. Similar to the TELEFOOD project, the water system project utilized all three forms of social capital – *bonding, bridging* and *linking* – to successfully access services for the community, but this time the first plank for the bridge was laid by a female.

## Suppositions from the Case Study

The findings of the Tumbasson case study help in understanding how the three heuristic forms of social capital actually work in a low-resource community and what are some of the possible outcomes. The case study showed how individuals gain social capital by participating in various forms of informal and formal networks. Through membership in these networks certain opportunities and benefits arise. Cleaver (2005) argued that the possibility of this occurring is based on certain fundamental assumptions. First, individuals in poor communities should possess a fair amount of resources that can be mobilized.  Second, there must be a certain level of social cohesion and trust among the residents.  Further, for this trust to evolve, there should be persistent social interactions and collective action in pursuit of a common goal with positive outcomes. Within this context, individuals are perceived as 'social entrepreneurs' who are consistently engaging in relationships, building trust, and creating norms in the anticipation that there are some tangible benefits for themselves, their families, or their communities (Cleaver 2005; Ellis 2000; Ostrom and Ahn 2003).

However, from the case study findings some of the more traditional assumptions in the social capital literature were challenged; bonding relations were not always created on the basis of trust, nor was trust an automatic outcome. Rather, the relational activities of members were for the most part a survival strategy.  Individuals understood that because of their socio-economic circumstances they needed to co-operate and help each other. In addition, the sharing of resources or the 'lend hand' practice was based on the expectation of reciprocity as it was very possible that anyone living in the same community could find themselves in a similar situation of need. Trust in both these situations may not have ensued or was desired.

The case study, however, did support the literature that suggested that where networks or groups have meagre resources then localized social capital can only help people 'get by'. In order to 'get ahead', parallel and vertical establishments of *bridging* and *linking social capital*, alongside *bonding social capital*, are required. The formation of associations with other networks, organizations and groups who shared some common purpose resulted in a greater pooling of resources, including access to information, technologies and services. This form of *bridging social capital* established with the surrounding community via the Caura Valley Village Council and Caura Farmers' Associations allowed the Tumbasson members to leverage power to approach government and non-governmental offices for assistance and resources. The voices of the poor became louder and chances to be heard greater as they advocated for better farm roads, electricity, water and health services for the entire Caura District that included the village of Tumbasson. *Bridging social capital*, in this scenario, resulted in greater success than if the villagers had tried to access resources and opportunities by themselves.

Interestingly, economic transactions only became possible through *linking social capital* when the TIC negotiated with the FAO for resources to assist the farming community with an income-generation project. This form of social capital, however, was only possible because one member of the community had a prior relationship with the FAO and was in good standing. This was a key factor in establishing *linking social capital*. In this instance, the relationship was a professional/business one, but in other examples *linking social capital* was possible because of political relationships. In fact, the history of the village is one built on male-dominated political networking over time that resulted in *bonding, bridging* and *linking social capital*. The continued political affiliations of individual men from the village with other men from the government, the opposition party and non-governmental agencies assisted the residents in manoeuvring within the power structures and social stratification systems of the Trinidadian society.

In regard to gender, the case study highlighted the impact of gender hierarchies on the ability of women to access social capital. First, although Afro-Trinidadian women were integral to the Black Power Movement, they were not included in the social network of individuals that initiated contact and received lands in Tumbasson. Moreover, having the nurturing and economic responsibility of children meant that they could not live in Tumbasson until it was more developed, and as such had little need for participating in *bonding social capital* in the village.

Similarly, their gender status in society did not give them access to key members of political organizations or development institutions to be the bridging force, except in one case. The men of Tumbasson, however, were aware that for the village to develop and stabilize, women had to have access to basic amenities, resources, and income generating activities of their own. As such, men with the social contacts and networks attempted to build bridges for the women. Once bridges were built, women took advantage of the opportunities and became major players in activities built through the *bridging* and *linking social capital*. In general, the case study illustrated the nuances, limitations and social exclusion implications of social capital usage based on social class and gender stratification.

## The Limitations of Social Capital in Poverty Reduction

The Tumbasson case study illustrates that in the real world the dynamics, process and outcomes of social capital are more complicated than the simple account described in the literature. It is very easy to oversimplify social capital and overlook issues of structural inequality, power differentials and the role of agency in society. Raúl Atria (2004) argued that if social capital is to be linked to poverty reduction then the social distribution of social capital also needs to be examined. Social capital, like human and economic capital, is normally distributed in stratified societies in such a way that not all groups are endowed with the same amount of it (549). As a result, Atria suggested that poverty studies look closer at the links between the distribution of both poverty and capital of all types.

Ironically, while the poor are more dependent on their ability to exercise agency to survive, structural disadvantages constrain their ability to use agency effectively and benefit from social capital (Cleaver 2005). At the same time, the social capital literature infers that any individual has the potential through collective action to foster economic growth and alleviate poverty. When structural inequalities, discrimination and forms of oppression are left out of the argument, the poor are made to look responsible for their own deficit of social capital. Further, the responsibility for poverty reduction shifts from governments and other institutions to the individual (Edwards et al. 2003; Schuurman 2003). This was shown to be the experience of the banana farmers in the region who lost their ability to take care of their domestic needs, including the education of their children, when the protected markets for bananas were taken away.

Similar examples were given in the previous chapters (four to six) of this book where discussions highlighted women's increased responsibilities in taking care of the elderly, the sick, and the economic burdens of the households as a result of structural adjustment policies in the Caribbean and elsewhere. Arguments that ignore structural and relational inequalities posit an apolitical approach in examining poverty, resource distribution, and the role of agency, and can easily lead to 'blaming the poor'.

In reality, the poor are increasingly frustrated by the difficulties encountered when using agency to effect change in more permanent and structural ways. Not only are there structural constraints but ideological ones as well. For example, the dominant worldview on what are appropriate channels and behaviours to survive everyday life are those of the non-poor. Within this social framework, the working and the poor are less able to negotiate and manoeuvre in their favour, and social capital actually reproduces inequality along race/ethnicity or caste, social class, gender and other social characteristics (Beall 2000). Within this structure, social capital in itself is not a good strategy for alleviating poverty. Cleaver (2005) labelled this the 'dark side' of social capital and argues that social capital can actually lead to the exclusion of certain groups while building the capacity of groups that possess strong anti-social norms.

Bourdieu (1986) reminded us that it is not always about the presence of social networks but also about the content, purpose and practices of the networks, groups and institutions. In other words, it is not what you know but who you know (Woolcock 2001). For example, access to certain clubs, organizations and networks requires an inside contact and sponsorship. Poor people do not form or are accepted in the same kinds of organizations and networks as the non-poor. More often than not, networks of the poor, like the ones in the case study, are about basic survival that includes bartering, exchanges of goods and services, lending and collective labour on special projects. Sometimes, non-poor groups and/or organizations participate in activities in poor communities, but these interactions are neither long-term nor are poor people encouraged to become members in such organizations and networks.

The social stratification of any society spurs groups, organizations and networks that are also socially, economically and politically stratified so that the poor and non-poor are separated. Thus, access to material and non-material resources are also differentiated by poor and non-poor. In reality, the poor will not have many material assets to offer and are usually socially excluded because their assets are not needed in the non-poor organizations and networks. By the same logic, communities with more resourceful social networks and organizations will naturally have a greater chance of fighting poverty (Moser 1996; Narayan 2002). Thus, while a social capital strategy for poverty reduction encourages associativity, Atria (2004) pointed out that the weakness of social capital has more to do with mobilizing capacity and access to resources.

Taken as a whole, networks, groups and organizations vary in resources and while some are heterogeneous and open in their membership, others are more exclusive. The question then arises: If the poor do not have adequate assets to form resourceful networks then how effective is social capital by itself as an instrument in poverty reduction? Similarly, if the poor are not given entry into the networks of the non-poor where there is more resourceful social capital, then to what extent can local social capital formation be an effective poverty reducing strategy (Oyen 2002)? Keep in mind that poor people do not form or participate in the same kind of organizations as the non-poor and, as such, are not privy to the resources that are necessary to drastically improve standard of living.

Research has shown that those who already have high incomes and/or access to resources are more likely to be included in networks with high social capital. In the same vein, Paul Collier (1998, 2000) observed that social capital is usually initiated and led by individuals from higher income brackets; groups, networks, organizations/clubs formed by such individuals are most likely to address the issues of higher-income people and attract membership from higher-income groups. The logic of these realities suggest that social capital instead of fostering social equality and social development enhances or maintains the social stratification of society and supports the status quo, even in times of economic growth, rather than address issues of inequality and poverty reduction (Narayan 2002; Narayan and Cassidy 2001).

As a rule, the poor are socially and economically excluded voluntarily or by coercion based on race/ethnicity, caste, social class, gender and other forms of discrimination. As the poor are denied entry to non-poor groups, organizations and networks, they are also ostracized from participation in political or civic life and experience what Oyen (2002) called 'political poverty'. This is a common practice in most societies because social stratification and differentiation results in the exclusion of the poor from important decision-making processes that directly involve them. Heterogeneity of networks, groups and membership, therefore, deepens or sustains the societal division of social capital between the rich and poor.

Thus, David and Malavassi (2004) are concerned that while social capital may be seen as a 'lubricant' for co-operation and pooling of resources, poverty reduction is still dependent on other forms of capital, particularly human and financial. Interestingly, the social capital literature that is dominated by the economic perspective does not adequately attest to these social-class issues or to race and ethnic differentiation, gender inequity, poverty and the role of women.

## Where is Gender in Social Capital?

Earlier chapters of this book described in detail the important role women play in staving off poverty in their homes and communities. The examples highlighted the adoption strategies that women use as they negotiate poverty-stricken living conditions. Poor women frequently rely on each other, their neighbours and family members. They have strong ties with kin and community. Circumstances also dictate that poor rural and urban women quickly establish women's networks that provide reciprocal support. For example, young urban mothers and/or single mothers readily create childcare networks among themselves and their supporters (Ciabaterri 2007).

The women in Tumbasson were no different; although they had spouses and partners in the rural village they lived, worked and supported their children by residing and co-functioning with their relatives in another community. They quickly joined the Caura Valley Village Council and formed their own women's group so as to work together to access training and other resources. They took care of the elderly and sick in their families and communities and like most Caribbean women they were the guardians and enforcers of the cultures and religions in their homes, community groups and social networks. They were never identified as leaders in any of these activities but their important roles in using social capital and, at the same time, operating within structural barriers that limited their access to *bridging* and *linking social capital* are often missed in the discourse on social capital (Kilby 2002). This is probably because researchers and policymakers are preoccupied more with how to measure rather than how to analyse social capital and poverty (Montano 2004).

In general, the social capital literature discusses the process, use and outcome of social capital as if it is a gender-neutral phenomenon (Molinas 1998; Silvey and Elmhirst 2003), as it does for issues of race, ethnicity and social class differentiations. Similar to the arguments made in the critique of the *feminization of poverty* perspective in chapter four, when social capital is treated in gender-blind ways, little attention is given to issues of gender power and hierarchy in the household, in networks, and in the broader society (Norton 2001; Silvey and Elmhirst 2003). By not addressing women's social and political exclusion from certain information and networks as well as the reciprocity that exist among powerful men, a gender-neutral approach can exacerbate women's disadvantages.

Moreover, the social capital literature is blinded to the existence and implications of gender inequalities and remains distinctively male biased (O'Neill and Gidengil 2006; Silvey and Elmhirst 2003). Hence, when economists and international development agencies such as the World Bank enthusiastically embrace the concept of social capital as an asset that can benefit women (Cameron and Gibson-Graham 2003), but does not delve into the reality of women's unpaid domestic activities as well as their economic role in the informal economy, then chances of success are slim.

Ironically, the World Bank has maintained this gender-blind approach to social capital although it has a Gender Unit to formulate 'women friendly' policies. This is not surprising as the new interest in social capital is based on the assumption that it can be a useful tool for women's empowerment, although it is centred on economic development, transactions, trade and market sales; areas that are male dominated and male centred (Cleaver 2005; Molyneux 1998; World Bank 2008a). For the World Bank and others, using social capital as a tool for economic development and women's empowerment is founded on the belief that women are proficient capitalists and successful entrepreneurs. This focus places the onus of empowerment on women and removes the role that systematic gender discrimination plays in the marginalization of women as a group (Cleaver 2005). Conversely, women are to be blamed for their own oppression and for not capitalizing on the social capital available to them. Here again, 'women's work' is defined using socially constructed masculine concepts where capitalism is linked to male modus operandi and as being economically more successful and important than 'women's work'. As such, women's work is not only undervalued but also not given as much support as 'men's work' (see also chapter five on female breadwinners).

Maxine Molyneux (1998) used the Latin American case study to draw a similar parallel and make some compelling arguments to explain why gender is absent from the social capital literature and process. First, she points out that the earlier studies of social capital were not only class biased in their focus but also centred on male in-groups such as Putnam's (2000) bowling clubs and other public spheres of activities. In reality, women's networks generally own fewer economic resources and rely more on time and labour exchanges that are more helpful for their domestic roles and responsibilities in the private spheres. As such, women are not positioned to take advantage of social capital efforts aimed at building economic resources, although historically they have been major players in the economic development of their societies. Women's networks are important social capital but they are undervalued, taken for granted and stereotyped as being naturally predisposed to reproductive rather than productive roles because of their sex. Under these circumstances, one can presume that certain types of social capital favour men's networks and intentionally or unintentionally exacerbate gender inequality.

To ensure that women have access to all types of social capital and that their economic resources are enhanced requires first redirecting the focus to women's networks. Women's capabilities to engage in political and economic activities also need to be strengthened along with their social responsibilities. Over the years, women's groups and networks have been established primarily through non-governmental organizations (NGOs). These networks and groups are built in solidarity with other women against common forms of oppression, domination and violence against women. Many include training programmes in skills building, technology use, education, health, childcare and social services and also advanced income-generating activities and credit programmes.

In general, women's groups and networks usually aim at generating social capital that benefits the individual, the household and the community in which women reside. Recently, some attention has been given to establishing political networks for women that involve training and mobilization, so that more women can be elected into political positions where their decision-making efforts can be enhanced. This holds true for governments as well as local, national, regional and international organizations/agencies. Similarly, the establishment of women and gender groups and units on university campuses throughout the hemisphere is useful in getting women's issues in academia as a valid discipline.

At the same time, caution must be taken not to romanticize or overestimate women's social networks and the issue of empowerment. Social capital like the *feminization of poverty* is not just a technical term but a political phenomenon (Montano 2004). Social capital has both positive and negative outcomes for women. However, the assumption that social capital is the universal remedy for poverty and that social capital alone can substitute for resources and policies that will assist women is misleading. This approach omits the impact of gender discrimination and gender inequity and ignores the negative impact of macro-economic policies and poor governance on women and the disenfranchised. Thus, the paradigm shift, albeit partially from the more orthodox theories on economic development to include social capital ignores gender as a limiting social factor.

The case study of Tumbasson along with the numerous examples given in the other chapters of the book show that social capital operates within a structural framework. It is driven by social relations of power that stratifies individuals and groups across race/ethnicity, caste and class and gender discrimination, and is used to exclude members of these groups from certain networks, resources, opportunities, human capacity, freedom and life chances.

## Social Exclusion and Social Capital

Discussions on social capital and its link to poverty go beyond the debate on how it can be counted as 'capital' and/or its consequences for women. Social stratification along class, race/ethnicity, gender, immigration status and other social features create power differences between the diverse set of subordinate and powerful groups as well as among the different subordinate groups that exist in a culturally mixed society. As such, even in instances where absolute poverty may not be a major issue, relative poverty and social deprivation generates stigmatization and discrimination that can result in social exclusion of individuals and communities from membership and/or association with non-poor networks, groups and organizations.

As chapter three on the socio-psychological dimensions of poverty shows, stigmatization associate human differences shared by a group with negative attributes that separates 'us' from 'them', and produces status loss. Social exclusion shared across vulnerable groups is a major barrier to the development of social capital networks. The findings and recommendations of these studies suggest that for social capital to be effective in poverty reduction there must be interventions that address issues of social exclusion. Interventions may include deliberate attempts to implement inclusionary social and economic policies that address economic 'catching up' to 'get ahead' as well as national civil and human rights frameworks to address discrimination based on gender, age, skin colour and nationality among other socially demographic features.

The term social exclusion is broad and has different meanings. Nevertheless, there is a general agreement that although inadequacy of income is a central component, social exclusion refers to a wider set of circumstances than income poverty (Sen 2000a; Bourguignon 1999; Rodgers et al. 1995). Within this understanding, social exclusion is not only linked to the unequal distribution of income and assets but to social deprivation and lack of voice and power in society, which are best reflected in the discussions with the most vulnerable groups in society. Interestingly, the social exclusion of people is not always linked to the inability of an individual to participate in the basic political, economic and social functioning of society, although this remains an underlying sentiment. Instead, a more concise explanation is the denial of equal access to opportunities relative to other groups in society and deprivation that are both tangible and non-tangible.

Further, social exclusion also results from the social interactions between groups who see themselves in relationships of powerful and subordinate (rich and not so rich) in society. Within these relationships exclusion is not an inevitable condition, but results from societal and cultural processes that have certain structural antecedents, including the impact of globalization. In some instances, economic growth can be perceived as both necessary and evil, as it can intensify social inequality rather than eliminate poverty. In these situations, the perception is that social exclusion is not just happening, but is being made to happen. Within this understanding, suggestions for improving the standard of living of those most affected include having those in authority accept the responsibilities and act to make it right as well as greater inclusion of civil society in the decision-making processes. Social inclusion policies are, therefore, extremely important if social capital is to have an impact on poverty alleviation. Such policies will have a direct impact on increasing people's well-being, promote equitable growth, and enhance social stability. It includes the fostering of social cohesion and the capacity of resource-poor households and communities to build social capital for residents to 'get ahead'.

Social inclusion policies also have a significant effect in reducing intergenerational poverty through the removal of barriers in education and employment, and providing opportunities for children of excluded groups to participate fully in the economy in ways their parents could not. Sustainable and healthy growth of any economy cannot rely solely on the injection of external investment; it must also include expanding economic opportunities of its own people. If not, households and families will breakdown, so too will the community and society. Social fragmentation of *the community* is the last indicator that living conditions are impacting negatively on everyone. A common view is that the social cohesion of the communities is declining because, in the first instance, when people experience economic difficulties, they must spend a lot of time trying to earn an income. As such, they do not have adequate time to help each other, socialize, to be neighbourly, or to engage in community activities.

The social fragmentation of a community puts the community at the risk of increased lawlessness, crime and violence. This is already observed in the increasing levels of crime, particularly in the more developed Caribbean countries like Trinidad and Tobago where the gini coefficient suggests a wide gap in income and wealth distribution. Social fragmentation is occurring as more communities are divided by social class and where wealth and poverty are also segregated into 'us' and 'them'. In these situations, poverty is more a disgrace than a sin.

## Summary and Conclusions

In sum, there are two startling and opposing debates about the role of social capital in poverty reduction. To a large extent, these relate to the disparate, and centre on the role of civil society, the resources that can be generated from different socio-economic communities, and the level of support supplied by government. The economic perspective espoused by the World Bank and some researchers is based on the belief that social capital can affect growth and that growth will reduce poverty (Collier and Gunning 1999). The social and human development perspectives question the extent to which interlocking disadvantages of poor individuals, families and communities hinder the use of social capital and agency to ameliorate poverty (Cleaver 2005).

Generally, of the different forms of capital that are important in poverty alleviation social capital is still the least understood (Grootaert 1998, 2001; Woolcock and Narayan 2000) and whether social capital can help in the alleviation of poverty remains undetermined. Nevertheless, case studies on social capital and poor communities, like the one cited in this chapter, suggest that understanding the dynamics of social capital and its role in helping poor individuals, households and communities cope with poverty is important. Within this approach, credence is given to human agency and the fact that while the networks, groups or communities of the poor may have less resources and greater structural barriers than the more affluent, they can still act collectively, though limiting and frustrating, to change their circumstances (Warren, Thompson and Saegert 2001). Individuals do have the capacity to negotiate their social experiences and adopt strategies of survival even under the direst of circumstances.

There is no doubt that social capital can be beneficial to poor individuals, households and communities. The underlying assumption is made that societies are built from social groups that determine attitudes, beliefs and values as well as access to resources, opportunities and power. Some research on social capital focuses on 'civic capacity' and 'community-building', shifting the attention from community needs to the capacity of communities to act and utilize the assets that they do possess or have access to through social relations with others (Gittell and Vidal 1998). Moreover, while the poor generally have less financial and other resources, they have a lower opportunity cost of time and are, therefore, more inclined to invest in social capital (Collier 1998, 2000). For example, since farm machinery and technology are often too costly for poor individuals and/or small farmers, sharing technologies and equipment as a form of social capital can help increase agricultural production and alleviate poverty (see Parthasarathy and Chopde 2006 study of farmers in India; Isham 2002 study of farmers in Tanzania; and Rajack 1996a sheep farmers in the Caribbean).

Michael Woolcock (2001) suggested that to better understand how social capital works, particularly in poverty reduction efforts, it is necessary to examine the different forms of social capital, *bonding*, *bridging*, and *linking social capital* and how they function and relate to each other. This will help us to understand the multidimensional nature of poverty and to differentiate as well as observe the interrelatedness of structural and relational constituents of poverty. More so, by centring on the role of agency and social networking, it forces us to examine issues of social exclusion and the lack of freedom to improve living conditions and the right to participate in markets, politics, civil and family life. It also forces us to examine how the exclusion of women affects their ability to lead a 'human' life. According to Sonia Montaño (2004, 347):

> From this relational point of view, what matters is that exclusion is disabling...the notion of social exclusion does not refer to simply being outside of something, but the fact that being outside makes it impossible to participate freely in the market, or in political decision-making, and in the family.

From this standpoint, social capital should not be studied solely on what it can do, but efforts must also be paid to what it cannot do. Similarly, the social capital of impoverished groups should be interrogated along with the social capital of the more affluent, governmental units, local, regional and international development and funding institutions. It is a concept that exists within the larger context of the unequal distribution of resources; to think otherwise is to create a false understanding of the concept and an impractical expectation of its use. In the end, the poor will continue to be blamed for their limitations, and gender issues marked as simply providing more resources to women.

# 8. Humanizing Poverty Research and Adopting Gender Approaches as We Move Forward

## The Problem

Poverty continues to be one of the world's most significant problems. At the global and regional levels, although there are fewer people living in extreme poverty, a significant number, close to three billion individuals, are still living on less than US$2.50 a day. At least 900 million go to bed hungry every night. Additionally, the social conditions of many remain appalling where, for example, the life expectancy in many African countries is age 58. In developing countries, maternal deaths are still unacceptably high and young girls and women are more likely to be sexually abused and experience chronic illnesses. Not only does poverty persist, but the gap between the industrialized North and the developing South is widening. The rich are getting richer, and various forms of gender discrimination make it more difficult for women to achieve gender equity.

Similar patterns are observed in Latin America and the Caribbean. The data show that poverty and indigence rates are the lowest in three decades, but the number of people who live under the poverty line is disturbingly high and estimated to be a little over 160 million for the region. What is even more alarming is that it is anticipated that there will be very little improvements for the estimated 66 million who currently live in dire poverty. Specific to the Caribbean, whereas the numbers may not appear as drastic as some of the countries in Africa and Asia, still, on average 20–40 per cent of the population in many Caribbean countries live below their country's poverty line, with an overall high of 78 per cent for Haiti. Equally disturbing is that while both economic growth and poverty reduction are slowly improving, the gap between the rich and poor in the Caribbean is also expanding accompanied by a burgeoning of social ills associated with poor living conditions. It is disturbing to think about mothers who cannot feed their families as well as how human dignity is taken away from a section of the population.

Caribbean governments have responded to the region's persistent poverty in several ways. First, together with the Caribbean Development Bank, they contracted poverty studies (CPAs) to be conducted along with surveys of living conditions (SLC). A few countries, like Barbados, Jamaica, and Trinidad and Tobago, now have their own national units to conduct ongoing surveys and poverty assessments. The data collected are used by individual governments to develop formal poverty reduction strategies that incorporate some of the recommendations specific to their country. The national strategies developed are usually comprised of transformative and ameliorative measures. In addition, regional governments have agreed with the United Nations to work towards achieving the *Millennium Development Goals,* and for the *Elimination of All Forms of Discrimination against Women.* They have also embraced the World Bank's *Poverty Reduction Strategies,* and where applicable, the Bank's *Pro-Poor Policies.* There are other specific Caribbean regional agreements focused on economic growth, sustainable development and food security.

The situation in the Caribbean, therefore, begs the question: why does poverty persist? Further, why are certain groups of households in the region not benefiting equally from the economic growth and human development that the region enjoys? The data show that conditions of impoverishment are experienced over generations in the same families. Are such households socially excluded from the resources and opportunities that are necessary to advance out of poverty? Equally important, what is it like to live under these circumstances and what do people do to survive? Why are women and female-headed households more likely to be affected?

In this book, women and female-headed resource-poor households were singled out because of the many controversial explanations of their lifestyles as well as the finger-pointing in the poverty literature. The fact of the matter is that female-headed households have been a fixed feature of the Caribbean landscape for a very long time and continue to be so. The poverty assessments conducted in the region did not find a direct link between poverty and head of households as the globally used *feminization of poverty* model suggests. The data did, however, indicate that single-female-headed households are more likely to fall below or near the poverty line, primarily because many of the women who head these households have low levels of education and skills training for the range of jobs that now require some level of technological knowledge. As a result, many women from resource-poor households work long hours in low-paying jobs. Ironically, these unsettling statistics exist in spite of women's overall advancement in education and professional employment. Further, Caribbean feminists and scholars argue that gender social relations and gender equity are still at odds with women's material gains.

The poverty statistics and the arguments made in this book make clear that the socio-economic benefits of society do not filter down to all women and female-headed households, but that there are social class and gender divides that are linked to persistent poverty among certain groups and households. While female-headed households struggle with harsh living conditions, they still do persevere and manage to continue to support their families, without much assistance from male partners or the state. How do they cope and what strategies are they adopting to survive? The women themselves, when asked, lament about their living conditions and daily hardships, but at the same time talk about the importance of having economic independence and autonomy, with or without a male partner. Some of the idiosyncrasies and strategies adopted by women were described and analysed in chapters three to six, but are rarely captured in both poverty studies and women and gender research.

In addition, the book critiques the current methodological and theoretical approaches that are being used in the region for not capturing all the dimensions of poverty. In particular, these approaches exclude the lived experiences of those we study, ignore issues of social exclusion, and lack in-depth gender analyses. As a result, while current poverty assessments are useful in making available important poverty statistics, the human side of poverty is lost. Consequently, they are inadequate by themselves in providing a deeper understanding of the nature and causes of poverty that are important theoretically and practically to poverty reduction and gender equity.

## Methodological and Theoretical Challenges

Currently, the bulk of data on Caribbean regional poverty can be found in two major sources of information: (i) reports from international and local funding institutions such as the World Bank and the CDB; and (ii) from international and regional developmental organizations such as ECLAC, IFAD, UNICEF, UNFAO, UNDP and others. The pieces of information presented in these reports are relatively accurate and useful to government policymakers. They collect data on living conditions through survey instruments, conduct quantitative data analyses, and present quantifiable information on poverty, including the extent to which poverty is prevalent among different groups, households and populations. Gender disaggregated data and income and wealth gaps are also reported. However, explanations of why social inequality and gender disparities and disadvantages exist are beyond the scope of these studies. Similarly, the lived experiences of women and men, as well as the dynamics within households, are sometimes reported through participatory poverty assessments and case studies, but are not fully analysed or utilized in policymaking.

The focal point of the country poverty assessments is understandable as their primary purpose is to provide measured descriptive and antidotal data for policymakers and governments. One of the major methodological and theoretical challenges in generating a deeper understanding of poverty in the Caribbean is, therefore, linked to fact that focus has been given to poverty assessments rather than to research on the social and gender dynamics of poverty. As a result, current poverty studies assess material deprivation through measures of income, employment, access to services and infrastructure, and other human development indices, but are limiting in the cognitive and relational aspects of poverty, and in gender analyses. Consequently, deeper understandings of the ideological aspects of poverty such as gender and social class discrimination, as well as social exclusion issues, are weak or missing. Additionally, while a lot of statistics are generated that describe the demographics of poverty, we know little about what it means to be destitute, struggling to make ends meet, or how it feels to be socially, economically and politically excluded. Moreover, current studies gather information on what people do not have, not what they do to survive. Both sets of information are important for poverty reduction strategies to be effective.

I am not suggesting that we do away with current country poverty assessments and surveys of living condition. Instead, I am making the call for Caribbean scholars to engage in more research focused specifically on why poverty exists and persists from the human and gender dimensions. These alternative and complementary research approaches should also utilize more micro-level studies and analyses that can best capture the role of human agency, the socio-psychological dimension of poverty, adopt stronger gender analyses, and explore how social exclusion and systemic networks impact social inequality and gender inequity. The information generated from micro-level data can produce social knowledge of the collective and be used for more effective and focused policy formulation and strategic planning. For example, the coping mechanisms used by women and men to survive their socio-economic environments, and how these are negotiated in the workplace, the community and in the home are all important in understanding how poverty is mediated by human beings. Such information is also valuable in understanding the dialectical relationship between the social relations of gender and power in the public and private domains of society.

Thus, the combination of country poverty assessments and more scholarly micro-level and gendered research will ensure that not only the statistics on people are available, but also the lived experiences and actions of those most affected will be known. By making human agency centre to understanding human conditions, poverty becomes a person and not just a statistic. Currently, some country poverty assessments include participatory approaches and case studies of individuals, households and communities. The findings from these efforts are presented as separate reports and some aspects are included in the main document. In such cases, policymakers are made aware of the voices of the poor, and what it means to be 'without'. It is uncertain whether these subjective findings influence policy or shape poverty reduction strategies. Some level of gender analyses are also done, but overall, the qualitative and gender data are more like 'add-ons' to the macro-level quantitative frameworks of the assessments.

## Re-Casting Women's Role in Understanding Poverty

The analyses and discussions in chapters three to six illustrated that simply documenting the statistics on women do not necessarily constitute knowledge on women, especially in patriarchal settings. This is more of an epistemic fallacy in which women's lived experiences are either invisible as was shown in the discussions on the socio-psychological dimensions of poverty in chapter three, or misinterpreted and distorted as was evident in the broad application of the *feminization of poverty* in chapter four. Women are treated as either 'victims', 'perpetuators' of social ills, strong 'matriarchs', or sometimes all three simultaneously. Current advancement by some women in education and professional employment has created new tensions and confusions. First, women who are less fortunate can now be viewed as being only a small group and their lived experiences trivialized. Second, the new data on women's overall achievements can be used to shift the blame of women's impoverishment from structural and ideological barriers to personal traits and preferences.

Third, because of this epistemic fallacy, women's activities, choices, and modus operandi is often found to be assessed in accordance to how similar or different they are to the norms of men. For example, chapter five explained how women farmers were discriminated and their work devalued because they were involved, by choice or de facto, in the food production and marketing sectors rather than in commercial agricultural production for trade in which men dominate. In the same chapter, the findings showed that assumptions were often made that women entrepreneurs would not be as successful because their primary objective was to provide high quality service that met people's needs, while making an income for themselves. This was interpreted as women not wanting to capitalize on their businesses through expansion, and hence women were not in need of high levels of financial and training assistance. The issue of women's choice of lifestyle as being abnormal and therefore dysfunctional is again observed in the discussions on the *feminization of poverty* in chapter four. The underlying assumption in this perspective is that poverty in single-female-headed households is due in part to women's conjugal union choices that are different from the andocentric and Eurocentric nuclear family norm. Women sometimes want to have children, but not necessarily legally marry the fathers of their children for both economic and emotional reasons.

The numerous examples in this book illuminate how women negotiate both the material and ideological facets of their lives daily. Patriarchy and value judgments of women are found in every institutional setting of society: in the workplace, the community and the households. Moreover, the value-laden judgments of women's choices and the labelling of their persona limit their opportunities to access resources and achieve social mobility. In other words, it affects what Amaryta Sen and Norman Girvan refer to as human capability and freedom of choice.

It is only through alternative epistemological positions and theoretical perspectives that are more women-centred can we understand and plan for women and female-headed households who continue to live in poor conditions. Their experiences and vision will provide the understandings necessary to develop ways to break the cycle of poverty in their families, and at the same time let them keep their dignity, economic independence, autonomy and the freedom of choice that they desire. Without household and gender analysis, the data provided in poverty assessments are vulnerable to simplistic analysis and binary conclusions that are not only limiting to understanding poverty and developing poverty reduction strategies but also to social and economic development overall. A gender analysis framework helps us to understand why some gender gaps close while others persist as well as how gender outcomes are linked to the structure and function of labour markets, and the formal and informal institutions embedded in society where women interact on a daily basis. It provides the theoretical leads that are best suited to analyse gender inequity and gender injustice.

Caribbean feminists and scholars have provided a skeletal research framework that can be used to study resource-poor women and female-headed households. Their research has not yet centred specifically on women's poverty, but the focus of many of their studies has been on low-income working women and women from resource-poor households. Some have gone a little further and made the link between women's health, sexuality, family, labour and education with poverty. However, there is an urgent need to further bring together women and gender studies with poverty research, as I have attempted to do in this book. In this regard, I make the plea for women and gender scholars to focus more directly on poverty among women and female-headed households, and for poverty studies to incorporate more feminist epistemologies and women's standpoints in their data collection and analyses. In both approaches, women must be seen as social actors who are emotional beings with a social consciousness. They do not simply respond but actively engage in a bargaining process over their identities, their living conditions, gender barriers, and their economic independence and autonomy. In other words, women are constantly negotiating the material and ideological relations of gender and power, in both the public and private spheres of their lives.

## Social Capital and Social Exclusion

Information on how resources are accessed, negotiated, and allocated in any society is directly linked to social relations of power not only between women and men but also between the rich and poor. The inclusion of this area of research in poverty studies speak to yet another important theme not often studied, that is, the 'power disadvantage of the poor'. This dimension is often neglected, in part, because it is highly political and an extremely sensitive issue. In chapter seven, this issue is addressed by discussing, at length, the role of social capital in a resource-poor community. The findings of the community-based research project revealed how a disenfranchised group of people can be empowered to enhance their lives and their community, but only within certain limiting parameters. It showed how social capital, a concept which is also gaining significance at the World Bank level, is not simply about traditional definitions of capital but involves human elements. Within this context, understanding how social networks, membership and affiliations can benefit some, and at the same time isolate others, is imperative.  If the concept of social capital is to be employed in poverty reducing strategies, and it should, then its capacity to build social equality within and across communities must be well understood and better incorporated into poverty reduction strategies.

The discussions and analyses in chapter seven are also valuable because they illustrate how micro-level analysis of a local community can produce findings that challenge dominant perspectives and help build scholarship based on local research and analyses. For example, the researchers of the Tumbasson study, (Trinidad) found that while popular literature emanating from Western studies advocates trust as a major factor in the access and use of social capital, it was not the case in this community. Instead, the basic survival needs of households, the understanding for interdependence as neighbours, and the social consciousness of a few individuals were the driving forces that brought people together. Through *bonding, bridging* and *linking* social capital, community members were able to negotiate poor living conditions and take steps to develop their community. The element of trust was never made clear by the residents, nor was it found to be either a determining factor or a barrier.

There is no doubt that greater emphasis needs to be placed on studying and analysing the usefulness and impact of social capital and to how it is used to manage social inclusion and exclusion. The addition of social capital in poverty studies directly addresses the relational aspects of poverty in the broader society. While the World Bank started this conversation, Caribbean governments, NGOs and CBOs are yet to comprehend how social capital works to both help and disadvantage certain individuals, groups and communities simultaneously. Current poverty data collection processes can include questions surrounding social networking to understand its impact on certain groups and communities. For instance, why are some old and new communities experiencing social fragmentation? Or on the contrary, what or who is responsible for cementing members of a 'troubled' community? Given that each neighbourhood is different and dynamics vary, surveys alone will not work but must be accompanied by case studies and community-level analysis, particularly when analysing and planning poverty alleviation strategies, economic growth and sustainable development.

Care must be taken not to let the dominant Western social capital literature lead in the analyses. Additionally, greater attempts must be made to include women and gender relations of power in the discourse. Currently, women's social capital, or lack thereof, is not well researched and documented. This important aspect of women's access to resources is weak or missing in the social capital literature, in poverty research, and in women and gender studies. Consequently, while some discussions ensue on gender barriers and social relations of gender, little is known about women's *bonding, bridging,* and *linking* social capital. In chapter three, where the socio-psychological dimension of poverty was discussed, women spoke about not having anyone to turn to. On the other hand, in the village of Tumbasson, the women did not need *bonding* social capital because they were not actually living in the community, but they did come together to form a women's group and exercised *bridging* and *linking* social capital to access resources to set up micro-businesses. They also participated in community-based organizations and took leadership roles where necessary.

Although in the case of the Tumbasson study, women's networking was not obvious, women do have their own forms of social capital. For example, chapters four and five talked about the reliance of women on female relatives in the extended family system and when women migrated, for exchanges of services. These included childrearing, taking care of elders or the sick, and sometimes just helping with the basic needs of others in their community or church. The case study of the women in Tumbasson did, however, highlight that women do not have the same access to organizations, institutions or key individuals as men. Similarly, in the discussion on gender barriers to finance and credit of female breadwinners in chapter five, it was shown that women more commonly use informal systems for loans such as the 'sou sou' or 'black box'. In all cases, women's access to social capital of any type used to improve the living conditions for themselves, their families and their communities.

More research efforts are, therefore, needed to examine the relationship between social capital, social inequality and gender inequity. Specific to women, further information on women's networks will assist in recommending strategies on what organizations need to be strengthened and in what areas. Moreover, not only should research look at women's networks and the social capital that can be acquired through these, but also how women and their organizations can be 'hooked' into other types of social capital where political, material and social resources can be equally accessed.

## Summary and Conclusions

In summary, researchers and policymakers who are interested in understanding human poverty and developing appropriate strategies should focus more on the lived experiences along with income, expenditure and social indicators. It is only by addressing all the dimensions of poverty, attacking it at all levels, and expanding analyses to include the cognitive, relational and gender aspects, that the payoffs to development and poverty reduction are likely to be the greatest, and where policy changes will make the most difference.

Specific to the Caribbean, country poverty assessments should be accompanied by more detailed and in-depth research on poverty in the region. Statistical measures of material deprivation supplemented by 'add-ons' of voices of the poor through descriptive narratives by women, men, youth, the elderly and the disabled, are a start. All three facets, the material, the cognitive and the relational, as well as their interrelatedness, must be studied at both the macro and micro levels. This would certainly ensure that issues of social inequality and gender inequity, both key elements as to why poverty persists over time and across generations of families in the Caribbean, are addressed. It will also make certain that human development is not left to a trickle-down effect from the affluent to those who are socially excluded and isolated, and who most likely do not have the social capital or human capacity to take advantage of the developments in society. In other words, poverty studies should take into consideration how agency and the ability to exercise freedom of choice by specific individuals, families, households, groups and communities are limited by structural and relational barriers.

In addition, by 'putting the people back in poverty studies' allows research approaches to not fall prey to local or imported stereotypes and stigmatizations. Instead, more micro-level analyses of households and gender issues will help in combating universalistic application of concepts and analytical tools that are not in sync with the socio-historical experiences of Caribbean women and men. The 'people-focused' approach and the use of micro-level qualitative studies will involve documenting and analysing the coping mechanisms, particularly those adopted by women. In the process, the way in which social relations of gender, gender power and women's identities mediate poverty reduction projects and programmes in households and in the broader society will be observed. This type of research approach and the information that it generates is not only important for developing more appropriate and effective poverty reduction policies and programmes, but it is also an important part of theory building on Caribbean poverty, households and gender.

As a whole, poverty studies that assess material deprivation are important and provide essential information and analyses on structural poverty. On the other hand, the focus on human emotions, rational choice, and social relations of power and gender, breathes oxygen into the mouths of those who are most affected and brings alive the issue of how poverty affects and is affected, by human capability and freedom of choice. Poverty is a person not a statistic; its persistence in societies that have so much to offer is a crime against humanity, and needs to be studied. However, if poverty studies are to be used for transformative reasons, then human agency must remain core to research and data collection. There must also always be a strong gender component because 'when a woman is poor, children are poor.'

## Missing Pieces: Future Research

Throughout the book, I kept referring to the multidimensional, multilevel, and multifaceted nature of poverty. As a result, one of the most difficult decisions in writing the book was what aspects of poverty to address and what can I leave out. Should it be women-centred or gender-focused? Outside country poverty assessments there is a serious lack of research on poverty that employs different methodological approaches and theoretical understandings. In lieu of this void, I decided to address what I thought were the most hidden dimensions of poverty – the human and gender factors. Ironically, not only are resource-poor individuals, households and communities socially excluded from society, but they are also left out of poverty studies.

Nonetheless, there are important research themes that are not included in this book and should be part of future research. Three of these are: (i) poverty and crime, (ii) the impact of impoverishment on children's well-being, and (iii) the impact of the tourist industry in the Caribbean. Hints of these areas were highlighted in the various narratives from the Country Poverty Assessment Reports, but are definitely worthy of more detailed research and analyses. Secondly, while the book discussed gender issues, it was to a large extent women-centred. Research on men-centred poverty is also important, albeit not at the expense of doing less research on women. Future research on how men's constant interaction with women affects the social construction of their reality and self-image is important, particularly how this impacts the ways in which they cope with poverty and family responsibilities.

Finally, my own intersectionality as a researcher, educator and social activist caused me to question the book's audience – should it be academics, educators, field workers, policymakers or the general public? After careful contemplation, it dawned on me that I always argue that women do not separate their different identities, based on race/ethnicity, gender, social class, and other social characteristics, so why not follow my own suppositions. As a result, the book is written for all categories of people interested in understanding the lived experiences and the humanity of those less fortunate as well as those who are actively engaged in working towards greater social equality and gender equity. It offers a combination of theory building and praxis and, as such, reflects who I am.

# Notes

## Chapter One

1. The indigence line is the estimated level of expenditure for an average adult to meet the minimum food requirements for a healthy existence.
2. Poverty line is based on the minimum cost of food and non-food requirements for an average adult. The poverty threshold, or poverty line, is the minimum level of income deemed adequate to purchase the essentials that an individual requires to live on a daily basis.
3. Poverty studies are conducted in different years for different countries. It is difficult to compare statistics across the region by year.
4. The GII ranges from 0 which is an indicator that women and men fare equally, to 1 which specify that women fare poorly in all three dimensions.
5. The 'new poor' was also identified in the CPAs as victims of natural disasters such as hurricanes.
6. In addition, the IMF and the World Bank created Poverty Reduction Strategy Papers (PRSPs) for specific countries that fall into the Heavily Indebted Poor Countries (HIPC). These must be initiated before a country could qualify for aid from most donors and financial institutions (see Factsheet PRSP, imf.org).
7. US$1/day is the international poverty line, while U $1.25/day is the World Bank's poverty line measure using the purchasing power parity (PPP) effect.
8. The Doha Round refers to the World Trade Organization's (WTO) trade negotiations aimed at reforming international trading systems. It was officially launched at the WTO's Fourth Ministerial Conference in Doha, Qatar, 2001.

## Chapter Two

1. The culture of poverty is a *social theory* that expands on the *cycle of poverty*. The term 'subculture of poverty' (later shortened to culture of poverty) made its first appearance in the ethnography *Five Families: Mexican Case Studies in the Culture of Poverty* (1975) by anthropologist Oscar Lewis.
2. Food poverty lines are based on a basket of goods, selected in such a way as to maximize one's nutrient intake at the lowest possible cost. The Caribbean Food and Nutrition Institute has developed software that is used. See the methodology section in CPA reports.
3. For comparative and policy related reasons, the World Bank established a poverty standard of US$1.25 to US$2 per person per day in developing countries – Africa, the Caribbean and Latin America. This figure varies for industrialized countries in Europe and North America and is based on some official absolute measure constructed.
4. HDI measures life expectancy, educational attainment (adult literacy, and combined primary, secondary and tertiary enrollment), and real GDP per capita (in PPP$US).

5.  The HPI measures human development in five areas: (i) percentage of adults that are illiterate; (ii) percentage of children under five who are underweight; (iii) percentage of people expected to die before the age of 40; (iv) the percentage of people without proper health care; and (v) the percentage of the population without access to safe water.
6.  See also 'the practice and experience of consciencization in Latin America' by Chambers (1994, 954) and Liebenberg and Stewart (1997, 97–98).

## Chapter Three

1.  A term used to refer to children whose parents have migrated and send clothes and other items for them in barrel containers, over many years.

## Chapter Four

1.  Male migration dominated in the Caribbean during the 1900s–1950s and led to an increase in female-headed households. Female migration increased in the post-war years and reached a peak in the 1990s.
2.  See the Barbados CALC (2010), the Social Survey of Jamaica (2008), the Analysis of the Survey of Living Conditions in Trinidad and Tobago (2005), and the CPAs conducted throughout the region.
3.  Botswana, Cote d'Ivoire, Ethiopia, Ghana, Madagascar and Rwanda.
4.  Bangladesh, Indonesia and Nepal.
5.  *De jure* refers to where women maintain their households alone because men have left the home and/or where women choose to remain female-headed households following conjugal breakdown or widowhood. *De facto* refers to female-headed households with men who are unable or unwilling to work.
6.  See Sakiki Fukuda-Parr (1999) on female-headed households in South Asia.

## Chapter Five

1.  Mass movement was observed during this period, but women shifted into non-agricultural wage jobs before slavery ended.
2.  Slave breeding was not actively encouraged in the Caribbean until the slave population in many of the territories declined.
3.  The WICP was developed by Caribbean women researchers in response to the idea that knowledge of women's experiences was being filtered through the methodologies and interpretation of men.  As such, the objectives of the WICP were to identify the subjective meanings of the social realities of women's experiences and develop a theoretical framework to analyse this reality.
4.  Share of women employed in the non-agricultural sector is the share of female workers in the non-agricultural sector (industry and services), expressed as a percentage of total employment in the non-agricultural sector.
5.  See tables 2, 3 and 4 in ILO 2001 Report.

## Chapter Six

1. Matrifocal refers to households that are headed by women and where women are central to the family's everyday life activities. Matrilineal refers to the practice where one's ancestry is determined through the maternal line.
2. Structural adjustment policies include: (i) cutbacks in public spending in order to balance government budgets and service past debts; (ii) fighting inflation by restricting the money supply (reduced incomes, devaluation of local currency, etc); (iii) increased privatization through selling of government enterprises in hopes of balancing government budgets and, at the same time, boosting business efficiency; and (iv) improved international balances by increasing manufacturing and agricultural production for export.
3. The case studies are taken from Rajack (1996) unpublished dissertation 'Neither Peasant nor Proletariat: The Paradox of Development for Caribbean Women and Men in Peasant Households,' PhD, University of Kentucky.

## Chapter Seven

1. See full report in 'The Participatory Approach for Integrated Community Development and Sustainable Livelihoods – Technical Report' (FAO: Trinidad, 2000).
2. The reported income earned, in 2000, from farming was low and averaged US$50 – US$100 per week with variations based on the growing season.
3. The project was conceptualized and designed as a joint project between the Tumbasson Improvement Committee (TIC) and the United Nations Food and Agriculture Organization (UN FAO), Trinidad.

# References

Agarwal, B. 1997. *Bargaining and Gender Relations: Within and Beyond the Household.* Discussion Paper. Food Consumption and Nutrition Division, IFPRI, Washington, DC.

——. 2001. Participatory Exclusion, Community Forestry and Gender: An Analysis and Conceptual Framework. *World Development 29*, no. 10:1623–48.

Aggarwal, V.S. 2012. Female-Headed Households and the Feminization of Poverty. *Research Journal of Social Sciences and Management* 2, no.4.

Alkire, S. 2007a. The Missing Dimensions of Poverty Data: An Introduction. *Oxford Development Studies.* Oxford, UK: Oxford University Press.

——. 2007b. Choosing Dimension: The Capability Approach and Multidimensional Poverty. In *The Many Dimensions of Poverty*, ed. N. Kakwani and J. Silber, 89–119. NY: Palgrave-MacMillan.

Allen, E. 2008. Women Entrepreneurs Spur Economic Growth. Interview in the *Washington Post.* Retrieved from http://voices.washingtonpost.com/small-business/2008/05/women_entrepreneurs_spur_econo.html.

Allen, E., N. Langowitz and M. Dean. 2008. Global Entrepreneurship Monitor (GEM): 2008 Report on Women and Entrepreneurship. Massachusetts: Center for Women's Leadership, Babson College.

Alleyne, F. 1994. Tenure, Credit and Agricultural Development in the Lesser Developed Countries of CARICOM. In *Proceedings from a Symposium on Land Tenure and Development in the Eastern Caribbean.* Barbados: CARIB Research Publication Inc.

Alsop, R., A. Fitzsimons and K. Lennon. 2002. Natural Women and Men. In *Theorizing Gender*, ed. Alsop, et al., 12–38. Cambridge: Polity Press.

Anand, S., and A. Sen. 1993. Human Development Index: Methodology and Measurement. *Human Development Report Office Occasional Paper 12.* New York, NY: UNDP.

Antrobus, P. 1990. Women Survival Strategies as a Model for Development. Special Issue: North-South Relations in the New World Order. *Socialist Review 20*, no. 3:14.

Atkinson, A. B. 1998. Social Exclusion, Poverty and Unemployment. In *Exclusion, Employment and Opportunity*, ed. A.B. Atkinson and J. Hills. CASE Paper 4. London: London School of Economics, Centre for Analysis and Social Exclusion.

Atria, R. 2004. Social Capital: The Concept, its Dimensions and Strategies for its Development. In *Social Capital and Poverty Reduction in Latin America and the Caribbean: Towards a New Paradigm.* Compiled by Raul Atria, Marcelo Siles, Irma Arriagada, Lindon J. Robison and Scott Whiteford, 545–53. An ECLAC and Michigan State University Publication.

Aymer, P. 2005. Caribbean Women: Travelers, Traders and Migrants Workers. *Ahfad* 22, no.1.

Bailey, W. 1998. *Gender and the Family in the Caribbean*. Proceedings of the Workshop on Family and the Quality of Gender Relations. March 5–6, 1997. UWI, Mona Jamaica: Institute of Social and Economic Research.

Baksh-Soodeen, R. 1998. Issues of Difference in Contemporary Caribbean Feminism. In *Rethinking Caribbean Difference*, ed. P. Mohammed. *Feminist Review* 59:74–85.

Barbados Country Assessment of Living Conditions. 2010. Volume 1: Human Development Challenges in a Global Crisis: Addressing Growth and Social Inclusion. Barbados: Caribbean Development Bank.

Barlette, P. 1989. Dimensions and Dilemma of Householding. In *The Household Economy: Reconsidering the Domestic Mode of Production*, ed. R.W. Wilk, 3–28. Boulder, CO: Westview Press.

Barriteau, E. 1994. *Gender and Development Planning in the Post-colonial Caribbean: Female Entrepreneurship and the Barbadian State*. Unpublished doctoral thesis, Howard University, USA.

——. 1996. Gender Systems and the Project of Modernity in the Post-Colonial Caribbean. Paper presented at the first SEPHIS Workshop on the Forging of Nationhood and the Contest over Citizenship, Ethnicity and History. New Delhi, India.

——. 1998. Liberal Ideology and Contradictions in Caribbean Gender Systems. In *Caribbean Portraits: Essays on Gender Ideologies and Identities*, ed. C. Barrow. 436–56. Kingston, Jamaica: Ian Randle Publishers.

——. 2001a. Before WID, Beyond GAS: Caribbean Women Creating Change. In *Stronger, Surer, Bolder, Ruth Nita Barrow,* ed. E. Barriteau and A. Cobley, 3–16. Social Change and International Development. Mona, Jamaica: UWI Press.

——. 2001b. *The Political Economy of Gender in the Twentieth-Century Caribbean*. New York: NY. Palgrave.

——. 2002. Women Entrepreneurs and Economic Marginality: Rethinking Caribbean Women's Economic Relations. In *Gendered Realities: Essays in Caribbean Feminist Thought,* ed. P. Mohammed, 221–48. Kingston, Jamaica: UWI Press.

——. 2003. Confronting Power, Theorizing Gender in the Caribbean. In *Confronting Power, Theorizing Gender: Interdisciplinary Perspectives in the Caribbean*, ed. E. Barriteau, 3–27. Kingston, Jamaica: University of the West Indies Press.

——. 2009. Confronting Power and Politics: A Feminist Theorizing of Gender in the Commonwealth Caribbean Societies. In *The Political Interests of Gender Revisited: Redoing Theory and Research with a Feminist Face*, ed. A. Jonasdottir and K. Jones, 122–49. Tokyo/New York/Paris: United Nations University Press.

Barros, R., L. Fox and R. Mendonca. 1994. *Female-Headed Households, Poverty, and the Welfare of Children in Urban Brazil*. Washington, DC: World Bank Publication.

Barrow, C. 1986. Caribbean Women, Agriculture and the Family. Paper prepared for UNESCO/ISER (EC) Seminar on 'Changing Family Patterns and Women's Role in the Caribbean'. Barbados: UWI, Cave Hill, November.

——. 1998. Caribbean Gender Ideologies: Introduction and Overview. In *Caribbean Portraits: Essays on Gender Ideologies and Identities*, ed. C. Barrow, xi–xxxviii. Kingston, Jamaica: Ian Randle Publishers.

——. 2010. *Caribbean Childhoods, 'Outside,' 'Adopted,' or 'Left Behind.'* Kingston, Jamaica: Ian Randle Publishers.

Barrow, C., M. de Bruin and R. Carr, eds. 2009. *Sexuality, Social Exclusion & Human Rights: Vulnerability in the Caribbean Context of HIV.* Kingston, Jamaica: Ian Randle Publishers.

Beall, J. 2000. Life in the Cities. In *Poverty and Development in the 21st Century*, ed. T. Allen and A. Thomas, 425–42. Oxford: Oxford University Press.

Beauboeuf-Lafontant, T. 2009. *Behind the Mask of the Strong Black Woman*: Voice and the Embodiment of a Costly Performance. Philadelphia, PA: Temple University Press.

Beckford, G. 1972. *Persistent Poverty: Underdevelopment in Plantation Economies of the Third World*. NY/London/Toronto: Oxford University Press.

——. 1984. Peasants and Rural Development in the Caribbean. In *Small Farmers in the Caribbean and Latin America*, ed. Ronald Parris. Published by the Centre for Economics and Social Studies of the Third World and the United Nations Educational and Scientific and Cultural Organisation.

Beckles, H. 1989. *Natural Rebels: A Social History of Enslaved Black Women in Barbados*. New Brunswick, NJ: Rutgers University Press.

Beneria, L. 1991. Structural Adjustment, the Labour Market and the Household: The Case of Mexico. In *Towards Social Adjustment: Labour Market Issues in Structural Adjustment*, ed. G. Standing and V. Tokman. Geneva: International Labour Organization.

——. 2011. Accounting for Women's Work: The Progress of Two Decades. In *The Women, Gender and Development Reader*, ed. N. Visvanthan et al., 114–20. London/New Jersey: Zed Books Ltd.

Beneria, L., and G. Sen. 1981. Accumulation, Reproduction and Women's Role in Economic Development: Boserup Revisited. *Signs* 7, no. 2:279–98.

Besson, J. 1998. Changing Perceptions of Gender in the Caribbean Region: The Case of the Jamaican Peasantry. In *Caribbean Portraits: Essays on Gender Ideologies and Identities*, ed. C. Barrow, 133–55. Kingston, Jamaica: Ian Randle Publishers.

——. 2003. Gender and Development the Jamaican Small-scale Marketing System: From the 1960s to the Millennium and Beyond. In *Resources, Planning and Environmental Management in a Changing Caribbean*, ed. D. Barker and D.M.F. McGregor, 11–37. Jamaica: The University of the West Indies Press.

Best, L. 1968. The Mechanism of Plantation Type Economics: Outlines of a Model of Pure Plantation Economy: A Comment. *Social and Economic Studies*, 283–326.

Black, M.L. 1995. My Mother Never Fathered Me: Rethinking Kinship and the Governing of Families. *Social and Economic Studies* 44, no. 1:49–71.

Blumberg, R.L. 1995. Introduction: Engendering Wealth and Well-Being in an Era of Economic Transformation. In *Engendering Wealth and Well-Being: Empowerment for Global Change*, ed. R.L. Blumberg et al., 1–14. Boulder, CO: Westview Press.

Boserup. E. 1970. *Women's Role in Economic Development*. London, UK: George Allen and Unwin Ltd.

Bourdieu, P. 1980. *The Logic of Practice*. UK: Stanford University Press.

——. 1986. The Forms of Capital. In *Handbook of Theory and Research for the Sociology of Education*, ed. J. Richardson, 241–58. New York: Greenwood Press.

Bourguignon, F. 1999. Villa Borsig Workshop Series 1999: Inclusion, Justice, and Poverty Reduction: Absolute Poverty, Relative Deprivation and Social Exclusion.

Bourguignon, F., and S.R. Chakravarty. 2003. The Measurement of Multidimensional Poverty. *Journal of Economic Inequality* 1, no. 1:25–49.

Bradshaw, S. 1996. Female-headed Households in Honduras: A Study of their Formation and Survival in Low-Income Communities. Unpublished PhD thesis, Department of Geography, London School of Economics.

———. 2002. *Gendered Poverties and Power Relation: Looking Inside Communities and Households*. Managua: ICD/Embajada de Holanda/Puntos de Encuentro.

Brenner, J. 1987. Feminist Political Discourse: Radical versus Liberal Approaches to the Feminization of Poverty and Comparable Worth. *Gender and Society* 1, no. 4:447–65.

Brereton, B. 1978. Gender Problems and Issues in Studying the History of our Women. In *Gender in Caribbean Development*, ed. P. Mohammed and C. Sheppard, 119–35. Trinidad: Women Studies Publications, UWI.

Brereton, B. 1979. *Race Relations in Colonial Trinidad*. UK: Cambridge University Press.

———. 1985. The Experience of Indentureship 1845–1917. In *From Calcutta to Caroni: The East Indian in Trinidad*, ed. J. La Guerre, 21–33. Trinidad: UWI Press.

Briggs, X. 1998. Brown Kids in White Suburbs: Housing Mobility and the Multiple Faces of Social Capital. *Housing Policy Debate* 9, no. 1:177–221.

Brizan, G. 1984. *Grenada: Island of Conflict*. London, UK: Zed Books.

Brown, J., and B. Chevannes. 2001. Redefining Fatherhood: A Report from the Caribbean. *Early Childhood Matters* 97:24–37.

Bryan, B., S. Dadzie and S. Scafe. 1985. *The Heart of the Race: Black Women's Lives in Britain*. London: Virago.

Buvinic, M. 1997. Women in Poverty: A New Global Underclass. *Foreign Policy* 108:38–53.

Buvinic, M., and R.G. Gupta, 1994. *Targeting Poor Woman-Headed Households in Developing Countries: Views on a Policy Dilemma*. Washington, DC: International Center for Research on Women.

Cameron, J., and J.K. Gibson-Graham. 2003. Feminizing the Economy: Metaphors, Strategies, and Politics. *Gender, Place and Culture* 10, no. 2:145–57.

CARDI. 1997. Socio-Economic Impact of the Caribbean Sheep Production and Marketing Project in Guyana, Barbados and Tobago. Trididad: CARDI/CIDA Publication.

Caribbean Centre for Money and Finance. 2013. *Caribbean Economic Performance Report, June 2013*. Central Bank of the Caribbean and the University of the West Indies.

Caribbean Development Bank. Basic Needs Trust Fund. n.d. http://www.caribank. org/programmes/basic-needs-trust-fund).

———. 1999. Country Participatory Poverty Assessment, Grenada. Retrieved from http://www.caribank.org/publications-and-resources/poverty-assessment.

———. 2005/06. Country Participatory Poverty Assessment, Saint Lucia. Retrieved from http://www.caribank.org/publications-and-resources/poverty-assessment.

———. 2006/07. National Assessment of Living Conditions, Cayman Islands. Retrieved from http://www.caribank.org/publications-and-resources/poverty-assessment.

——. 2007. Country Participatory Poverty Assessment, Antigua and Barbuda. Retrieved from http://www.caribank.org/publications-and-resources/poverty-assessment.

——. 2007/08. Country Participatory Poverty Assessment, Grenada. Retrieved from http://www.caribank.org/publications-and-resources/poverty-assessment.

——. 2007/08. Country Participatory Poverty Assessment, Saint Kitts and Nevis. Retrieved from http://www.caribank.org/publications-and-resources/poverty-assessment.

——. 2007/09. Country Participatory Poverty Assessment, Anguilla. Retrieved from http://www.caribank.org/publications-and-resources/poverty-assessment.

——. 2008/08. Country Participatory Poverty Assessment, Dominica. Retrieved from http://www.caribank.org/publications-and-resources/poverty-assessment.

——. 2008/09. Country Participatory Poverty Assessment, Barbados. Retrieved from http://www.caribank.org/publications-and-resources/poverty-assessment.

Carr, R. 2009. Social Exclusion, Citizenship and Rights: Grappling with Vulnerability in the Epidemic of HIV. In *Sexuality, Social Exclusion & Human Rights*, ed. C. Barrow, M. de Bruin, and R. Carr, 71–94. Kingston, Jamaica: Ian Randle Publishers.

Casserly, C. 1998. *African-American Women and Poverty: Can Education Alone Change the Status Quo?* NY: Garland Publishing, Inc.

Catells, M., and A. Portes. 1989. World Underneath: The Origins, Dynamics and Effects of the Informal Economy. In *The Informal Economy: Studies in Advanced and Less Developed Countries*, ed. M. Catells, A. Portes and L. Beneton, 11–37. Baltimore: John Hopkins University Press.

Cecchi, C., L. Molinas and F. Sabtini. 2009. Social Capital and Poverty Reduction Strategies: The Case of Rural India. In *Changing Identity of Rural India: A Socio-Historic Analysis*, ed. Elisabetta Basile and Ishita Mukhopadhyay, 65–95. London, UK: Anthem Press.

Chafel, J.A. 1997. Societal Images of Poverty. *Youth and Society* 28:432–63.

Chambers, R. 1994. The Origin and Practice of Participatory Rural Appraisal. *World Development* 22:953–69.

Chant, S. 1985. Single-Parent Families: Choice or Constraint? The Formation of Female-Headed Households in Mexican Shanty Towns. *Development and Change* 16:635–56.

——. 1997a. *Women-Headed Households: Diversity and Dynamics in the Developing World*. Houndmills, Basingstoke: Macmillan.

——. 1997b. Women-Headed Households: Poorest of the Poor? Perspectives from Mexico, Costa Rica and the Philippines. *IDS Bulletin* 28, no.3:26–48.

——. 1999. Women-Headed Households: Global Orthodoxies and Grassroots Realities. In *Women, Globalization and Fragmentation in the Developing World*, ed. H. Afshar and S. Barrientos, 91–130. Houndsmills, Basingstoke: MacMillan.

——. 2001. Female Household Headship, Privation and Power: Challenging the 'Feminization of Poverty' Thesis. Working Paper No. 01-09b. Princeton: Center for Migration and Development, University of Princeton.

——. 2003a. *Female Household Headship and the Feminization of Poverty*. Gender Institute Working Paper Series, 9, London School of Economics.

———. 2003b. The Engendering of Poverty Analysis in Developing Countries: Progress Since the Decade for Women and Priorities for the Future. *Issue 11, November 2003*. Gender Institute.

———. 2006. Re-thinking the 'Feminization of Poverty' in Relation to Aggregate Gender Indices. *Journal of Human Development* 7, no. 2:201–20.

Charlton, S.E. 1984. *Women in Third World Development*. Boulder, CO: Westview Press.

Chase, V. 1988. Farming Systems Research in the Eastern Caribbean: An Attempt at Analyzing Intra-Household Dynamics. In *Gender Issues in Farming Systems Research and Extension*, ed. S. Poats, M. Schmink and A. Spring, 171–82. Boulder, CO: Westview Press.

Chen, M.A. 2007. Rethinking the Informal Economy: Linkages with the Formal Economy and the Formal Regulatory Environment. DESA Working paper (46). Washington, DC: UN Department of Economic and Social Affairs.

Chevannes, B. 2001. *Learning to be a Man: Culture, Socialization and Gender Identity in Five Caribbean Communities*. Mona, Jamaica: University of the West Indies Press.

Ciabaterri, T. 2007. Single Mothers, Social Capital, and Work-Family Conflict. *Journal of Family Issues* 28, no.1:34–60.

Chiappori, P.A. 1988. Nash-Bargained Household Decisions: A Comment. *International Economic Review*, 29, no. 4:791–96.

———. 1992. Collective Labor Supply and Welfare. *Journal of Political Economy* 100, no. 3:437–67.

Clark, C. 1990. Emotions and Micropolitics in Everyday Life: Some Patterns and Paradoxes of Place. In *Research Agendas in the Sociology of Emotions*, ed. T.D. Kemper, 305–33. NY: State University of New York Press.

Clarke, E. 1957. *My Mother who Fathered Me – A Study of the Family in Three Jamaican Communities*. London: George Allen and Unwin Ltd.

Cleaver, F. 2005. The Inequality of Social Capital and the Reproduction of Chronic Poverty. *World Development* 33, no. 6:93–96.

Cole, J. 1994. Socio-political Problems of the Tenurial System in Saint Lucia. Proceedings from a Symposium on Land Tenure and Development in the Eastern Caribbean. Barbados: CARIB Research Publication Inc.

Coleman, J.S. 1988. Social Capital in the Creation of Human Capital. *American Journal of Sociology* 94, Supplement, S95-S120.

———. 1990. *Foundation of Social Theory*. Cambridge, MA: Harvard University Press.

Collier, P. 1998. Social Capital and Poverty. *Social Capital Initiative, Working Paper*, No. Washington. DC: World Bank.

———. 2000. Ethnicity, Politics and Economic Performance. *Economics and Politics* 12, no. 4:225–45.

Collier, P., and J.W. Gunning. 1999. *The Microeconomics of African Growth*. Washington, DC: World Bank.

Collins, J. 1988. The Household and Relations of Production in South Peru. *Comparative Studies in Society and History* 28, no. 4:651–71.

Collins, P.H. 1991. *Black Feminist Thought: Knowledge, Consciousness, and the Politics of Empowerment*. New York: Routledge Press.

Conniff, M.L. 1985. *Black Labor on White Canal: Panama 1904–1981*. Pittsburgh, PA: University of Pittsburg Press.

Corner, L. 2002. Time Use Data for Policy Advocacy and Analysis: A Gender Perspective and Some International Examples. Paper presented at the National Seminar on Applications of Time Use Statistics, UNIFEM Asia-Pacific and Arab States, Regional Programme for Engendering Economic Governance, UNDP Conference Hall, Delhi, October 8–9, 2002. Retrieved from http://www.unifem-ecogov-apas/ ecogov apas/EEGProjectsActivities/TimeUseMeeting.

Cornwall, A. 2001. Making a Difference? Gender and Participatory Development. IDS Discussion Paper 378, Brighton: Institute of Development Studies.

Dasgupta, P. 1988. Trust as a Commodity. In *Trust Making and Breaking and Co-operative Relations*, ed. D. Gambetta. Thousand Oaks, CA: Sage Publications.

——. 2000. Economic Progress and the Idea of Social Capital. In *Social Capital: A Multifaceted Perspective*, ed. Partha Dasgupta and Ismail Serageldin, 325–424. Washington, DC: World Bank.

Dasgputa, P., and I. Serageldin. 2000. *Social Capital: A Multifaceted Perspective*. Washington, DC: World Bank.

Dauber, R., and M. Cain, eds. 1981. *Women and Technological Change in Developing Countries*. (AAAS Selected Symposium) Boulder, CO: Westview Press.

David, M.B., and L.M.O. Malavassi. 2004. Social Capital and Rural Development Policies: Starting Point or Finishing Point? Chapter XIV in *Social Capital and Poverty Reduction in Latin America and the Caribbean: Towards a New Paradigm*. Raúl Atria and Marcelo Siles (Compilers). New York: United Nations. Davis, F.G. 1981. Economics and Mobility: A Theoretical Rationale for Urban Black Family Well-being. In *Black Families*, ed. H.P McAdoo, 127–38. Thousand Oaks, CA: Sage.

De Albuqureque, K., and J.L. McElroy. 1982. West Indian Migration to the United States Virgin Islands. *International Migration Review* 16, no. 1:61–101.

Deere, C., H. Safa and P. Antrobus. 1997. Impacts of Economic Crisis on Poor Women and their Households. In *The Women and Gender Development Reader*, ed. N. Visvanathan et al., 267–76. London/NJ: Zed Books.

Deosaran, R. 2000. *Psychonomics and Poverty: Towards Governance and a Civil Society*. St Augustine, Trinidad: The University of the West Indies Press.

Deveaux, M. 1996. Feminism and Empowerment: A Critical Reading of Foucault. In *Feminist Interpretations of Michel Foucault*, ed. S. Heckman, 211–38. PA: The Pennsylvania State University Press.

Donham, D. 1990. *History, Power and Ideology: Central Issues in Marxism and Anthropology*. Cambridge: Cambridge University Press.

Doss, C. 2012. Intra-Household Bargaining and Resource Allocation in Developing Countries. *World Development Report 2012: Gender Equality and Development*, Background Paper. A World Bank Publication.

Douglas-Ricketts, S. 2002. Free Zone Garment Workers: How do they Cope? *Social and Economic Studies*, 51, no. 4. UWI, Mona: SALISES.

Dreher, M., and R. Hudgins. 2010. Maternal Conjugal Multiplicity and Child Development in Rural Jamaica. In *Family Relations 59*, December, 495–505.

D-REP. 1998. Dominica Rural Enterprise Development Projects: Baseline Survey. Published by Kairi Consultants and the Caribbean Development Bank.

Dubois, W.E.B. 1909. *The Negro American Family*. Atlanta, GA: Atlanta University Press.

Duncan, N. 1994. Mechanisms of Impoverishment in the Caribbean: The Role of Bretton Woods's Institutions and Caribbean Non-Governmental Organisations' Recommendations. Unpublished Papers, Barbados: UWI.

Dunn, L. and H.S. Dunn. 1999. Employment, Working Conditions and Labour Relations in Off-Shore Data Service Enterprises: Case Studies of Barbados and Jamaica.Working Paper, No. 86. Geneva: ILO.

Dunn, L. and A. Mondesire, A. 2009. Regional Special Topic Monograph on Gender and Development Issues, from Analysis of the 2000 Round Census Data of Eighteen Caribbean Countries. Prepared for the CARICOM Secretariat.

Durkheim, E. 1933. *The Division of Labor in Society.* New York: The Free Press.

——. 1951. *Suicide.* Trans. J.A. Spalding. Toronto: Free Press/Collier-Macmillan.

Dwyer, D., and J. Bruce. 1988. *A Home Divided: Women and Income in the 'Third World'.* Stanford: Stanford University Press.

Economic Commission for Latin America and the Caribbean. 2000a. *Equity, Development and Citizenship.* Bogotá: Economic Commission for Latin America and the Caribbean.

——. 2000b. Male Marginalization in the Caribbean. In *Gender Dialogue* Issue 1.

——. 2005. *The Millennium Development Goals: A Latin American and Caribbean Perspective.* Santiago, Chile: ECLAC.

——. 2009. *The Social Panorama View of Latin America, 2010.* Santiago, Chile: ECLAC.

——. 2012a. *Development Paths in the Caribbean,* LC/CAR/L. 401. Santiago, Chile: ECLAC.

——. 2012b. *Macroeconomic Report on Latin America and the Caribbean.* Santiago, Chile: ECLAC.

Edwards, M.R. 1980. Jamaican Higglers: Their Significance and Potential. In *Monograph 7*, University College of Wales, Centre for Development Studies. Swansea, Wales.

Edwards, R., J. Franklin and J. Holland. 2003. *Families and Social Capital: Exploring The Issues.* Families and Social Capital ESRC Research Group Working Paper No. 1, London South Bank University, UK.

Eitzen, D.S., and K. Eitzen Smith. 2009. *Experiencing Poverty: Voices from the Bottom.* Boston: Pearson Education Inc.

Ellis, F. 2000. Rural Livelihoods and Diversity in Developing Countries. *Journal of Development Economics* 70, no. 1:248–52.

Ellis, P., ed. 1986. *Women in the Caribbean.* London/New Jersey: Zed Books.

——. 1988. The Institutional Framework. In *Caribbean Women in Agriculture.* A Food and Agriculture Organisation of the United Nations (UNFAO) Publication.

——. 2003. *Women, Gender and Development in the Caribbean.* London, New Jersey: Zed Books.

Elmelecha, Y., and H.H. Lub. 2004. Race, Ethnicity and the Gender Gap. *Social Science Research* 33, no. 1:158–82.

England, P., and N. Folbre. 2002. Involving Dads: Parental Bargaining and Family Well-Being. In *Handbook of Father Involvement: Multidisciplinary Perspective*, ed. C. Tamis-LeMonda and N. Cabrera. Mahwah, 387–408. NJ: Lawrence Erlbaum Associates.

Engle, P. 1995. Father's Money and Parental Commitment: Guatemala and Nicaragua. In *Engendering Wealth and Well-Being: Empowerment for Global Change*, ed. R.L. Blumberg et al., 1–14. Boulder, CO: Westview Press.

Evans, A. 1988. Gender Relations and Technological Change: The Need for an Integrative Framework of Analysis. In *Gender Issues in Farming Systems Research and Extension*, ed. Poats et al., 37–48. Boulder, CO: Westview Press.

Everts, S. 1998. *Gender and Technology: Empowering Women, Engendering Development*. New York, London: Zed Press.

Folbre, N. 1984. Cleaning House: New Perspective on Household and Economic Development. Paper presented at the XII International Congress of the Latin American Studies Association, Albuquerque, New Mexico.

Ezeala-Harrison, F. 2010. Black Feminization of Poverty: Evidence from the U.S. Cross-Regional Data. *The Journal of Developing Areas* 44, no. 1:149–66.

Flap, H.D. 1991. Social Capital in the Reproduction of Inequality. *Comparative Sociology of Family, Health and Education* 20, no. 6:179–202.

———. 1994. No Man is an Island: The Research Program of a Social Capital Theory. Presented at the World Congress of Sociology, July, Bielefeld, Germany.

Flap, H.D., and B. Volker. 2004. *Creation and Returns of Social Capital: A New Research Program*. London and New York: Routledge.

Food and Agriculture Organisation, United Nations. 2000. The Participatory Approach for Integrated Community Development and Sustainable Livelihoods: Tumbasson Village, Trinidad. Technical Report submitted to the Food and Agriculture Organisation of the United Nations, Trinidad.

———. 2006. *Agriculture, Trade Negotiations and Gender*. FAO Agriculture Report. Rome: UNFAO.

———. 2008. *The State of Food Security in the World 2008*. FAO Agriculture Report, Rome: UNFAO.

———. 2010. *The State of Food in Security in the World: Addressing Food Insecurity in Protracted Crises*. Rome, Italy: UN FAO/WFP.

———. 2010–2011. *The State of Food in Security in the World: Women in Agriculture – Closing the Gender Gap*. Rome, Italy: UN FAO/WFP.

———. 2012. *Women's Contribution to Agriculture. Social and Economic Development*. Department, FAO. Retrieved from http://www.fao.org/docrep/009/a0493e/a0493e03.htm.

Forde, N.M. 1988. *Caribbean Women in Agriculture*. Food and Agriculture Organisation of the United Nations, Rome: UNFAO.

Foner, N. 1975. Women, work, and migration: Jamaicans in London. *Urban Anthropology* 4, no. 3:229–49.

Fox, J., and J. Gershman. 2000. The World Bank and Social Capital: Lessons from Ten Rural Development Projects in the Philippines and Mexico. *Policy Science* 33, nos. 3–4:399–420.

French, J. 1988a. Defining Productive Women in Agriculture: The Case of Jamaica. *Caribbean Women in Agriculture*. Food and Agriculture Organisation of the United Nations, Rome: UNFAO.

———. 1988b. Women in Caribbean Agriculture Research/action project: Overall Report. Trinidad: Caribbean Association for Feminist Research and Action (CAFRA) Publication.

Freire, P. 1968/1970. *Pedagogy of the Oppressed*. NY: Continuum Press.

Frazier, F. 1966. *The Negro Family in the United States*. Chicago: University of Chicago Press. (First Printed in 1939).

Fukuda-Parr, S. 1999. What Does Feminization of Poverty Mean? Or is it Just Lack of Income. *Feminist Economics* 5, no. 2:1999, 99–103.

Fuller-Rowell, T.E., G.W. Evans and A.D. Ong. 2012. Poverty and Health: The Mediating Role of Perceived Discrimination. *Journal of the Psychological Science*, 23, no. 7.

Fuwa, N. 2000. The Poverty and Heterogeneity Among Female-Headed Households Revisited: The Case of Panama. *World Development* 28, no. 8:1515–1542.

Gafar, J. 1998. Growth, Inequality and Poverty in Selected Caribbean and Latin American Countries with Emphasis in Guyana. *Journal of Latin American Studies* 30, no. 3:591–617.

GEM. 2008. Report on Women and Entrepreneurship. Authors: I. Elaine Allen, Amanda Elam, Nan Langowitz, and Monica Dean. MA: Center for Women's Leadership, Babson College.

George, S. 1990. *A Fate Worse Than Debt*. New York, NY: Grove Weidenfeld.

———. 2007. Down the Great Financial Drain: How Debt and the Washington Consensus Destroy Development and Create Poverty. *Development* 50, no. 2:4–11.

Gerson, J., and K. Peiss. 2000. Boundaries, Negotiations, Consciousness: Reconceptualizing Gender Relations. In *The Gendered Society Reader*, ed. M. Kimmel, 118–31. NY/Oxford: Oxford University Press.

Gidengil, E., and B. O'Neil. 2006. Removing Rose Colored Glasses: Examining Theories of Social Capital Through a Gendered Lens. In *Gender and Social Capital*, ed. Brenda O'Neill and Elisabeth Gidengil, 1–14. New York, London: Routledge.

Gill, M., and J. Massiah. 1982. *Women, Work and Development*. Institute for Social and Economic Research Publication, Cave Hill, Barbados, UWI.

Gimenez, M. 1999. The Feminization of Poverty: Myth or Reality? *Critical Sociology* 25, 336.

Girvan, N. 1997. *Poverty, Empowerment and Social Development in the Caribbean*. Jamaica: Canoe Press, University of the West Indies.

Gittell, R., and A. Vidal. 1998. *Community Organizing: Building Social Capital as a Development Strategy*. Thousand Oaks, CA: Sage.

Goffman, E. 1963. Stigma and Social Identity. In *Stigma: Notes on the Management of Spoiled Identity*. NJ: Prentice-Hall.

Gomes, P. I. 1984. Some Notes on the Small Farmer in the Anglo-Caribbean. In *Small Farmers in the Caribbean and Latin America*, ed. R. Parris. Published by the Center for Economic and Social Studies of the Third World and the United Nations Educational and Scientific and Cultural Organisation.

———. 1985. *Rural Development in the Caribbean*. Jamaica: Heinemann Educational Books Caribbean Ltd.

Gonzalez de la Rocha, M. 2001. From the Resources of Poverty to the Poverty of Resources: The Erosion of a Survival Model. *Latin American Perspectives* 28, no. 4:72–100.

Goulet, D. 1989. *The Uncertain Promise: Value Conflicts in Technology Transfer.* New York: New Horizons Press.

Green, V. 1974. *Migrants in Aruba.* The Netherlands:Van Gorcum.

Grootaert, C. 1998. Does Social Capital Help the Poor? A Synthesis of Findings from the Local Level Institutions Studies in Bolivia, Burkina Faso and Indonesia. Local Level Institutions Working Paper No. 10, Social Development Department. Washington, DC: World Bank.

———. 2001. Social Capital: The Missing Link? In *Social Capital and Participation in Everyday Life*, ed. Eric M. Uslaner, 9–29. New York, London: Routledge.

Gunder Frank, A. 1966. The Development of Underdevelopment in Latin America. *Monthly Review Press.*

———. 1967. *Capitalism and Underdevelopment in Latin America.* Monthly Review Press.

Guyer, J. 1981. Household and Community in African Studies. *Journal of African Studies Review* XXIV, nos. 2/3:87–137.

Hagenaars, A. 1991. The Definition and Measurement of Poverty. In *Economic Inequality and Poverty: International Perspectives*, ed. L. Osberg, 134–56. Armonk, NY: M.E. Sharpe.

Halpern, D. 2005. *Social Capital.* Boston, MA: Polity.

Halperin, R.H. 1994. *Cultural Economies: Past and Present.* Austin: University of Texas Press.

Hanifan, L. 1920. *The Community Center.* Boston: Silver, Burdett & Company.

Harley, S. 1997. Speaking Up: The Politics of Black Women's Labor History. In *Ethnicity and Class*, ed. E. Higginbotham and P. Romero, 28–51. CA: Sage Publication.

Harewood, J. 1975. *The Population of Trinidad and Tobago.* CICRED Series.

Heckman, S. 1990. *Gender and Knowledge: Elements of a Post-modern Feminism.* Boston: Northeastern University Press.

Henry, H., and A. Mondesire. 1997. Poverty Alleviation and Reduction Programmes: The Commonwealth Caribbean Experience. In *Poverty Empowerment and Social Development in the Caribbean*, ed. Norman Girvan, 101–36. Kingston, Jamaica, UWI: Canoe Press.

Henriques, F. 1953. *Family and Colour in Jamaica.* London: Eyre & Spottiswoode.

Henry-Lee, A., and E. Le Franc. 2002. Private Poverty and Gender in Guyana and Barbados. *Social and Economic Studies* 51, no. 4.

Henshall, J.D. 1986. Gender Roles in the Caribbean Small Scale Agriculture. Paper presented at the Conference on Gender Issues in Farming Systems Research and Extension. Feb–March.

Hooks, B. 1990. Choosing the Margins as a Space of Radical Openness. *Yearnings: Race, Gender and Cultural Politics.* Boston: South End.

Humphrey, J. 1985. Gender, Pay and Skill: Manual Workers in Brazilian Industry. In Haleh Afshar, ed. *Women, Work and Ideology in the Third World.* London, UK: Tavistock, 214-31.

Iceland, J. 2003. *Poverty in America: A Handbook.* Berkeley, CA: University of California Press.

———. 2005. Measuring Poverty: Theoretical and Empirical Considerations. *Measurement* 3, no. 4:199–225.

IICA. 1996. *Women Small Farmers in the Caribbean*, ed. Brenda Kleysen. Trinidad: The Inter American Institute for Cooperation on Agriculture (IICA) and the Inter-American Development Bank (IADB).

ILO. 2001. SEED Working Paper 19, 2001– Series on Women's Entrepreneurship Development and Gender in Enterprises — WEDGE.

——. 2003. *Global Employment Trends for women*. International Labor Office.

International Labour Organization (ILO) Office for Women. 1981. Women, Technology and the Development Process. In *Women and Technological Change in Developing Countries*. (AAAS Symposium), ed. R. Dauber and M. Cain. Boulder, CO: Westview Press.

International Institute for Labour Studies. 1996. Retrieved from http://www.ilo.org/inst/lang--en/index.htm.

International Fund for Agriculture Development (IFAD). 1999. *The Issue of Poverty Among Female-Headed Households in Africa*. Rome: IFAD.

International Monetary Fund. 2013. *World Economic Outlook: Hope, Realities and Risks*. Washington, DC: IMF.

ISER. 1982. Research Papers on Caribbean Women. Institute for Social and Economic Research, Barbados: The University of the West Indies, Barbados.

Jackson, C. 1996. Rescuing Gender from the Poverty Trap. *World Development* 24, no. 3:489–504.

Kabeer, N. 1994. *Reversed Realities: Gender Hierarchies in Development Thought*. London: Verso.

——. 1995. Targeting Women or Transforming Institutions? Policy Lessons from NGO Anti-Poverty Efforts. *Development in Practice* 5, no. 2:108–16.

——. 1996. Agency, Well-being and Inequality: Reflections on the Gender Dimensions of Poverty. *IDS Bulletin* 27, no. 1:11–21.

——. 1997. Editorial, Tactics and Trade-offs: Revisiting the Links between Gender and Poverty. *IDS Bulletin* 28, no. 3:1–25.

——. 1998. Jumping to Conclusions? Struggles over Meaning and Method in the Study of Household Economics. In *Feminist Visions of Development: Gender Analysis and Policy*, ed. C. Jackson and R. Pearson. London/New York: Routledge.

——. 1999. Resources, Agency, Achievements: Reflections on the Measurement of Women's Empowerment. *Development and Change* 30, no. 3:435.

——. 2003. *Gender Mainstreaming in Poverty Eradication and the Millennium Development Goals: A Handbook for Policy-makers and Other Stakeholders*. London: Commonwealth Secretariat.

Kairi Consultants, Ltd. 2007. *An Analysis of the Survey of Living Conditions (2005), Trinidad and Tobago*. Submitted to the Ministry of Social Development, Trinidad and Tobago.

Katz, M. 1989. *The Undeserving Poor: from the War on Poverty to the War on Welfare*. NY: Pantheon Press.

Kempadoo, K. 2004. *Sexing the Caribbean: Gender, Race, and Sexual Labor*. NY: Routlege.

Kilby, P. 2002. Social Capital and Civil Society. Canberra: National Centre for Development Studies at ANU. Retrieved from http://www.fdc.org.au/files/pk-sc-cs.pdf. 1–15.

Kleysen, B. 1996. *Women Small Farmers in the Caribbean*. Costa Rica: IICA and IDB Publication.

Kudson, B., and B. Yates. 1981. *The Economic Role of Women in Small-Scale Agriculture in the Eastern Caribbean, St Lucia*. Barbados: Women and Development Unit Publication.

Lagro, M., and D. Plotkin. 1990. Women Traders in Saint Vincent and the Grenadines: The Agricultural Traders of Saint Vincent and the Grenadines, Grenada, Dominica and Saint Lucia. Consultant Report. Port-of-Spain, Trinidad: UNECLAC.

Larmer, B., and K. Mosses. 1996. The Barrel Children. *Newsweek* 127, no. 8:45, February, 19.

Lashley, J. 2010. *Women Entrepreneurs in the Caribbean: A Study of the Structures and Challenges that Exist and the Opportunities for Enhanced Support*. The Caribbean Council.

Lehtinen, U. 1998. *Underdog-Shame – Philosophical Essays on Women's Internalization of Inferiority*. Doctoral thesis, University of Gothenburg.

Leo-Rhynie, E., B. Bailey and C. Barrow, eds. 1997. *Gender: A Caribbean Multi-Disciplinary Perspective*. Jamaica: Ian Randle Publishers.

Lewis, D. 1993. Going it Alone: Female-Headed Households, Rights and Resources in Rural Bangladesh. *European Journal of Development Research* 5, no. 2:23–42.

Lewis, G. 1993. Black Women's Employment and the British Economy. In *Inside Babylon: The Caribbean Diaspora in Britain*, ed. W. James and C. Harris, 73–96. London: Verso.

Lewis, O. 1959. *Five Families: Mexican Case Studies in the Culture of Poverty*. NY: Basic Books Inc.

———. 1963. *The Children of Sanchez*. New York: Random House Publishers.

Lewis, W.A. 1955. *Theory of Economic Growth* (University Book). London, UK: Allen & Unwin.

Lin Chih, A., and D.R. Harris, eds. 2008. *The Colors of Poverty: Why Racial and Ethnic Disparities Persist*. NY: Russell Sage Foundation.

Lin, N. 1999. Social Networks and Status Attainment. *Annual Review of Sociology* 25, 467–87.

———. 2001. *Social Capital: A Theory of Social Structure and Action*. Cambridge: Cambridge University Press.

———. 2008. Building a Network Theory of Social Capital. In *Social Capital: Theory and Research*, ed. N. Lin, K. Cook and R.S. Burt, 3–29. New Brunswick, New Jersey, London: Aldine Transaction.

Lipman-Blumen, J. 1984. Resources and Contributions: Maintaining the Gender Power Ration. *Gender Roles and Power*. NJ: Prentice-Hall Inc.

Louden, J. 1988. Incorporating Women into Monitoring and Evaluating Farming Systems Research and Extension. In *Gender Issues in Farming Systems Research and Extension*, ed. Poats et al., 87–98. Boulder, CO: Westview Press.

Lowenthal, D. 1972. *West Indian Societies*. New York, London, Toronto: Oxford University Press.

Louat, F., M. Grosh and J. va der Gaag. 1993. Welfare Implications of Female Headship in Jamaican Households. LSMS Working Paper Number 96, Washington, DC: The World Bank.

Mack, G. 1974. *The Land Divided*. Location/Octagon Books.

Mathurin-Mair, L. 1975. *The Rebel Woman in the British West Indies during Slavery*. Jamaica: Institute of Jamaica for the African-Caribbean Institute of Jamaica 1975.

———. 1986. The 1986 Elsa Goveia Memorial Lecture: Women Field Workers in Jamaica during Slavery. Jamaica: The University of the West Indies Press.

Mantz, J. 2007. How a Huckster Becomes a Custodian of Market Morality: Traditions of Flexibility in Exchange in Dominica. *Identities: Global Studies in Culture and Power*, 14:19–38.

March, C., I. Smyth and A. Mukhopadhyay. 1999. *A Guide to Gender-Analysis Frameworks*. London: Oxfam.

Marcoux, A. 1997. The Feminization of Poverty: Facts, Hypothesis and the Art of Advocacy. Posted in *SD dimensions* Report from the Sustainable Development, Food and Agriculture Organisation. Rome: UNFAO.

———. 1998. The Feminization of Poverty: Claims, Facts and Data Needs. *Population and Development Review* 24, no. 1:131.

Marshall, W. 1985. Peasant Development in the West Indies since 1838. In *Rural Development in the Caribbean*, ed. P.I. Gomes, 1–14. Jamaica: Heinemann Educational Books Caribbean Ltd.

Massiah, J. 1984. *Employed Women in Barbados: A Demographic Profile, 1946–1970*. Institute of Social and Economic Research. Mona, Jamaica: UWI.

Massiah, J., ed. 1986. Women in the Caribbean Project: An Overview. *Social and Economic Studies* 35, no. 2:1–29.

Mathurin, L. 1974. *A Historical Study of Women in Jamaica from 1655 to 1844*. Doctoral thesis, University of the West Indies, Mona, Jamaica.

McElroy, M. 1992. The Policy and Implications of Family Bargaining and Marriage Markets. Paper presented at the IFPRI-World Bank Conference on Intra-Household Resource Allocation: Policy Issues and Research Methods. IFPRI, Washington.

McElroy, M., and M.J. Horney. 1981. Nash-Bargained Household Decisions: Towards a Generalization of the Theory of Demand. *International Economic Review* 22, no. 2:333–49.

———. 1990. Nash-Bargained Household Decisions: Reply. *International Economic Review* 31, no. 1:237–42.

McNay, L. n.d. The Foucauldian Body and the Exclusion of Experience. *Hypatia* 6:125.

McLanahan, S., and E. Kelly. 1999. *Feminization of Poverty: Past and Future*. MacArthur Research Network, Working Paper.

McLanahan, S., A. Sorenson and D. Watson. 1989. Sex Differences in Poverty. *Signs: Journal of Women in Culture and Society* 15, no. 11:102–22.

Medeiros M., and J. Costa. 2006. Poverty among Women in Latin America: Feminization or Over-representation? *Working Paper* No. 20. Report Published by the International Poverty Center of the United Nations Development Programme.

———. 2008. What do we mean by the Feminization of Poverty? One Pager, July 2008, No. 58. Published by the International Poverty Center of the United Nations Development.

Melville, J. 2002. The Impact of Structural Adjustment on the Poor. Paper prepared for the Eastern Caribbean Central Bank, Seventh Annual Development Conference, Basseterre, St Kitts and Nevis, November 21–22.

Menjivar, R., and J.D. Trejos. 1992. *La Pobreza en America Central*. 2nd ed. San Jose: FLACSO.

Micklewright, J. 2002. *Social Exclusion and Children: A European View for a US Debate*. Center for Analysis and Social Exclusion, Paper No. 51. London: London School of Economics.

Mingione, E. 1991. *Fragmented Societies: Sociology of Economic Life beyond the Market Paradigm*. Translated by Paul Goodrich. Cambridge, MA: Basil Blackwell Ltd.

Mintz, S. 1955. The Jamaican Internal Marketing Pattern: Some notes and hypotheses. *Social and Economic Studies* 4:95–103.

———. 1974. *Caribbean Transformation*. NY: Aldine Publishing Company.

Moghadam, V. 1997. *The Feminization of Poverty: Notes on a Concept and Trends in Women Studies*. Occasional Paper No. 2. Normal: Illinois State Univ.

———. 2005. The 'Feminization of Poverty' and Women's Human Rights. *SHS Papers in Women's Studies/Gender* No. 2. UNESCO.

Mohammed, P. 1998. Towards Indigenous Feminist Theorizing in the Caribbean. *Feminist Review* 59:6–33.

Mohammed, S. 1998. Migration and the Family in the Caribbean. *Caribbean Quarterly*, Vol. 44, nos. 3 and 4:105–21.

Molinas, J. R. 1998. The Impact of Inequality, Gender, External Assistance and Social Capital on Local-level Cooperation. *World Development* 26, no. 3:413–31.

Molyneux, M. 1998. Analysing Women's Movements. In *Development and Change 29*, no. 2:219–45.

———. 2001. *Women's Movements in International Perspective: Latin America and Beyond*. Houndsmills, Basingstoke: Palgrave.

Momsen, J.H. 1988. Changing Gender Roles in Caribbean Peasant Agriculture. In *Small Farming and Peasant Resources in the Caribbean*, ed. Brierley, J.S and H. Rubenstein. Winnipeg: University of Manitoba, Manitoba Geographical Studies 10, 83–100.

———. 1991. *Women and Development in the Third World*. London, New York: Routledge.

———. 1993. *Women and Change in the Caribbean*. London: James Currey Ltd.

———. 1998. Gender Bias in Development. In *The New Third World*, eds. A. Gonzalez and J. Norwine, 93–111. Boulder, CO: Westview Press.

Montaño, S. 2004. Policies for the Empowerment of Women as a Strategy in the Battle against Poverty. In *Social Capital and Poverty Reduction in Latin America and the Caribbean: Towards a New Paradigm*. Compiled by Raúl Atria, Marcelo Siles, Irma Arriagada, Lindon J. Robison and Scott Whiteford, 337–52. An ECLAC and Michigan State University Publication.

Moore, H. 1994. *Is there a Crisis in the Family?* Geneva: World Summit for Social Development, Occasional Paper No. 3.

———. 1996. Mothering and Social Responsibilities in a Cross-Cultural Perspective. In *Good Enough Mothering? Feminist Perspectives on Lone Motherhood*, ed. E. DSilva, 58–74. London: Routledge.

Moser, C. 1989. The Impact of Structural Adjustment at the Micro-Level: Low Income Women, Time and the Triple Role in Guayaquil, Ecuador. In *Invisible Adjustment*. vol. 2. New York: UNICEF Americas and the Caribbean Office, 137–62.

——. 1993. *Gender Planning and Development: Theory, Practice and Training*. London: Routledge.

——. 1996. *Confronting Crisis: A Comparative Study of Household Responses to Poverty in Four Poor Urban Communities*. Washington, DC: Environmentally Sustainable Development Studies and Monographs Series No. 8.

Moynihan, D.P. 1965. *The Negro Family: The Case for National Action*. Washington, DC: US Department of Labor, Office of Policy Planning and Research.

Muthwa, S. 1993. Household Survival, Urban Poverty and Female Household Headship in Soweto: Some Key Issues for Further Policy Research. Paper presented in seminar series 'The Societies of Southern Africa in the 19th and 20th Centuries: Women, Colonialism and Commonwealth.' Institute of Commonwealth Studies, University of London, November 19.

Narayan, D. 1997. Voices of the Poor: Poverty and Social Capital in Tanzania. In *Environmentally and Socially Sustainable Development Network, Studies and Monographs, Series* No. 20. Washington, DC: World Bank.

——. 2002. Bonds and Bridges: Social Capital and Poverty. In *Social Capital and Economic Development: Well-being in Developing Countries*, ed. Sunder Ramaswamy. Cheltenham, UK: Edward Elgar.

Narayan, D., et al. 2000. *Voices of the Poor: Can Anyone Hear Us*. Oxford, UK: Oxford University Press.

——. 2001. *Voices of the Poor: Crying Out for Change*. Oxford, UK: Oxford University Press and the World Bank.

Narayan, D., and M. Cassidy. 2001. A Dimensional Approach to Measuring Social Capital: Development and Validation of a Social Capital Inventory. *Current Sociology*, 49:59–102.

Narayan, D., and L. Pritchett. 1999. Cents and Sociability: Household Income and Social Capital in Rural Tanzania. *Journal of Economic Development and Cultural Change* 47, no. 2:871–97.

Nash, J. 1978. The Aztecs and the Ideology of Male Dominance. *Signs* 4:349–62.

National Research Council. 1995. *Measuring Poverty: A New Approach*, ed. C.F. Citro and R.T. Michael. Washington, DC: National Academy Press.

Neckel, S. 1996. *Status and Shame*. Frankfort: NY Campus.

Netting, R. 1993. *Smallholders, Householders: Farm Families and the Ecology of Intensive, Sustainable Agriculture*. California: Stanford University Press.

Nicholson, L., and M. Garvey. 2006. *Survey of Family-owned and Women-owned Businesses in Jamaica*. Mona School of Business, The University of the West Indies, Jamaica.

Norton, A. 2001. The Market for Social Capital. *Policy* (Autumn): 40–44.

Ocampo, J.A. 2004. Social Capital and the Development Agenda. In *Social Capital and Poverty Reduction in Latin America and the Caribbean: Towards a New Paradigm*. Compiled by Raúl Atria et al., 25–32. An ECLAC and Michigan State University Publication.

Okin, S.M. 1991. *Justice, Gender, and the Family*. Published by Basic Books.

Olwig, K.F. 1993. The Migration Experience: Nevisian Women at Home and Abroad. In *Women and Change in the Caribbean*, ed. Janet H. Momsen, 150–66. Bloomington, IN: Indiana University Press.

Ostrom, E., and T-H. Ahn, eds. 2003. *Foundations of Social Capital*. Cheltenham, UK: Edward Elgar.

Overholt, C., et al., eds. 1985. *Gender Roles in Development Projects: A Casebook*. West Hartford, CT: Kumarian Press.

Oyen, E. 2002. Social Capital and Poverty Reduction: Which Role for the Civil Society Organisations and the State? Published by the United Nations Educational, Scientific and Cultural Organisation (UNESCO).

Palmer, P. 1983. The Racial Feminization of Poverty: Women of Color as Portents of the Future for all Women. *Women Studies Quarterly* 11, no. 3.

Pankhust, H. 2002. Passing the Buck? Money Literacy and Alternatives to Savings and Credit Schemes. *Gender and Development* 10, no. 3:10–21.

Parmasad, K. 1983. The Hosein Riots of 1884, Trinidad. Master's thesis, Faculty of Arts and General Studies, The University of the West Indies, Trinidad.

Parthasarthy, D., and V. Chopde. 2006. Building Social Capital: Collective Action, Adoption of Agriculture Innovations and Poverty Reduction in the India Semi-Arid Tropics. Paper presented at the Annual Conference of the Global Development Network.

Patterson, O. 1967. *The Sociology of Slavery: An Analysis of the Origins, Development and Structure of Negro Slave Society in Jamaica*. USA: Fairleigh Dickinson University Press.

Payer, C. 1975. The Debt Trap: the IMF and the Third World. Institute of Development Studies Bulletin 7, no. 1:32–33.

Pearce, D. 1978. The Feminization of Poverty: Women, Work and Welfare. *Urban and Social Change Review* 11:28–36.

———. 1983. The Feminization of Ghetto Poverty. *Society* 21:70–74.

Peterson, J. 1987. The Feminization of Poverty. *Journal of Economic Issues* 21, no. 1.

Portes, A. 1998. Social Capital: Its Origins and Applications in Modern Sociology. *American Review of Sociology* 24:1–24.

———. 2000. The Two Meanings of Social Capital. *Sociological Forum* 15, no. 1:1–12.

Portes, A., M. Castells, and L. Benton. 1989. *The Informal Economy: Studies in Advanced and Less Developed Countries*. Baltimore, MD: John Hopkins University Press.

Portes, A., and P. Landolt. 1996. The Downside of Social Capital. *The American Prospect* 26:18–21.

Prendergast, P., and H. Grace. 2006. Bringing the Male Voices, Perspectives and Issues to the Gender Agenda: The Task of Male Organisations in the Caribbean. *Caribbean Quarterly* 52, no. 2/3 (June–Sept): 14–21.

Pressman, S. 2003. Feminist Explanation of Poverty. *Journal of Economic Issues* 37, no. 2:353–61.

Pretty, J., et al. 1995. *A Trainer's Guide for Participatory Learning and Action*. London, UK: International Institute for Environment and Development.

Putnam, R.D. 1993. *Making Democracy Work: Civic Transitions in Modern Italy*. Princeton, NJ: Princeton University Press.

———. 1995. Tuning In, Tuning Out: The Strange Disappearance of Social Capital in America. *Political Science and Politics* 28:1–20.

———. 2000. *Bowling Alone: The Collapse and Revival of the American Community*. New York: Simon & Schuster.

Quisumbing, A.R., L. Haddad and C. Pena. 1995. Gender and Poverty: New Evidence from 10 Developing Countries. *FCND Discussion Paper 9*. Washington, DC: International Food Policy Research Institute.

Rajack, T. A. 1990. Extension Planning for Women in Agriculture as it Relates to National Agricultural Policies. Proceedings from the Fourth Multi-disciplinary Seminar by the Women and Development Studies on Alternative strategies for Agricultural development: An Analysis of women and gender issues. UWI Trinidad.

——. 1991. *The Historical and Contemporary Role of Female Sugar Cane Workers in Trinidad*. M. Phil. thesis, Department of Agriculture Extension, The University of the West Indies, Trinidad.

——.1991a. The Farm and Home Management Approach to Caribbean Agricultural Development. Paper presented at the Caribbean Food Society Symposium, Dominica.

——. 1996. *Neither Peasant nor Proletariat: The Paradox of Development for Caribbean Women and Men in Peasant Households*. Unpublished doctoral thesis, University of Kentucky, USA.

——. 1996a. Social Impact Assessment of the Caribbean Sheep Production and Marketing Project: Barbados, Guyana and Tobago. Technical Report submitted to the Canadian International Development Agency and the Caribbean Agricultural Research and Development Institute.

——. 1997. Lessons to be Gained from Having a Social and Gender focus in the Technology Generation and Transfer Process. Trinidad: CARDI/CIDA Report.

——. 1998. Case Studies, Illustrations and Detail Examples of Rural Women in Dominica, St Lucia and Trinidad and Tobago. Extension Manual on *Strengthening Extension Services to Rural Women*. Trinidad: UNFAO-UN/CEPAT, Report, Extension Department, The University of the West Indies.

——. 1999. Burying the Myth of the East Indian Woman on the Sugar Plantation. Book Chapter in *Matikor*, ed. R. Kanhai, 181–93. Trinidad: The University of the West Indies Press.

Rajack, T.A., and F. Deare. 1993. Traditional Sheep Farming in Tobago: Focus Group Interview. CARDI/CSP/M Project Document. Trinidad: CARDI.

Rajack, T.A., and A. Hosein. 1993. Social/gender Experience in the CARDI/CIDA Caribbean Sheep Production and Marketing Project. Proceedings from the Regional Small Ruminant Workshop. Barbados.

Rajack-Talley, T.A. 2004. Afro-Caribbean Women's Resistance to Race, Class and Gender Domination. *International Journal of Africana Studies* 10, no. 2.

Rajack-Talley, T.A. 2015. The Role of Small Producers, Family Farms and Women Farmers in Sustainable Food Production Systems and Food Security. In *Sustainable Food Production Practices for the Caribbean* Vol 1, 1–33, ed. W. Gunpat and W. Isaac. Kingston, Jamaica: Ian Randle Publishers.

Rajack-Talley, T.A., and L. Best. 2015. The Feminization of Poverty and the Black Family: Ideological and Methodological Contestations. In *The Black Family and Society – Africana Studies* Vol. 6, 87–102.

Rajack-Talley, T.A., and C. Talley. 2000. The Role of Farming Women in Caribbean Agriculture: A Historical and Contemporary Perspective. *Caribbean Journal for Agriculture and Natural Resources* 2, no. 2:4–13.

———. 2005. Eurocentrism and the Afro-Caribbean Family. *The GRIOT*, 24 (1).

Rainwater, L. 1966. The Crucible of Identity: The Lower Class Negro Family. *Daedalus* 95:268–64.

Ramazanoglu, C. 1993. *Up Against Foucault: Explorations of Some Tensions Between Foucault and Feminism*. Psychology Press.

Razvi, S. 1999. Gendered Poverty and Well-Being: Introduction. *Development and Change* 30, no. 3:409–33.

———. 2000. Gender Poverty and Well-Being. *Development and Change: Special Issues*. NJ: Wiley Press.

Reddock, R. 1985. The Indentureship Experience: Indian Women in Trinidad and Tobago, 1845–1917. In *Women Plantation Workers: International Experience*, ed. Jain and R. Reddock. Oxford, UK: Berg.

———. 1988. Women and the Slave Plantation Economy in the Caribbean. In *Retrieving Women's History*, ed. S. Jay Kleinberg. Oxford and New York: Berg.

———. 1994. *Women, Labour and Politics in Trinidad and Tobago: A History*. London, UK: Zed Books.

———. 1998. Contestation over National Culture in Trinidad and Tobago: Considerations of Ethnicity, Class and Gender. In *Caribbean Portraits: Essays on Gender Ideologies and Identities*, ed. C. Barrow, 414–35. Kingston, Jamaica: Ian Randle Publishers.

———. 2004. *Interrogating Caribbean Masculinities*. Mona, Jamaica: University of the West Indies Press.

Reddock, R., and J. Huggins. 1988. The Case of the Sugar Industry in Trinidad and Tobago. In *Women in Caribbean Agriculture*. Food and Agriculture Organisation of the United Nations (UNFAO).

———. 1997. Agriculture and Women's Place: The Impact of Changing National Policies on Women's Agricultural Work in Trinidad and Tobago. In *Gender: A Caribbean Multidisciplinary Perspective*, ed. E. Leo-Rhynie, B. Bailey and C. Barrow, 324–46. Kingston, Jamaica: Ian Randle Publishers.

Retzinger, S.M. 1991. *Violent Emotions, Shame and Rage in Marital Quarrels*. London: Sage Publications.

Reynolds, T. 2001. Black Mothering, Paid Work and Identity. *Ethnic and Racial Studies* 24, no. 6:1046–1064.

Richardson, B.C. 1983. *Caribbean Migrants: Environment and Human Survival on St. Kitts and Nevis*. Knoxville, TN: University of Tennessee Press.

Robb, C.M. 2002. *Can the Poor Influence Policy? Participatory Poverty Assessments in the Developing World*. 2nd ed. Published by the International Monetary Fund and the World Bank.

Roberts, D., et al. 2009. *Sex, Power and Taboo: Gender and HIV in the Caribbean and Beyond*. Kingston, Jamaica: Ian Randle Publishers.

Rodgers, G., C. Gore and J.B. Figueiredo, eds. 1995. *Social Exclusion: Rhetoric, Reality, Responses*. Institute of International Labour Studies, Geneva: ILO.

Rodgers, H.R. 1987. Black Americans and the Feminization of Poverty: The Intervening Effects of Unemployment. *Journal of Black Studies* 17, no. 4:402–17.

———. 1990. *Poor Women, Poor Families: The Economic Plight of America's Female-Headed Households*. NY: M.E. Sharp Inc.

Rodman, H. 1971. *Lower Class Families: The Culture of Poverty in Negro Trinidad*. London: Oxford University Press.

Rodney, W. 1974. *How Europe Underdeveloped Africa*. Washington, DC: Howard University Press.

Rogers, B. 1980. *The Domestication of Women: Discrimination in Developing Societies*. London/New York: Tavistock Publications.

Roopnarine, J. 2013. A Closer Look at Caribbean Fathers. *Trinidad Express*, May 22, 2013.

Roopnarine, L. 2003. Indo-Caribbean Migration: From Periphery to Core. *Caribbean Quarterly*, 49, no. 3:30–60.

Rubenstein, H. 1980. Conjugal Behaviour and Parental Role Flexibility in Afro-Caribbean Village. *Canadian Review of Sociology and Anthropology* 17, no. 4:330–37.

Ruggles, P. 1990. *Drawing the Line: Alternative Poverty Measures and their Implications for Public Policy*. Washington, DC: Urban Institute.

Safa, H. 1995. *The Myth of the Male Breadwinner: Women and Industrialization in the Caribbean* (Conflict and Social Change Series). Boulder, CO: Westview Press.

Safa, H., and P. Antrobus. 1992. Women and Economic Crisis in the Caribbean. In *Unequal Burden: Economic Crisis, Persistent Poverty and Women's Work*, ed. L. Beneria and S. Feldman, 49–82. Boulder, CO: Westview Press.

Sawicki J. 1986. Foucault and Feminism: Toward a Politics of Difference. *Hypatia* 1:26–32.

———. 1988. Identity Politics and Sexual Freedom. In *Feminism and Foucault: Reflections on Resistance*, ed. I. Diamond and L. Quinby. Holliston, MA: Northeastern.

Samman, E. 2007. Psychological and Subjective Well-Being: A Proposal for Internationally Comparable Indicators. *OHIP Working Paper Series 5*.

Scheff, T.J. 1990. *Microsociology, Discourse, Emotion and Social Structure*. Chicago, IL: The University of Chicago Press.

Schuurman, F.J. 2003. Social Capital: The Politico-Emancipatory Potential of a Disputed Concept. *Third World Quarterly* 24, no. 6:991–1010.

Scott, J.L. 1994. Afro-Caribbean Women Entrepreneurs: Barriers to Self-employment in Toronto, *Canadian Women Studies* 15, no. 1:38–41.

———. 2003. Shame in Self and Society. *Symbolic Interaction* 28, no. 2:147–66.

Seidman, S. 1994. *Contested Knowledge: Social Theory in the Postmodern Era*. 3rd ed. Oxford: Blackwell Publishers.

Sen, A. 1985. *Commodities and Capabilities*. Amsterdam: North-Holland Press.

———. 1987. *Standard of Living*. Cambridge, MA: Harvard University Press.

———. 1990. Gender and Cooperative Conflicts. In *Persistent Inequalities: Women and World Development*, ed. I. Tinker, 123–49. New York/Oxford: Oxford University Press.

———. 1992. *Inequality Re-Examined*. Cambridge, MA: Harvard University Press.

——. 1993. Capability and Well-Being. In *The Quality of Life*, eds. Sen, A. and M. Nussbaum, 30–53. Finland: United Nations University.

——. 1997. *Social Exclusion: A Critical Assessment of the Concept and its Relevance.* (mimeo), Asian Development Bank.

——. 1999. *Development as Freedom*. NY: Knopf.

——. 2000. A Decade of Human Development. *Journal of Human Development* 1, no.1:17–23.

——. 2000a. Social Exclusion: Concept, Application, and Scrutiny. Published by the Governance and Social Development Resource Center (GSDRC).

Sen, G. 1999. Engendering Poverty Alleviation: Challenges and Opportunities. *Development and Change* 30, no. 3:685–92.

——. 2011. Subordination and Sexual Control: A Comparative View of the Control of Women. In *The Women, Gender and Development Reader*, ed. N. Visvanthan et al., 154–61. N. London/New Jersey: Zed Books Ltd.

Shepherd, V., B. Brereton and B. Bailey. 1995. *Engendering History: Caribbean Women in a Historical Perspective*. London: James Currey/ Jamaica: Ian Randle Publishers.

Sidel, R. 1996. *Poor Women; Public Welfare; Family Policy; Women Heads of Households United States*. NY: Penguin Books.

Silver, H. 1994. Social Exclusion and Social Solidarity: Three Paradigms. *International Labour Review* 133:531–78.

Silvey, R., and R. Elmhirst. 2003. Engendering Social Capital: Women Workers and Rural-Urban Networks in Indonesia's Crisis.*World Development* 3:865–79.

Simey, T. 1946. *Welfare and Planning in the West Indies*. Oxford: Clarendon Press.

Smith, R.T. 1956. *The Negro Family in British Guiana*. London: Routledge.

——. 1988. *Kinship and Class in the West Indies – A Genealogical Study of Jamaica and Guyana*. New York: Grove Press.

Smith, J., I. Wallerstein and E. Hans-Dieter. eds. 1984. *Households and the World Economy*. CA: Sage.

Soares, J. 2009. The Myth of Poverty Alleviation- Part 2. *Abeng Magazine*. Retrieved from http://www.abengnews.com/2009/01/24/the-myth-of-poverty-alleviation-part-2.

Sookram, S., and P. Watson. 2008. The Informal Sector, Poverty and Gender: The Case Study of Trinidad and Tobago. *Journal of Eastern Caribbean Studies* 42, no. 2:111–28.

Spring, A. 1988. Linking FSR/E and Gender: An Introduction. In *Gender Issues in Farming Systems Research and Extension*, ed. Poats, et al., 1–18. Boulder, CO: Westview Press.

St Bernard, G. 2003. Major Trends Affecting Families in Central America and the Caribbean. Paper prepared for the United Nations, Division of Social Policy, Department of Economics and Social Affairs Program on Family.

St Hill, D. 2003. Women and Difference in Caribbean Gender Theory: Notes Towards a Strategic Universalist Feminism. In *Confronting Power, Theorizing Gender*, ed. E. Barriteau. Kingston, Jamaica: UWI Press.

Stiglitz, J. 1998. *Towards a New Paradigm for Development: Strategies, Policies, and Processes*. Given at the 1998 Prebisch Lecture at UNCTAD, Geneva.

Stuart, S. 1996. A Comparative Perspective of the Caribbean and the Developed World. *Gender and Development* 4, no. 2:28–34.

Tangney, J.P., and R.L. Dearing. 2002. *Shame and Guilt*. London: Guildford Press.

Taylor, P. 1999. Democratizing Cities: Habitats Global Campaign on Urban Governance. *Habitat Debate* 5, no. 4:1–5.

Temkin, K., and W.M. Rohe. 1998. Social Capital and Neighbourhood Stability: An Empirical Investigation. *Housing Policy Debate* 9, no. 1.

Terjesen, S., and J.E. Amorós. 2010. Female Entrepreneurship in Latin America and the Caribbean: Characteristics, Drivers and Relationship to Economic Development. *European Journal of Development Research* 22:313–30. doi:10.1057/ejdr.2010.13.

Thompson, P., and E. Bauer. 2000. Jamaican Transnational Families: Points of Pain and Sources of Resilience. *Wadabagei: A Journal of Caribbean and its Diaspora* 3, no. 2:1–36.

Tickamyer, A., and C. Talley. 1994. Economic Restructuring and Household Survival Strategies: Linking Labor Markets and Income Sources for Different Social Groups. Paper presented at the Rural Sociological Society Meetings, Portland, Oregon.

Thomas, C.Y. 2002. *Designing and Implementing Development Policy: The Shift to Holistic Approaches and Social Policy Frameworks*. Transition Issue 31. University of Guyana, Georgetown.

Thomas, M., and E. Wint. 2002. *Report on Inequality and Poverty in the Eastern Caribbean*. Prepared for the ECCP Seventh Annual Development Conference in 2002, 7. Table 2.

Tinker, I. 1990. *Persistent Inequalities: Women and World Development*. Oxford: Oxford University Press.

Townsend, P. 1970. Measures and Explanations of Poverty in High Income and Low Income Countries: The Problems of Operationalizing the Concepts of Development, Class and Poverty. In *The Concept of Poverty Working Papers on Methods of Investigation and Lifestyles of the Poor in Different Countries*, ed. P. Townsend. London: Heinemann Educational Books.

———. 1979. *Poverty in the United Kingdom*. London: Penguin, Harmondsworth.

———. 1985. A Sociological Approach to the Measurement of Poverty: A Rejoinder to Prof. Amartya Sen. Oxford, UK: Oxford University Papers, 37.

United Nations Children's Fund (UNICEF). 2012. Report on the State of the World's Children. Retrieved from http://www.unicef.org/publications/.

———. 2006. Poverty Begins at Home? Questioning Some (Mis) Conceptions about Children, Poverty, and Privation in Female-Headed Households. Prepared by Sylvia Chant for UNICEF.

United Nations Development Project. 1991. *The Human Development Report*. NY: UNDP.

———. 1995. *Human Development Report*. Oxford: Oxford University Press, 4.

———. 1995a. *Copenhagen Declaration and Programme of Action: World Summit for Social Development*. New York: United Nations.

———. 1995b. *The World's Women 1995: Trends and Statistics*. New York: United Nations.

———. 1997. *The Human Development Report*. NY: UNDP.

———. 2001. *The Human Development Report*. NY: UNDP.

———. 2009. *Country Assessment Report – Jamaica: Enhancing Gender Visibility in Disaster Risk Management and Climate Change in the Caribbean.*

United Nations Economic and Social Council. 2006. *State of the World's Indigenous People*, ST/ESA/328.

United Nations. 1996. *Food Security for All: Food Security for Rural Women.* Geneva: International Steering Committee on the Economic Advancement of Rural Women.

———. 2000. *The World's Women 2000: Trends and Statistics.* New York: United Nations.

Varley, A. 1996. Women Headed Households: Some More Equal Than others? *World Development* 24, no. 3:505–20.

Waggle, U. 2002. *Rethinking Poverty: Definitions and Measurement.* UNESCO Publication, Oxford, UK: Blackwell Publishers.

Walby, S. 1990. *Theorizing Patriarchy.* Oxford: Blackwell Publishers.

———. 1997. *Gender Transformations.* London, UK: Routledge.

———. 2001. From Community to Coalition: The Politics of Recognition as the Handmaiden of the Politics of Redistribution. *Theory, Culture and Society* 18, nos. 2–3:113–35.

Warren, M.R., P. Thompson and S. Saegert. 2001. The Role of Capital in Combating Poverty. In *Social Capital and Poor Communities*, ed. Warren, Thompson and Saegert New York: Sage Publications.

Wetengere, K. 2011. Is the Adoption of Farm Technology Gender Neutral? The Case of Fish Farming in Morogora Region, Tanzania. *International Journal of Ethics* 7, no. 1:19–24.

Whitehead, A., and M. Lockwood. 1999. Gendering Poverty: A Review of Six World Bank Africa Assessments. *Development and Change* 30, no. 3:525–55.

Wilk, R.W. 1989. Decision Making and Resource Flow within the Household: Beyond the Black Box. In *The Household Economy – Reconsidering the Domestic Mode of Production*, ed. R.W. Wilk, 23–52. Boulder, CO: Westview Press.

Williams, S., J. Seed and A. Mwau. 1994. *The Oxfam Gender Training Manual.* UK and Ireland: Oxfam.

Willis, K. 2003. Women's Work and Social Network Use in Oaxaca City, Mexico. *Bulletin of Latin American Research* 12, no. 1:65–82.

Wilson, W.J. 1987. *The Truly Disadvantaged: The Inner City, the Underclass and Public Policy.* Chicago: University of Chicago Press.

Wiltshire-Brodber, R. 1986. *The Caribbean Transnational Family.* Barbados: University of the West Indies, Institute of Social and Economic Research.

———. 1998. *The Caribbean Transnational Family.* Barbados: University of the West Indies, Institute of Social and Economic Research.

Woolcock, M. 1998. Social Capital and Economic Development: Towards a Theoretical Synthesis and Policy Framework. *Theory and Society* 27:151–208.

———. 2001. The Place of Social Capital in Understanding Social and Economic Outcomes. *Canadian Journal of Policy Research* 2, no. 1:11–17.

Woolcock M., and D. Narayan. 2000. Social Capital: Implications for Development Theory, Research, and Policy. *The World Bank Research Observer* 15:225–49.

World Bank. 1994. *Enhancing Women's Participation in Economic Development*. Washington, DC: World Bank.

——. 1997. Social Capital: The Missing Link? Chapter 6, *Expanding the Measure of Wealth*. Retrieved from http://web.worldbank.org.

——. 2001. World Development Report 2000/2001 – Attacking Poverty, Vol. 1.

——. 2002. *Integrating Gender into the World Bank's Work*. Washington, DC: World Bank.

——. 2008. *World Development Indicators Report*. Washington, DC: World Bank.

——. 2008a. World Bank and Gender Equity at a Glance. Retrieved from http://web.worldbank.org/WBSITE/EXTERNAL/TOPICS/EXTGENDER/0.

——. 2013. *Poverty Data Report*. Washington, DC: World Bank.

Yelvington, Kevin. 1995. *Producing Power: Ethnicity, Gender, and Class in a Caribbean Workplace*. Philadelphia, PA: Temple University Press.

Zavaleta, D. 2007. The Ability to go Without Shame: A Proposal for Internationally Comparable Indicators on Shame and Humiliation. *OPHI Working Papers* 3.

# Index

CPSIA information can be obtained
at www.ICGtesting.com
Printed in the USA
BVOW10s0232240716
456580BV00010BA/139/P